THROWN AW...
OTHER BOOKS ... THIS SERIES

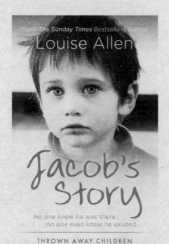

From *The Sunday Times* Bestselling Author
Louise Allen

Jacob's Story

No one knew he was there...
no one even knew he existed

THROWN AWAY CHILDREN

Witness to things a child should never see.
'She has closed herself off from the world'

Eden's Story
Louise Allen

THROWN AWAY CHILDREN

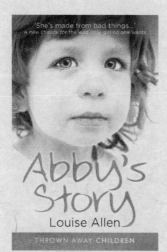

'She's made from bad things...
A new chance for the wild little girl no one wants

Abby's Story
Louise Allen

THROWN AWAY CHILDREN

The shocking true tale of a broken life

Stella's Story
Louise Allen

THROWN AWAY **CHILDREN**

The cases I reveal in my books are all based on true experiences, but I have changed names and some details to protect their identities as they go on to build new lives and families of their own.

THROWN AWAY CHILDREN

Sparkle's Story

Louise Allen

with Theresa McEvoy

MIRROR BOOKS

MIRROR BOOKS

1

Published in Great Britain and Ireland in 2023 by
Mirror Books, a Reach PLC business,
5 St Paul's Square, Liverpool, L3 9SJ.

www.mirrorbooks.co.uk
@TheMirrorBooks

Print ISBN 9781915306555
eBook ISBN 9781915306562

Design and production by Mirror Books.

Printed and bound in Great Britain by
CPI Group (UK) Ltd, Croydon, CR0 4YY

Cover image: Shutterstock
(Posed by model)

Contents

FOREWORD

When I was a child I had short, boyishly-cropped hair. I wore a lot of my older, adopted brothers' hand-me-downs. I played with their trains and action men. I also had a Girl's World. I do not remember wearing gender-specific clothes. Most expectant parents received gifts of yellow for the unborn babies. Blue and pink wasn't a 'thing'. Or at least not so much of a thing. Pink was just a colour, not a symbol.

There are many theories about when pink began being marketed in earnest to young girls: perhaps as early as the 1920s, 1940s or 1950s. I have a memory that it really took off in the 1980s. For me, this seems like the boom years of manufacturing pink plastic toys, and a time when most clothes for girls were suddenly pink and sparkly.

Girls who rejected this, or perhaps their parents who didn't want to be part of it, were made to seem like they were 'difficult'. It seems absurd. We do strange things as a society, and often to our girls. We have a long, long way to go in our understanding and our approach to gender.

PART ONE

I

Luke

Luke pours Lois another drink, making a pretence of measuring the vodka out before tipping it on top of the melting ice cubes at the bottom of the glass. He sloshes a further dash of the spirit on top, pouring freehand from the bottle.

Why not? It's Tuesday night.

He wipes the drop that has landed on the worktop with his finger and then dabs it on his tongue. No point in wasting the good stuff. He adds a splash of orange juice and another couple of ice cubes from the bag nestling in the freezer, right between the oven-cook sweet potato fries and the ready-made frozen Mojito poptails.

The children are busy cooking themselves individual chicken tikka masala dinners in the microwave. Sparkle is in charge, letting the younger ones stab into the plastic lids with a fork but overseeing that they cook them for the right amount of time.

Cormac sits on a stool with a plate on his lap, already eating. He makes the too-hot sound, his mouth a small round 'o', but he doesn't complain. He knows better. The microwave dings to signal that Cahira's masala is also ready. Sparkle serves herself last.

Good job that they all like it because stacked up in the fridge are nine more identical tikka masala ready-made meals from Lidl. They were on special offer and it was such a good deal that Luke took the lot. He'll save them for the kids though, seeing as it's going down so well with them. He and Lois can make themselves something later on tonight if they feel like eating. Bacon sandwiches, maybe.

Sparkle has them well in hand. She's a good kid, thinks Luke. The vodka is making him feel relaxed and cheerful. Sparkle makes sure that Cormac and Cahira get home OK on the days when Granny and Grandpops aren't able to get to the school to meet them all, seeing them over the five big roads that are dangerous to cross. The grandparents live forty-five minutes away by car and it would be a big ask for them to do the school run every day.

But then, they're the ones who made schooling difficult in the first place.

Luke would have been perfectly happy with the school around the corner, but no, his mother's middle-class snobbishness means that they have to travel to the other side of town every day. It was Alexa, not him, who made the decision. She was the one who spent hours scrutinising all the local Ofsted reports before selecting the best school in the area, instigated a meeting with the head-teacher, and somehow made sure that they all got in, even though they were way beyond the catchment area.

So *they* should be the ones doing the school run every day. Not him.

And the children really like it when their grandparents are there, he knows. It's good for children to spend time with their grandparents.

'You like it when Granny's here, don't you?' he says, even though they haven't seen the grandparents at all today. In the vodka fuzz he speaks his thoughts as they come into his head.

'Sure,' says Sparkle.

'Granny always makes sure we've had our dinner,' Cahira says.

'I'm making sure you're fed, aren't I?' Sparkle says, sounding slightly put out.

'Yes, but she doesn't do packets,' Cormac joins in. 'She says they're bad for you,' he parrots, shovelling another hot forkful into his mouth.

'You don't seem to be doing too badly with that packet,' Sparkle says, indicating the tikka masala, still defensive.

'Granny always makes sure Max has been fed, too,' Cahira adds.

Max is their bouncy Springer Spaniel.

'He has too much energy,' says Luke.

'Who?' says Sparkle.

'Max!' says Luke, exasperated that Sparkle can't follow his train of thought.

He causes all sorts of problems in the household, that dog. Sometimes Luke wishes they hadn't got him at all. But Lois wanted a damn puppy and so Luke did the good thing and got her the damn puppy. Anything for a quiet life.

'He doesn't have enough walks,' says Sparkle.

'And whose fault is that?' says Luke.

'He shouldn't be left out in the garden so much. He's a working dog. He needs walking at least twice a day. That's what Granny says.'

'You take him for a walk, then.'

Sparkle shrugs. 'I've already got plenty to do.'

She might be a good kid, and help with looking after the younger two, but she has too much to say for herself at times for an 11-year-old. Now being one of those times. But she's right, Luke thinks. Granny and Lois had another huge argument about Max this week and how much exercise the dog gets. Max probably should be taken for a walk more often, but it's not Luke's job. He bought the bloody dog.

He's done his bit. He shouldn't have to take it for a walk as well.

'Granny and Grandpops are starting their retirement. They won't do so much complaining about how we live our lives.'

'Should we get them a card?' Sparkle asks.

Give Sparkle her due, he thinks, the girl is thoughtful about things like that. It wouldn't have occurred to Luke to give them a card. Besides, the insistence on retirement is a further annoyance which means that, far from getting more help with childcare, Lois and Luke might actually get less support from his folks, which hardly seems fair.

Words from the last row he had with his mother float back to him.

'We've got lives of our own, Luke. Things we want to do in this next phase of our lives. We're not going to become the children's carers.'

'But it was you who insisted that they went to that school.'

'To give your children the best education possible. God knows they need it.'

'What's that supposed to mean?'

But he doesn't need to ask. The answer is always something negative about Lois. She drinks too much. She neglects the children. She should never have had children in the first place. She doesn't take care of the house. She doesn't take care of the dog. She doesn't take care of herself. She can't cook. She has no class. He's heard it all before. He hears it every time he has anything to do with his mother and stepfather. The same old, worn arguments. He's spent many years defending Lois against their various accusations. The fact is, no woman was going to be good enough for him in their eyes.

Anyway, if his parents are going to be difficult about the school run and childcare, he'll find a different solution. He's clocked a family who have recently moved close to the school and has already earmarked them as potential free babysitters. The mum looks like one of those mums who would want to take care of everyone, a matronly sort who might feed his children and do some running around if he gets on the right side of her. He knows the type. Things would sort themselves out. They always did. Meanwhile, there was tonight to think about.

'Right, hurry up kids. Let's get the bedtime routine going ay-sap. You all need an early night tonight.'

Sparkle raises one eyebrow. He's always wondered how she can do that.

She tilts her head towards the drink in his hand. 'I think it's you that needs an early night.'

'Now, now. Mind your cheek, young lady!'

He heads towards the sitting room, where Lois is, and hands over the drink. The truth is, he does want an early night – with her.

'Thanksh,' she says, slurring the end of the word a little.

Good, thinks Luke. Exactly how he wants her to be:

drunk. Drunker than him. Relaxed enough to be up for the fun and games he has in store later. He watched a new porn film last night after Lois had fallen asleep and it's given him a few ideas to try out with Lois tonight. They both enjoy a bit of role play but Lois is always more up for it when she's had a few. He's excited just thinking about it.

Neither of them has a drink problem, exactly. It's just a good way to pass the day when the kids are at school. Life is more fun that way. It gives everything a little bit of an edge. Lois used to say that it was medicinal. Goes nicely with a little bit of weed when they're gaming. Though Lois does seem to get more out of control these days than she used to. And have worse hangovers. He might need to slow down a bit on how much he's giving her.

He notices that Lois already seems quite slumped over in the armchair. He hopes he hasn't overdone the vodka. It was part of a nice three-piece suite once, that armchair. A gift from Luke's parents that had been bought from IKEA. It's seen better days now, though. His parents also bought him the house, concerned that he couldn't offer enough security to the children when he wasn't able to hold down a job. It's never been a case of not being able to, he tells himself. Not wanting to, yes. It was far easier to be at home doing things he wanted to. Not needing to, also yes. When his parents have always bailed him out financially there's no real reason to sit in some deadbeat office all day. Only an idiot would put themselves through that if they didn't *have* to. And Luke is many things, but he is certainly not an idiot.

Far from it.

He could probably make a career out of gaming, actually. He's thought about it. It's not so far-fetched. People do.

But back to the matter in hand. He doesn't want to put off his little sexual fantasy for another night. He's been thinking about it all day. It involves a bit of dressing up, so Lois will need to be up for it. He spends a lot of money online buying various accessories to help enact his fantasies. His latest fetish is dressing as a woman, but not just any woman. He enjoys dressing up as Lois herself. He likes them both to wear exactly the same clothes and has bought a long black wig which he spent some time cutting to the same length as Lois's hair.

Tonight there's a new twist to the sex game. He's got it all planned out, explained earlier to Lois how she needs to have her hair. Not that she looks capable of sorting out her hair in that state. Perhaps he should give her something to eat, to soak up a bit of the alcohol. Sparkle always comments on how thin she is.

As if reading his mind, Sparkle shouts through from the kitchen where she's rinsing the dinner plates.

'Has Mum eaten tonight?'

He doesn't mind the thinness. It makes her more girlish, somehow. More like the 14-year-old girl she was when he first met her, rather than the 27-year-old woman she is now.

'Not yet. Has anyone not eaten their masala? She could have a bit of that. Or a bacon sarnie.'

She does look like she needs a bit of pepping up. Damn. He really hopes he hasn't overdone it tonight.

At that moment, Cahira and Cormac troop in ready for their blast of CBeebies on the iPlayer before bed.

'Where's the remote?' Cormac searches around.

'Under Mum,' Cahira says, reaching to pull it from where it has become wedged between her mother and the side of the armchair.

'I feel sick,' Lois mutters as she comes to for a moment.

She levers herself up from the armchair.

'What is it, Babe? I'll get it. Sit back down.'

But Lois is strangely persistent. She walks into the kitchen where Luke has left the empty vodka bottle on the window sill by the backdoor and makes a lunge for it.

'Again? You fucking bastard, you fuckin-' she slurs and waves the bottle in the air, and the rest of the words get lost.

'Something is very wrong with Mum,' Sparkle says, looking accusingly at Luke.

That tickles him. 'No more than usual,' he chuckles, as if he has made a great joke. Then he watches with further amusement as Lois attempts to navigate walking back into the lounge.

'Hey,' he calls out as she drops the bottle onto the carpet. It bounces once and then spins under the sofa. 'Watch out!'

Lois seems oblivious. Like she's in some kind of trance.

There is more purpose to her actions than the usual alcoholic stupor might allow. She heads to the corner of the room where Luke's mother has set up a crafting area for the kids after a trip to Hobbycraft.

He watches as Lois picks up a pair of scissors. What on earth is she doing?

She stumbles out into the hall. Luke shrugs.

Then he hears Sparkle screaming. 'Stop it, stop it, stop it!'

Cahira and Cormac stop squabbling over whether it should be Truckstar Smackdown or Just Dance.

'Help! Quick, come quick,' Sparkle screeches.

The cry is so desperate that there is a frenzied dash into the hall.

'Please stop cutting, stop cutting!'

Cutting? Luke wonders what on earth is going on. What stupid thing is she doing now?

He stands in the frame of the doorway to the hall, the children ahead of him. In front of the set of vintage mirrors, another gift from Luke's mother, stands Lois. She holds her arms aloft, and her dressing gown sleeves have slipped back to reveal the series of cuts on her arms that he doesn't like the children to see.

'Mummy, what are you doing?' Cormac shouts.

Cahira joins in the screaming. 'No! Stop!'

But it's too late.

A large pile of raven hair is already forming on the floor around Lois's feet.

'Oh shit,' Luke says.

He wants to cover his eyes, and his ears. The sight and the noise are unbearable. Max, pacing outside, starts barking at all the disturbance. His bark turns into a howl, joining the cacophony of pain.

Luke knows he must act. And fast.

He does what he always does when he doesn't know what to do.

He phones his mother.

II

Mobile in hand, Luke paces up and down in the kitchen, away from the hair horror-show in the hallway. It is three rings before Alexa answers. Just as Luke knew she would.

His mother always answers within three rings. Or calls him straight back.

Deep down he understands that they have some kind of weird mutual dependency, that they both feed and draw from. They need each other. Luke knows that his mother still feels guilty about his early years. Knows that she was in the wrong, and wants to right that wrong. At the time Luke's father died of cancer when Luke was six years old, his mum was already having an affair. That generated a lot of mixed-up feelings. Everything she has done since then has been atonement for the mistakes in his early childhood. The man began to stay in the house at almost the same time as the urn with his father's ashes did, and promptly began to sexually abuse Luke.

When Alexa found out she ended the relationship straight away, and then tried to make up for what had happened by doing everything she could to make life easier for Luke. She was what might be described as a 'curling parent', like the broom-sweepers who compete at the Winter Olympics, clearing the ice so that the stone can slide freely. Luke knew that Alexa had always cleared the path ahead of him so that he didn't have to think or act for himself.

So he didn't. And still doesn't. Whenever he needs to he milks her guilt for all it's worth.

'It's a mess, Mum. I think Lois is having some sort of breakdown. The children are a mess. My world is a mess.'

'I'll be with you in an hour.'

Lois is immovable, wielding the scissors as if they are a weapon, refusing to move from the hallway. There is no talking to her. Each time he tries to talk her back into the sitting room or upstairs she tells him to leave her alone, defending her position in the mirrored hallway like a warrior at a guard-post.

It is Sparkle who manages to coax the younger children upstairs. They have all shut themselves in Sparkle's room. He can hear the sounds of the TV.

Alexa is as good as her word. The familiar dark blue Jaguar draws up and he watches as his mother parks five houses away from the house.

Bill stays in the car. Of course.

No doubt he's used the same excuse he always does, that things are probably better if he doesn't come in.

He's right, too. Things have never really settled down since Lois told Bill in no uncertain terms to 'fuck off' one day. It was probably Lois' reaction to being told that the dog could do with a walk.

Shit. There are people in the street. The shouting and screaming from the house has gathered a small crowd. Nosy neighbours prying into his business. That's all they need.

He lets his mother in through the front door, giving a quick two fingers to the crowd.

'Those poor bloody kids. Social never do anything,' a voice from the street says. He recognises the woman from two doors down. An interfering type, arms folded, lips pursed.

'What's it got to do with you?' Luke can't resist saying, slamming the door and shutting them all out. Things will be okay now that his mother's here.

'Now, Lois, I need you to calm down,' Alexa says.

Lois, it seems, has no intention of calming down. 'Go away, you fucking freaks,' she screams.

'Alright, alright. Just let me have the scissors.'

Then Lois opens her mouth and instead of more words, she just keeps screaming and shaking.

Luke covers his ears.

When it seems as if there can be no more breath in her to scream, she starts shivering more. She holds the scissors at her throat. 'I'm going to do it, I'm going to do it.'

'Silly child. Give those here and let's sit down with a cup of tea and talk about it. You aren't going to do anything with those scissors. We both know that.'

The point of the scissor blade is pressed into Lois' neck, leaving a white mark from the pressure.

'Take one step closer and I fucking will,' Lois breathes. Her voice is hoarse from all the screaming.

Far from being a soothing balm, Alexa's arrival seems to have added fuel to Lois' flames.

There's a knock at the door, adding to the chaos.

'Go away and mind your own business,' Luke shouts out.

'It's me, you idiot.'

The voice is Bill's, or, as the children know him, Grandpops. 'The police are on their way,' he says.

Luke feels he has no choice but to let his stepfather into the house. He reaches across and opens the door, and tries to see the scene from Grandpops' point of view. It doesn't look good. Lois holding the scissors at her throat. Her hands shake violently and she has returned to her threat, as if she is in some sort of video loop, repeating over and over, 'I'm going to do it, I'm going to do it.'

Alexa nods grimly to her husband and indicates up the stairs with a tilt of her head. Luke watches helplessly as Grandpops goes up, treading around piles of clothes and shoes that have gathered on each step. Luke still doesn't know what to do, how to respond. This is his home. What right do they have? He has never felt so out of control. He tries again to talk Lois down from this heightened state.

'Please, Lois. What are you doing? What's the matter?'

Lois seems to stare through him, as if he isn't there at all. Luke grabs at his own throat as if he is finding it difficult to breathe. The atmosphere itself feels poisonous. Perhaps it's the ketamine. He can't remember if he's given Lois any yet tonight. Could that be causing some kind of psychosis? It can't be just the vodka.

Bill's footsteps can be heard on the landing above. He is heading for Sparkle's bedroom, where the children are.

'Grandpops!' The children cry out, delighted, as ever, to see their grandfather, even in the midst of all this mess. Luke fully expects Bill to bring them trooping down, but instead he hears the sound of the bedroom door closing and Bill stays upstairs. There is a dragging noise, as if a piece of furniture is being pulled across the floorboards. Then the television is turned up even louder.

Everything seems to be happening in slow motion. The front door is still open and Luke notices a neighbour, Pat from across the road, with her mobile phone recording the whole scene: Lois' maniacal screaming, the locks of hair on the floor, the scissors, Alexa trying and failing to calm her down, pleading with her to put down the scissors, the repeated threat that Lois will 'do it'.

'Two years of this shit!' Pat shouts. 'Two years of watching your nonsense. Those poor kids. You're a disgrace to this street. I hope they lock you up and throw away the key!'

He isn't sure whether the neighbour means that Lois should be locked up or him. Either way he doesn't want to hear any more.

'Fuck off,' he snarls, slamming the door in her face, and time speeds back up to normal. Whatever normal is.

And then he hears the sirens. Several sets of sirens in the distance. It takes a few more minutes, but an ambulance and two police cars pull into the street.

Luke can see through the hall window the two paramedics who are walking towards the house. Behind them, the police attempt to persuade the audience to go home.

He opens the door again to let the paramedics in, stepping out of the way so that they can get past.

'Go away, go away!' Lois screams.

The paramedics raise their arms in a gesture of passivity and step backwards. Luke thinks for a moment that they might just go away and leave him alone. Then he hears them mention 'crisis team.'

The flashing lights and sirens only seem to have encouraged even more neighbours and passers-by to join the crowd, in spite of the police's efforts to disperse them.

'There's three children in that house!' Pat shouts out.

This new piece of information seems to change things. Far from going away, the police now seem to want to come inside, but Lois has other ideas. She dashes to the kitchen and grabs a knife from the draining board. She waves it around wildly, threatening the paramedics and police officers with it, while still holding the scissors to her own throat.

'Crisis team are 50 minutes away,' one officer announces, after speaking into his phone.

Lois is bleeding from the neck. 'I want to die!' she says. 'He's the reason.'

Then she looks at Alexa. 'And her. It's always been her.'

'Would you like them to leave?' the paramedic asks.

'Yes.' Lois's voice is a whisper.

Another police car and an ambulance have arrived in the street.

'Sir, can I ask you to sit in the police car with us?' the first officer addresses Luke.

'Why? Am I being arrested?'

'No sir, but we need to do what's best here to make everyone feel safe. You heard what she said. And you, please, Miss.' The paramedic steps aside to clear the way for Alexa to leave too.

Luke looks to the door and begins walking, a bit like a rock star going on stage. He is calm. He has resigned himself to whatever now lies ahead.

His mother, though, is outraged.

'Luke, remember whose house this is! I will not be spoken to in this manner!' But even his mother is no match for two policemen when the strong arm of the law is a force at her back.

From the car, Luke can still see what is going on, even if he can no longer influence it.

The paramedic seems to be asking Lois to step outside, too.

Lois is still holding the knife and the scissors, but looking less scared and more exhausted.

He hears Lois ask, 'Have they gone?'

The paramedic asks for the knife again.

Lois raises it back in the air. 'I want to kill them. I hate them. They've destroyed my life.'

From his position in the car, Luke can hear the police officers communicating. He hears the words 'sectioning' and 'consent'. A doctor has arrived. They try to persuade Lois to come outside the house.

Lois shakes her head. 'Not until they're gone.' She looks straight at the car with Luke and Alexa in it.

The police officer and paramedic look at each other and both nod. The officers return to the parked car and open the driver and passenger doors.

'Right, you two. We're going to go for a little drive.'

Luke looks ahead as they pull away, so he doesn't see Lois crying quietly as she is taken through the sectioning process.

PART TWO

I

Louise

The children are acting more than a little strangely today. Jackson just rushed back out of the room the minute he saw me, and Lily giggled and shut the door of her room when I went past. I think I know why.

It's my birthday, as it is on this day in June every year.

I don't expect a fuss, nor do I want one. To be honest, I find birthdays, and the other occasions throughout the year when we're expected to be happy on demand, just a bit too much pressure. A homemade card and a box of chocolates is more than good enough for me. I've managed to scale back

Mother's Day to a single card between them and one little present, with no other special treatment, which suits me just fine.

As a child I never had a birthday party of my own. I went to other children's houses when I was invited to their birthday parties, but the complex situation in the household in which I grew up meant that I understood birthday parties were very definitely for other people, and not for me. My own childhood birthdays usually consisted of the resentful presentation of a paper bag with an item from the PDSA charity shop. Sometimes, if my adopted mother was feeling particularly generous, I got a small, individual cake. I never heard my friends sing *Happy Birthday* to me. There was no out-of-tune building towards '*Happy birthday dear Lou-we-eese*'. Having never been encouraged to make a fuss, I just don't put birthdays up there as a priority. Not my own, anyway. It still feels strange to be the centre of attention for no reason other than it being a particular day of the year.

I did try it once. I was in my twenties and I decided to see what it was like. A friend of mine, Shena, organised a party for me and I enjoyed it. Or at least I think I did. I can't be sure because I don't really remember. I ended up having so much to drink in order to cope with the social pressure that I have almost no recall of the whole occasion. I have pretty much tried to ignore it since.

Not so when it comes to the children's birthdays. I probably over-compensate for the lack of fuss that was made of me by trying to give them lots and lots of treats to make them really special.

Still, the children seem to be behaving in this peculiar way and it's giving me a bad feeling. I am beginning to suspect that they and Lloyd are up to something.

'Make sure you choose something nice to wear today,' Lloyd says, eyeing my pyjamas dubiously.

'Don't I always wear something nice?' I ask, probably sounding a bit put out, but it's because I'm really suspicious now. What have they done? A surprise party? I think that might be my worst nightmare. Perhaps the children have decided to do for me what I try to do for them. Oh, it's *awful*. I don't know how I'm going to navigate the day without upsetting someone.

I hate this feeling. I don't want to be ungrateful to people I love who want to do something lovely for me, but I am almost certain that something is going on, and that I won't like it. My simple little birthday feels compromised. I don't understand why my wishes can't be taken into account for things like this.

I clear away the breakfast things as Jackson dashes in and back out of the kitchen for a second time. What on earth is he up to?

I empty the kitchen bin, taking the bag outside to the rubbish. When I come back inside a beautiful bouquet of flowers has appeared on the table.

I look around to find Lloyd, or someone, to give me

some help as to what to do. It hasn't been presented to me, so that leaves the question in my mind, 'Are they even for me?'

How am I supposed to know? It would be presumptuous to assume that they were for me. I make the decision to leave the bouquet on the table as if I haven't even seen it. I head upstairs to get in the shower and do my hair and obviously, now that I've had the directive, find something nice to wear. I look out of the window. It's not sunny, but there's enough suggestion of blue sky to indicate that it could be later. I decide to go for one of my maxi style dresses, that I turned up at the hem because I couldn't stand the length - I felt swamped. So now it has become a sort of between-the-knee-and-ankle maxi. More than a midi. I'm going to call it a 'mixi-length.' Who knows? It might catch on.

I decide to get over myself and, whatever I do, make sure that I avoid feeling in any way sorry for myself. I swear that self-pity represents taking the lid off the bottle for a squeeze of melancholy. That would be totally inappropriate. I am a grown woman and to indulge myself with a bit of childish 'it's not fair' sulking when I have so much joy in my life would be ridiculous.

I hang the proposed mixi-dress up on the outside of the wardrobe door, and rummage to find a pair of Vans in a mustardy brown to go with the vintage patterned colours in the dress. I decide on a big back-combed bun with loose bits hanging down.

And some bright red lipstick. Never mind what Vincent will have to say about that.

My youngest son does seem to have a bit of a problem with my make-up. He doesn't understand why I wear it. I have explained that it is about self-expression, and that I did – and still do – love all things clothes, fashion and glamour. That is my choice, not someone else's decision to make.

His perspective is that 'girls should be natural' because 'that's how he likes them.' There were quite strong views about loose, long hair and no make-up.

Good for him. I did have to explain that I wasn't, in fact, girlfriend material, I was his mother, and that he could keep his judgy views to himself.

In Vincent's defence he did once make a T-shirt that said 'I'm a feminist'. In the town where we live that's quite a bold thing for a young man to openly say. It shouldn't be, of course, but things don't always seem to move on fast enough here. There are a number of our acquaintances, for example, who still appear shocked when I speak up about the financial independence that Lloyd and I cultivate and enjoy.

Likewise, there are some in the community who have a definite, if outdated, view on what constitutes 'man's work' and 'woman's work'. As far as I'm concerned this was all sorted out in the Edwardian era, but some attitudes from that time seem to remain. Personally, I couldn't give a hoot who does or knows what.

Since the flooding in recent years I have become a

'drain-spotter'. It requires more anorak than a train-spotter and means that I have developed an ability to more-or-less instantly diagnose the health of most of the drains I pass when I walk down the roads of my town. Like the revelations about financial independence, it leads some individuals in the area to question how appropriate that kind of knowledge is for someone of my sex.

I try to be amused rather than aggravated.

Before I was married and found that Lloyd likes sorting out the car, I did it all. I am more than capable of putting up a shelf; just see any home that I lived in prior to matrimony. Still, I continue to fight the cause of feminism in this household. Our roles and responsibilities are, to my mind, fairly divided. Lloyd now does the cars, most of the decorating, and the bins. He is also, drum roll please, the main cook. This has not always been the case.

In the early days of our relationship I just assumed that 'female' role of cooking. But I gradually began to notice that Lloyd took more interest in cooking, and seemed to gravitate towards the kitchen if he needed to decompress after a day's work. I didn't take a great deal of persuading away from the stove; it's never been an enjoyable pastime for me, so I absolutely encouraged and supported this method of relaxation. Years later I eat well and hardly ever cook. Voila!

More than once Lloyd has had to be on the receiving end of a 'we can see who wears the trousers in your house,' kind of comment, usually from male associates.

It's obvious to me that we both do, but I get to wear rather lovely dresses too. Sorted.

Jackson runs along the corridor holding something. He darts out of my way without making eye contact.

I definitely think that they have organised a surprise party. God help us.

Right, clothes and make up are all laid out and decisions made about clothing. Time for the morning ablutions. The hallway is empty again and I haven't seen Lily for a while. I wonder what she's up to and give a quick tap on her door.

She shouts, 'Get out!'

I see hair straighteners fly across the floor, and a hand appears from nowhere to push the door shut. Yes, something is definitely going on.

I continue along to the bathroom for my shower. Under the pounding water I think about the day. Normally my family gives out cards and presents at the breakfast table. So far, nothing. Part of me is mildly disappointed. I normally receive a new perfume or SOMETHING! I know I don't want a fuss, but to not even have acknowledgement feels weird. It is making me completely on edge. This, I know, is why surprises are often not a good idea for children from traumatic childhoods. Or adults, for that matter. We expect so little and actually feel quite happy with that. All this over-thinking and second-guessing is very stressful.

I carry on getting ready, even though I don't quite know what I'm getting ready for, and I enjoy that bit. I work my hair up in what I hope resembles Elizabeth Taylor from the 1950s: a kind of big bun on the top. I ringlet the sides with my curling tongs that I bought when I had Covid and was in bed feeling poorly. It seemed a productive use of that time to plan my next season's looks. I should confess that I have only used the tongs twice since I got them. In a post-Covid world there never seems to be the time, but today I'm pleased to see that I look 'done.'

The others, however, are taking ages. I'm all dressed up and ready for whatever is about to commence, but the children are still very much in the preparatory stages. Both bathrooms are belting out different music, creating quite the cacophony of sound. Jackson is into Kate Bush, and *Running Up That Hill* is on repeat. I think it's the third time that I've heard the lyrics right through in the last fifteen minutes. I don't mind Kate Bush, but I'm starting to think that no, I don't wanna feel how it feels, nor do I wanna know, know that it doesn't hurt, thank you very much. Vincent seems to be into Gangster Rap music, which is quite the new development. I walk along the hallway through the sound-clash only to realise that there is a third contribution on the airwaves. As if she didn't want to be left out, there is a sudden blast of the distinctive vocals of Yungblud at decibels. Oh my. I make a quick escape back down to the kitchen where it is at least quieter. But still radiating strangeness because what do I find in there? Lloyd ironing a shirt.

'Wow, you look nice.'

And I feel it, too. Though I don't want to touch anything or crease my rather fabulous dress, and my eye is stinging from the tinted moisturiser. Ignoring that, I feel a million dollars. Or a good proportion of that, anyway.

The flowers are still on the table. Lloyd dashes over to them and lifts them up in the air like a sporting trophy. He shouts all the children's names.

Good luck with that, I think. They'll never hear anything over their music.

Lloyd offers the flowers to me and I behave like I have never seen them before in my life.

'Oh, how lovely!'

It's a big bouquet and one that deserves a big vase, but my huge blue jug, a favourite car-boot prize, that would have been just perfect for this lot, was recently sacrificed when the boys were teaching the dogs to catch a ball. Indoors.

Instead of dwelling on that particular loss, I reach up to the top shelf of the pantry cupboard and pull down three medium-sized vases. I decide I will separate the bouquet out and spread flowers through the house. They are stunning. And suddenly my often-chaotic domestic interior takes on something of the aspect of a show home. It's amazing what a few flowers can do. Combined, I suppose, with the feeling of having taken greater control of the house in the last few months since we decided to take a little break from fostering. Our last longer-term foster children were young twins, Max and Mia. They were exhausting to be around and we had intended to have a break when they left, but found ourselves looking after a teenage boy for a month. That was hard work, too. Not because of anything Christopher himself did, but because the social worker didn't seem to know his left hand from his right and was hugely arrogant. We tried to support and offer some advice about the young man's college choices. I taught in FE and HR for over twenty years and have a bit of experience. I used to write course content and was heavily involved in recruitment. But, like so many social workers, he seemed to think that my background counted for very little.

In fact, the social worker actually very nearly messed up Christopher's education choices because he mixed up the colleges by mistake and wouldn't admit it. I had to intervene, and did manage to speak to a nice woman from admissions who phoned up the other college and recruited him back to do the course that he actually wanted to do: Uniformed Services. He had been toying with the idea of joining the army and wanted to learn more about the various choices. His social worker, for some reason, heard that as Mechanical Engineering, which isn't what he wanted at all. It was sorted out in the end, but all very wearing.

So, our decision to take a break was caused not so much by the children, but by the tiresome prospect of having to deal with professionals from various agencies who are meant to be working *for* the children. Sometimes, the children are the easy bit.

But actually, I'm enjoying not having the pressure. I think we all are. If we had a challenging child in our home we wouldn't easily be able to get dressed up and go out for the day. Nor would we be able to have friends round for dinner as we have done recently. It has been something of a novelty to feel like normal people, behave as a regular family. Though 'normal' and 'regular' are broad terms. Another benefit of not having an additional child is that we can all fit in one car. Again, this has a pleasing freshness. I normally have to follow behind in the little old car with one or two of the children while others get to ride in Lloyd's nice flash vehicle. It will be nice to be driven for a change. Wherever that might be to.

Finally, the children are ready, and don't they all look fabulous.

If ever there was an advertisement for freedom of expression, then here it is, standing right in front of me.

Jackson seems to be paying homage to anime, his favourite cartoons. He is in baggy black joggers and a hoodie that makes him look like some sort of demon slayer. Vincent, by contrast, is an explosion of colour. He sports mauve Vans socks that he got for Christmas. So keen does he seem to be to show the world his designer socks that he has rolled his jeans up to his calves. His trainers are bright white and blue, and though his hoodie is white, it is adorned with a brightly coloured motif. Lily is dressed like a fan of Yungblud, or rather, like Yungblud himself. She has an alarming amount of black eyeliner on her face, and red, red lips. She wears black brothel creepers and a pair of luminous pink socks. Her nails are painted in clashing multi-colours and her hair has been straightened and then bent by the straighteners into kinks. To be fair, I seem to remember wearing a similar look myself in the early 80s when I was a massive fan of The Cure and Siouxsie and the Banshees. Though forty years ago the style was somehow 'bigger'. I remember backcombing mine first to get the height, then spraying clouds of hairspray. I can well believe it was the 80s' hair generation that destroyed the ozone layer.

They all look amazing in their own way. I love the fact that they all do their own thing. They each have their own style tribe. With me in my patterned mixi-dress we must make quite the picture.

Lloyd brings the car around to the front door. He looks like he belongs in a different group. He seems to be dressed as a country gentleman, topped off with a shirt and tie. This I can't work out at all. He hates ties and shirts. On our wedding day he was so uncomfortable in his wedding garb that he bore a closer resemblance to a trussed-up chicken desperate to escape than to a happy groom. Generally he wears T-shirts, or in the winter T-shirts with a jumper on top.

The dogs look mildly peeved that they aren't part of the party. I tell them to lie down and know that they will be fine for a little while.

We clamber into Lloyd's flash car and drive out to the

motorway. I see signs for Bristol and wonder if that's where we might be heading. I'm still not allowed to know, apparently. We pass the turning for Bristol, so that's not it. Suddenly the penny drops. We're off to a gallery and restaurant. I know exactly where we're going and I'm pleased. It's lovely, but I still oscillate between the feeling of hating the pressure of surprises and the pride in my little darlings for their fantastic idea.

As we get out of the car, I recognise another car already parked. It's Millie, Lloyd's daughter, my step-daughter and her partner Mitchell. Millie looks fantastic in her 1970s dress that coordinates with her dark pink hair. She seems to have acquired more tattoos since the last time I saw her, as does Mitchell. Both look freshly inked. We head towards the gallery and restaurant. As we walk in I start to recognise many more faces.

Oh. My. God!

There are loads of people here. What is this?

Have they made all this effort for me? Why would they do that?

I am given a glass of champagne which goes down rather fast, and then another. We wander around the gallery looking at a mixed show of regional artists. Some I like very much. Others remind me of first-year degree work. After a few years you know when you come across something that you have already seen somewhere before.

The children are thrilled with the whole thing and their

part in keeping it all a surprise. They keep scrutinising my face and I know that they're checking to make sure that I'm happy. Which I am. I give them lots of squeezes and hugs. Lloyd looks jovial as he chats away to guests, some we haven't seen for years. It is quite the social occasion.

Lunch is delightful. I have fish'n'chips posh-style, which means that my chips are beautifully placed in a little wire basket. The fish is cooked in the lightest, crispiest batter I have ever tasted. I look out across the table and realise while it is so lovely to see people, I need a minute to myself. I'm a little overwhelmed. It's time to head for the loo and take a few minutes to compose myself. I head out to the garden. It's nice to have some fresh air and it's much quieter.

There are only a few people outside on phones or having a cigarette or both. I walk around the plant beds, inhaling the lovely smells, or at least the ones that don't contain plumes of fag and vape smoke. There is sage and lemon mint amongst mauve lupins. All rather beautiful and I totally lose myself for a few moments. I think I'm probably a little tipsy from the champagne. This suspicion is confirmed as I nearly trip over the hose pipe which runs across the fine gravel path.

I stand with both hands on my hips surveying the scene, almost as if I'd done the gardening myself. I try to take it all in and think just how lucky I am to have such a wonderful life and family.

My phone rings.

'Louise Allen?'

It's either a dentist or Children's Social Care. Given the scarcity of NHS dental appointments, it must be a social worker. Sure enough, Suzanne introduces herself. She sounds more mature than most, so I guess that she must be a manager.

She tells me about a young girl, only 11 years old, who needs to be moved away from a residential home because some older girls are bullying her.

'Poor little thing,' I say.

That's how they get us, reel us in like dozy fish on the hook.

'Her name is Sparkle and it's her birthday today.'

And of course, I'm hooked. I am so pathetic.

I like her name, 'Sparkle'. It's unusual and I wonder how she got it. But we also share a birthday. A Gemini who has suffered childhood trauma just like me.

Oh, pull yourself together, Louise, another part of me thinks. I'm easily suckered.

But after a few champagnes, I'm not going to be able to say 'no' to helping a child in a tricky situation. At the same time I know I can't make a promise about this without talking to Lloyd and the children. After all, we're on a fostering break.

'I'll get back to you,' I say. 'I've got to go. It's my birthday and we're out having lunch.'

'Oh, it's your birthday too? Happy birthday.' She pauses. 'Then really, it was meant to be.'

II

By the time we reach home we're all tired.

Lily is exhausted. But she has done very well indeed. Foster children can't always keep it together at their foster family's events. I'm proud of her. In the past we have experienced door slamming, showing off, sulking and rudeness. On some occasions guests have had to go home. Not a good advert for fostering, but it's an honest reflection of what can happen. Any kind of routine change can be a challenge, and a family party can bring to the surface all sorts of emotions and memories. But today I am very proud of all my children and Lily especially. I watched her holding conversations with people she didn't know very well. She was polite, and remembered to inquire about how people are and how their families and lives are, just as I have encouraged her to. Everything she has done today has been underpinned with good manners and thoughtfulness. Good on her.

I'm having these thoughts as I make the mistake of

checking my emails. It's a habit when I return to the house. It doesn't matter what time of day it is, I still have that leftover optimistic childhood feeling of hope and what-if. Hope that I will receive an amazing job offer, or that a film director has read one of my books and wants to make a Hollywood film, or the Tate Gallery wants to do my retrospective.

You never know. We can all dream.

Instead there are four emails from the local authority, all about Sparkle.

The first is the referral itself. Pages of names and dates, comments from social workers and generally lots of people's thoughts about this young woman. Her grandparents are cited. I recognise their surname, Wilbury, for some reason, but I don't know why. I wonder if I've met them at some point. Or perhaps it's just a common surname. Their address is given. They're located a little way away, north-east of here. I wonder if we are actually meant to see this much detail. It seems like a lot of sharing in a time of concern about data protection.

But in some ways it's very useful. Popular perception has it that the north-east part of the county is where the money is. There are media sorts, posh schools, good restaurants and antique shops.

That's it! Antique shops. That's why I recognise the name: Wilbury's Antiques. It's an amazing emporium of curiosities. I have bought a few bits and pieces from there over the years.

I can picture it: it's massive. Room after room of amazing finds. The lady who owns it usually sits behind four huge glass cabinets of costume jewellery, all laid out on dark blue fine velvet. The last time I went, the upstairs was full of chairs in all conditions. They hung down from the ceiling, suspended on wire, along with an enormous Penny Farthing bicycle. I remember that I took the boys there when they were young and they loved it too. I walked around saying, 'Don't touch anything,' every five minutes. I remember the owners quite distinctly. They looked like they belonged on the *Antiques Roadshow*, not because of their age, more their look. Mr Wilbury wore a striped boating jacket and round straw hat. I think, if I'm not misremembering, he played the banjo.

'Lloyd, Lloyd, guess what?'

I tell him who the grandparents of Sparkle are and he lights up.

In the nicest possible way, I have to confess that my husband is something of a snob. He loves antiques and history, and the people most often involved with these activities are people with wealth and credentials.

I print off a copy of the referral to carry on reading through it. Words do different things on the page to the screen. We can soak it in. The children have all disappeared upstairs now that Mum's birthday duty is officially finished. They are free to be themselves and get back to swearing and gaming in the boys' case. Lily will be pouring over pictures of kittens, and of Yungblud, wondering if he will ever notice her.

Oh well, I'll let them get on with being young and confused by life.

It's still my birthday so I open a bottle of Cava and offer no explanation whatsoever to Lloyd. He laughs, finding it amusing that I am so anarchic today.

We go over the referral. I read some of the important bits out loud.

The residential home doesn't get a good rap. I note the name of the company that runs the home and recall hearing some bad stories about them in the past.

We also looked after one little girl years ago who was at one of their homes. Natalie was in a terrible mess when she first arrived with us. Her hair was matted and she hadn't washed for weeks. I know that I didn't like the look of the bruises on her arms. The explanation from the managers when I enquired how she got them was, 'lively play'.

Perhaps not much has changed. It didn't sound like it was a good environment for Sparkle. From the notes in the referral she comes across as a sensitive girl. And of course, now that we know who her grandparents are we feel that we practically know her. In my mind's eye, banjo-playing Mr Wilbury is like an old friend. It's telling that I can't think what his first name is though. I've probably never known it.

The parents sound a bit odd to me, but I'm sad to hear that her mum, Lois, is described as suffering from mental health issues.

I read on, and begin to notice similarities with another

young mother I know. I worked directly with her in the past. She was addicted to prescription medicines. She was originally prescribed painkillers for a sore neck after she fell down an escalator. Somehow, that led onto other prescriptions for sleeping pills, then tablets for depression. She's still addicted, ten years later, and I can't believe that her doctors prescribe them to her after all this time.

Around five years ago I spoke to a journalist friend who was trying to investigate a pattern of young mums addicted to opioids. As far as I know, the company involved managed to close her work down. She also received threats, though she could never prove where they came from. Whoever was responsible broke into her home and did some weird stuff that made her stop her research. I don't remember all the details exactly.

Reading about Lois makes me wonder if something similar was – or is – going on for her along these lines. After a few years as a foster carer you develop the foster carer's sixth sense about certain cases.

You can't prove anything, of course. If you could, then the perpetrators would already be in prison. It's not so simple. It's more like a heavy feeling that something is not right, with an instinct of what that 'not right' might mean. It's a whiff of something wrong that turns into a hunch. That makes it very difficult to act on. If you say anything to anyone official, say a social worker, they will close you down without any evidence.

Yet some police work begins with these kinds of feelings.

It must do. My instinct says that an important piece of the puzzle is missing from this document. Something isn't quite right about this family. It doesn't quite add up.

The good news is that the other siblings at least seem to have been put into a good placement. I know carers who work for the independent fostering agency named on the form and they regularly sing their praises. It sticks in my mind because, particularly at the moment, there doesn't seem to be much to sing praises about in social care. That level of positivity is rare.

I compose a quick email in reply to the person who sent the referral to say that we are potentially interested in supporting Sparkle. It's the weekend, so I don't expect to receive a response until Monday. I sit on the sofa with my feet on the ottoman with my Cava. I'm two sips in when Lloyd walks in with my phone.

'It's the social worker.'

As he hands me the phone I see that the screen shows 'Caller ID withheld'.

That means it is indeed a social worker, or the school, or the police.

'Hello? Louise Allen here.'

The voice on the other end of the line is young and male. He introduces himself as Richard. I don't recognise his name. I must have missed that off the referral.

He sings Sparkle's praises. 'I can't tell you how amazing she is!'

Probably because of the bubbly I've had today, I can't resist asking, 'How long have you known Sparkle?'

'Umm, I should say, oh, perhaps a good month or so.'

I know that, in reality, that will amount in real terms to a small number of hours in her company, maybe five at the most. He will have no doubt spent some extra hours on top of that to do the administrative work around her case, but I would truly doubt that he has spent more than a day in her company.

What do we know about anyone? What can we know of anyone in such a short space of time? I have people in my circle of friends and acquaintances that I've known for a long time that I'm still trying to figure out. It's a reason that many job interviews last several days; so that potential employers can attempt to get to know someone.

Nevertheless, I listen to what he has to say. It mostly revolves around how much Sparkle is struggling at the residential home. There have been some incidents with the other girls and she can't settle. The memory of Natalie, the little girl we looked after all those years ago, is uppermost in my mind.

I mouth a message to Lloyd: we should go and meet her soon.

He nods.

I listen to Richard talk on. Just the way he speaks about Sparkle and her family leads me to decide that he sounds too young to understand the world. That must be the Cava talking. I'm not usually quite so dismissive of age. I have met plenty of young people who are brighter, smarter and more intuitive than most people my age. I remind myself that Richard is only doing his best to be helpful under probably very difficult circumstances, and that is to his credit. He gives me the number of the residential home, The Maples, and I pause for only a moment before I am tapping the numbers in.

A woman called Marcie answers the phone within a couple of rings. She explains that she is the manager and, before I know it, I'm arranging to meet Sparkle in the morning.

III

It's a Saturday, so Lloyd will need to stay at home with the children. This will be a solo mission. The journey is over two hours each way.

I think about another glass of Cava to celebrate because, well, it's my birthday after all; but settle instead for a large glass of water.

It was the right move. I wake up without too much of a hangover from birthday indulgences. Making myself actually drink the water before I fell asleep has worked a treat.

I am soon up and moving about with purpose. First I let the dogs out and watch them as they do their yoga stretches. Their movements never fail to amuse me. I try a few myself. I put my fingers at the top of the door frame and let my whole body stretch, enjoying the lovely release afterwards. The action also releases a memory, one from secondary school. Our caretaker's wife used to run keep fit classes for 'all the gals'. I can see her clearly: dyed black hair and a range of astonishing leotards. I remember a particular exercise that appealed to all the 'gals' just as we were on the verge of puberty. It was the 'I must, I must, I must improve my bust' routine where we pulled and stretched our upper bodies, each trying to imagine what our breasts would look like one day, and hoping desperately to be endowed with a large bosom. Reader, I was; so thank you, Mrs Caretaker. It worked a treat.

Breakfast consists of my daily egg. This morning it is poached on a small slice of brown bread, lightly buttered beneath a scrape of Marmite. Delicious! Apparently, an egg in the morning is a way of stopping the afternoon fatigue. The 4pm droop is no longer a problem since I've been eating eggs this way. It works for me. While I'm eating I make some mental notes about the day ahead. I wonder about what linen to put on her bed. I have a lively rainbow-coloured duvet set that looks great, but I have no idea what her tastes might be. What if she's emo and likes black or blood red?

I remind myself that I can always change it and decide I will go for the rainbow.

The rest of the house sleeps on. I knew that my little cherubs would be tired after yesterday's celebrations. I enjoy the peace as I do the bed and make a few further preparations in the room for Sparkle. Job done.

Since I know it was Sparkle's birthday yesterday I plan to collect a box of chocolates at the garage. I didn't see anything on the referral that said 'allergies' so I think it will be OK. She may be allergic to the residential home, by the sounds of things.

I know that I'm not supposed to be bringing Sparkle home today, or at least that's not the plan. Still, my foster carer's sixth sense says something different, which is why I have already prepared the room. Even though I didn't discuss a time frame with Richard, I know that when a placement has broken down everyone wants it to end as soon as possible. All being well, I suppose it should be some time next week. Still, it's always best to be prepared. I mean, I didn't hear Richard say anything that sounded like, *whatever you do, do not take Sparkle back to yours*, so I'll keep an open mind and play it by ear.

I'm dressed and ready to roll by 9.30am. Given that it's a Saturday, the main roads shouldn't be too bad. But I might as well get going. It won't hurt to arrive early. Given our little break from fostering, I've missed this buzz before a new arrival.

I drive along one particular A road and remember to slow down. Two speeding tickets are a healthy deterrent. I acquired both because I was on my own listening to music and singing along to it, oblivious. The last time I simply didn't notice my speed because I was singing along, with some gusto, to *Livin' on a Prayer* by Bon Jovi. Weirdly, when that was a hit in the mid 80s I was an art school snob and would definitely not admit to liking anything that wasn't cool. Somehow all these years later I realise that I know most of the lyrics to Bon Jovi, Bruce Springsteen, Whitney Houston and Tina Turner, even though they're artists that I never would have chosen to buy albums of. Music has a funny quality of osmosis.

I check the speedometer and make sure that it stays firmly below 70mph, turning the radio down a notch to make sure. It's a nice journey and the countryside is pretty. I feel absolutely no older than I felt the day before my birthday.

The hours and miles zip by and I soon arrive at the postcode area for the residential home, though there is no sign for 'The Maples'. I try a couple of lanes, driving up and down looking carefully at signs and names.

An old man is walking his dog. I slow further and wind down the window.

'Good morning, I don't suppose you could help me. I'm looking for 'The Maples'. Do you happen to know where it is?'

The man tuts. 'That place, huh? I don't know why anyone would want to go there. Bloody dump if you ask me.'

I refrain from pointing out that I haven't asked him for his opinion on it, only the way there. All the same, that's not a good reaction.

He points a few lanes in the other direction and tells me to look for an old rusty tractor parked opposite the entrance. It's a long lane up to the office and house. As I head off I catch him in my rearview mirror, shaking his head.

His directions are accurate. Sure enough, I see a tiny little sign: 'The Maples'. It's an ensemble of buildings, some old, some new and one that looks like it's still under construction. Not a maple tree in sight. I drive along to a spot that looks sensible to park in, and head over to what looks like an office. It's in an old prefab and it's all locked up. I look around, slightly at a loss for where to go next. Suddenly a woman appears from out of nowhere. I put her somewhere in her late twenties or early thirties. She wears big brown glasses and her hair is pulled back sensibly away from her face. The pale blue works polo shirt she sports is rather tight fitting on her. The stretched branch and maple leaf logo looks like a hand grabbing her boob.

'Are you Louise?' she asks.

'I'm Louise,' I confirm. 'Lucky for you!' I say, thinking that I could be anyone.

She doesn't get my attempt at a joke, which is fair enough because it wasn't a very good one. I don't get the impression that she is the sharpest tool in the box, though she seems polite.

'I'm Marcie.'

She leads me towards a house that looks like it was built in the 1960s. It has large sliding doors at the back which is the way we go in. The garden is nice. Partly laid to lawn with some well-tended borders and flowerbeds.

'Would you like a cup of tea?' Marcie asks.

Of course I say yes. My tongue's hanging out after yesterday's celebrations and this morning's drive. I ask to use the loo and she points me in the right direction. I feel a bit depressed as I walk through the house. I'm not entirely sure why. Maybe it's because this house is not too dissimilar to the one I grew-up in in Oxford, and that doesn't hold happy memories for me. I do my best to shake off those thoughts. There is the enticing smell of toast in the air. I find my way back to Marcie who has made me a rather nice-looking cup of builder's tea. Just the right amount of milk, and a decent colour.

'So, Sparkle,' she says. 'She was staying in one of our other houses but had to be moved here last night after another fight with the other girls.'

I swallow… and wonder what we have agreed to. Then remind myself that even though I have made up a bed, I haven't signed anything. This is only an introductory visit.

'Oh, that doesn't sound good.'

Marcie looks genuinely upset. 'Sparkle's a nice girl. She's a good kid, but can't cope with the other girls.'

'Okay. Is there anything else that I should know?'

She sighs. 'Not really.'

Which sounds to me as though there is, but instead of pushing her I ask if there are other girls in this house.

Marcie nods.

'Perhaps it's time I met Sparkle,' I suggest.

As soon as I say the words I hear an almighty ruckus.

A young person is shouting and swearing, and stomping down the stairs. She is followed by a member of staff, easily recognised by her pale blue polo shirt that matches Marcie's.

I watch quietly at the side of the door in the kitchen. They have no idea that I'm here.

'Don't you fucking walk away from me when I'm speaking to you.' I'm shocked to hear the care worker swear at the young person, who I can only assume is Sparkle.

The mood is tense and toxic. The care worker is in quite a rage.

Not good, not good, I think to myself.

I watch, gobsmacked, as the care worker grabs Sparkle's arm and pulls her quite aggressively.

I look at Marcie, expecting her to intervene. She merely looks embarrassed, as she should be.

I stand still, doing nothing, as this is not my situation to manage. I don't know what has happened prior to this event, but I do know that the care worker should know how to restrain someone safely. And anyway, what I have just seen isn't at the level of needing restraint. They still have no idea that I'm there, and Marcie seems to be turning into a chocolate teapot before my eyes.

Sparkle comes flying into the kitchen and shouts, 'Go away!'

The care worker advances past me, towards her.

'Didn't you hear me? I said, just leave me alone!'

I watch in horror as Sparkle snatches a knife from the knife rack mounted on the wall and turns to face us all, wielding the weapon menacingly.

IV

I can't be quiet anymore.

Aside from the fact that this is all wrong (has no one done a basic risk assessment? Why would you leave a set of knives in easy reach of girls with behaviour challenges?), I'm now in a dangerous situation myself.

'Sparkle? Hello, I'm Louise. I've come to meet you and see if you'd like to move into my house.'

All factually correct, and a sharp reminder to all that my journey here has an element of gravitas that I think it is time to remember. I step forward and go to shake her hand, as if that's a perfectly normal thing to do when someone is waving a knife at you.

The flame in her eyes dies down. She puts the knife down on the side and holds her hand out.

'So, why don't you give me a tour?'

'Oh, that's a good idea,' Marcie says, lamely. But she does at least move the knife back out of reach of Sparkle.

I'll report back to Richard on Monday about everything I have seen here. And my mind is made up: I'm not leaving this girl here.

Sparkle duly takes me for a walk around the grounds. I say 'grounds' as if we were walking through the estate of *Downton Abbey*. The reality is we walk up a few dead ends, past a large farm gate with a sign that says *Keep Out*, and a dumping area containing a load of broken pieces of furniture and a few mattresses leaned up by a wall. It isn't a very inspiring location. There is nothing here that says the children are valued. Nothing inviting.

Sparkle is clearly still angry, but it is a much calmer kind of anger.

I don't blame her for being angry. This place is a dump. The man with the dog was right. It isn't a place for a young person to grow and flourish. The only thing growing is in Marcie's garden. She might be good at caring for plants, but she evidently doesn't let the children have access to them. Nor does she seem to apply that nurturing instinct to the people she is supposed to be responsible for. I know I haven't been here long enough to judge properly, but I've seen more than enough to make me very concerned indeed.

'Can I see your room?' I ask. 'If you want to show me?'

We head back inside, past Marcie and the other care worker in the kitchen who are drinking tea. Mine was abandoned somewhere during 'knifegate'. Never mind, Sparkle and I can stop for a drink on the way home.

We head upstairs. I see a small, dark room with not much in it. On automatic pilot I go to the window and pull back the curtains. 'You youngies are all the same, brides of Dracula.'

She smiles at this and then, for some reason, seems to find it funnier as she thinks about it. She sputters out a laugh. She must have been desperate for that laugh, I think.

I look out of the window and see a paddock. It's a nice view of a lovely space, but it looks like it belongs to the farm with the *Keep Out* sign. I suppose that just emphasises all the things that Sparkle and these girls don't have, and don't have access to. What an unfair world it is.

'There were ponies in that field when I got here,' Sparkle says, as if she can read my mind. 'I thought-' she breaks off. 'I thought I would be able to ride them,' she says, helplessly. 'Stupid.' She laughs again. But this time it is bitter laughter.

I look at her and sigh. 'Sparkle, would you like to leave today?'

She looks at me as if I've told her that she's won the lottery. Her eyes look as if they might balloon right out of her head. Then she nods enthusiastically, still with bulging eyes.

'Right. Start packing.'

It won't take her long.

I get my phone out of my bag and text Lloyd. *Sparkle's coming home to us today – can you do the usuals and get the children ready?*

So, things not good there? comes the almost immediate reply.

No. Hands full now. I'll tell you properly later.

I suggest to Sparkle that she stays there in her room whilst I speak to Marcie. 'What's the other care worker called? The one who came down the stairs with you?'

That's a very euphemistic way to describe the scene I witnessed. Still, no point in adding any fuel to Sparkle's fire.

'She's called Deena.'

It takes me only a few minutes to negotiate a leave plan with Marcie and Deena, the full details of which will follow in the post.

When I get back upstairs, Sparkle is sitting on her bed, ready to go. She jumps up when I knock on the open door.

I notice how tired and thin the duvet cover looks and think with some primal 1950s housewife pride (that only serves to remind how complex the female position is these days), that at least Sparkle will be sleeping beneath a lovely clean crisp cotton duvet tonight, and her room will be clean and bright and welcoming. Unlike this pit.

We say a very quick goodbye, during which both staff have the decency to look a little bit sheepish. Sparkle stands by my side. The lines, it seems, have already been firmly drawn.

And that is that.

I help Sparkle put her meagre belongings in the boot of the car and we drive away from The Maples. For good, if I have anything to do with it. I notice that she doesn't look back.

V

'Sorry about the knife. I wouldn't have-, I mean, I don't usually do stuff like that.'

'I didn't think you did, or you wouldn't be sitting in my passenger seat now.'

Sparkle nods. I'd love to know more about what happened, but it's not my business, and why should Sparkle tell me anything when we've only just met. I know enough not to push her to try to talk about anything heavy on the journey home. We steer clear of difficult subjects, though she is happy to talk about some things. I keep things as light as I can and ask very general questions, just learning a little bit about who she is. I start with her name.

'Sparkle's a cool name. I've never met another Sparkle.'

'I think it makes me sound like a My Little Pony.'

'Oh. I think it's unique. And it makes you sound like you have a fire inside you. I like that.'

She shrugs.

I wonder how the name was chosen for her, but she doesn't say any more about it. Foster carers know that we need to get out our tweezers and begin teasing the information out carefully – strand by strand – from the spider's web of confusion and anger that a child feels, to get to the truth. It doesn't matter that there are things I really want to know about; she is in charge of her story. She will tell me about her name, and her life, when she's ready. If at all.

I think Sparkle does very well, actually. Being in a car for two hours chatting away with someone who is basically a stranger, she must feel some degree of safety. Feeling safe is the most important emotion to aim for with all children, as far as I'm concerned. From a place of safety, all else can grow.

She is polite and articulate and has an older-than-her-years wisdom about the world when she speaks.

I ask her about her favourite foods.

'I like the chicken tikka masala that you microwave. We ate those a lot. And Fray Bentos tinned pies. I used to cook them with mashed potatoes for Cormac and Cahira.'

Her answers don't suggest a particularly broad or varied diet. But that is no surprise with a child in care. It also sounds as if she has done quite a lot of the cooking.

'Mum was always on some fad diet,' she explains. 'Once it was only ginger tea and fruit and she ended up in hospital.'

When we take a comfort break at a service station I text Lloyd with the things that she likes so that he can nip out and stock up before we get back. I can well anticipate Lloyd's reaction to buying ready-meals. He's not a fan of processed foods. Nor am I. More importantly, Lloyd does an amazing Masala dish from scratch. He makes flat breads which we all tear strips from and use to scoop up the magic thick red sauce. Of course, he makes a version for Lily without any meat and has well-learned how to keep a separate set of utensils so that no cross-contamination can occur into her vegetarian diet. Perhaps we can wean Sparkle onto the home-made stuff.

She doesn't say much else about her mother, but the few comments she does make suggest that she doesn't think very highly of her. In fact, she sounds more like a parent, perhaps talking about her teenage daughter at university who isn't eating properly and burning the candle at both ends. She is equally disparaging about her father. 'He only likes gaming.'

Then 'something happened' which meant she had to go and live with her grandparents.

'How did you like that?' I ask, gently.

She looks away, out of the passenger window.

'We liked it there. I did. We all did to begin with. We ate nice food. And grandpops is alright.'

Sometimes it is what is left unsaid that gives the biggest clues.

'And your gran?'

Sparkle tightens her lips and says, 'okay.' Then, after a pause, 'But it didn't work out,' she says, darkly. 'So I ended up there. Where you saw.'

'And now a new chapter,' I say, trying to lift the mood.

She really does seem quite mature and articulate for her age. I also manage to glean that she has done not just the cooking but the lion's share of caring for her two younger siblings. She misses them, and hasn't seen them since she was put into care. That is not right or fair, and will be one of my first items on the Sparkle to-do list.

When there is a lull in our conversation, I say, 'I should prepare you for Lily.' I am thinking about the fight that Marcie described and the way she spoke about Sparkle not being able to handle the other girls. I want them to have a good introduction to one another. It will be good if they can be allies. I explain a little about Lily's situation: that she has been with us for a few years now as a long-term foster child. I don't want Lily to feel usurped in any way by Sparkle's arrival; equally, I need Sparkle to feel welcome into our family dynamic.

It turns out I needn't have worried. Lily and Sparkle are only a year and a half apart in age and seem to like the same things, according to the quick checklist that Lily bombards Sparkle with as she walks through the door. It includes Yungblud. They hit it off straight away. The boys are, perhaps understandably, a little less excited.

'Another girl,' Vincent had moaned last night, and was backed up by a conciliatory raised eyebrow from his brother. But they do manage to come down and say hello without too much awkwardness. Though Vincent doesn't seem to be able to look Sparkle in the eye. He's at an age where girls terrify him. He had a girlfriend but forgot some of the rules and didn't speak to her at school one day. Consequently, she dumped him. He still keeps drawing penises everywhere. It's been going on for some time now.

When the bathroom mirror steamed up yesterday I saw a great big penis and balls staring back at me. Jackson is, thankfully, more or less coming out of this stage, though he still does it occasionally. I can tell which illustrations belong to whom because Vincent names his while Jackson's have eyes. Freud would have a field day with these two. I'm assuming that they are curious about sex and terrified at the same time, so it's all going on for them. It's no secret that girls' brains on the whole develop faster and earlier than boys. It's painfully apparent at times here.

Lily's excitement, on the other hand, is palpable. Lloyd tells me later that she went into overdrive on hearing the report that Sparkle was actually on her way back today. She immediately dashed to the shops in town and bought some sweets and a fragrant diffuser as a welcome gift.

'I've put some things on Sparkle's bed,' she whispers to me. 'Can I show Sparkle her room?'

'Of course you can. On you go, you two.'

I love that she is so enthusiastic, and that she wants to make another foster child feel welcome. Having been in that position once herself, she no doubt remembers what it's like to arrive in a strange home. But, in a house of foster-brothers,

I also know that Lily has always loved the idea of having a sister. Sparkle is the closest to her in age of any girl that we have fostered in a while.

I haven't seen Lily this engaged by anything other than her hair for months. She sweeps round to Sparkle's bedroom door like the concierge at a New York hotel.

'Perhaps you could help carry her b-' I start to say. But no chance of that, since the new best friends forever have dashed off to do the grand tour, leaving muggins here to bring things in. I resist saying, 'Will that do m'lady?' when they return briefly to the hall so that Lily can point out the front door. The very exciting front door that Sparkle has only just stepped through.

There's no stopping Lily. She points out every feature and detail available. The two paintings by my mentor and friend, Douglas. 'He was a Fine Artist,' she says, and I can hear the mental capitalisation of his title. 'And the dog's named after him.'

She even explains the composition of the telephone. 'You can tell it's Bakelite if you rub it, and get the smell.'

I'm quite sure that Sparkle doesn't need to 'smell' our telephone on arrival at the house, but Lily evidently thinks otherwise.

'That's a mirror,' she says, stating the bleeding obvious and pointing to the large frame on the sideboard. 'It's got a carved eagle at the top.'

It has indeed, and that always makes me think of the

Third Reich, but it was here when we bought the house so I have learned to live with it.

'Look, there's us!'

It's a lovely sight. The two of them reflected back, already arm in arm.

I have no idea where this Lily the estate agent has come from, but she seems to be doing a good job of selling the house to Sparkle who is making all the right noises.

There has been no sign of Lloyd so far. I hope he will appear soon. I can see through the window and the gap in the wooden barn where we keep the cars that his car is not there. He must still be at the supermarket.

Lily flings open the middle hallway door and unleashes our two little beasts: Douglas and Dotty. On the vet's advice my little darlings have been in boot-camp regime. This is mostly for Dotty's benefit. She has put on a lot of weight lately, so much so that we have begun to call her 'the loaf'. She is moving into comfortable middle-age in dog years which might be one reason, but I also think the children must be feeding them on the sly, trying to curry favour. Each seems to want to be the one most loved by the dogs. They have a lot to learn. Dogs will do anything for food and love anyone that feeds them. Which is why they love me the most. Obviously.

Sparkle likes the dogs, dropping straight down to their level to greet them. She chats to them in a baby voice, something that the boys tell me off for. I make no comment when they do it. I'm playing the long game. I shall simply wait for them to grow up and have their own dogs and babies, and then enjoy listening to them use baby-talk.

Next, Lily ushers Sparkle out into the garden for a tour of the sheds. Maybe she's not ready to be an estate agent just yet. When they get back to the kitchen I suggest that it might be time to have a drink and something to eat.

'Don't worry, Louise, I'll sort out something for me and Sparkle,' Lily says. I try to react as if this is a perfectly normal thing for Lily to offer to do. She really has transformed into the hostess with the mostess. I am quietly amused by the whole scenario. My arms and legs might drop off and Lily wouldn't notice, but her sudden attentiveness to Sparkle's every need is amazing. She fixes them each a glass of diet coke with ice and lemon. I need to show Lily how to slice the lemon properly, but now is not the moment. She's basically put half of a serrated lemon in the glass that is floating on top like a buoy at sea. Once a slice or two of Lidl's finest shortbread has been consumed, off they go for the rest of the tour.

So far so good. Sparkle seems at ease.

I listen as Lily takes Sparkle into the main sitting room where many of my own paintings hang, calling it the 'gallery'. She explains a little about some of the paintings, and I'm quite touched as she zooms in on the oil painting of Ron and Penny.

Ron and Penny are special. They are two foster carers

who I would put up there as fostering gods. Between them they had their own children as well as looking after hundreds of other people's. They recently looked after some refugee boys and young men. They became famous, not because of receiving an honour from the Queen for their brilliant dedication, but for being the foster carers of Ahmed Hassan, the Iraqi teenager who made a bomb on their kitchen table and took it to Parsons Green underground in 2018 with the intent of causing serious harm. It was described as an act of Jihadist terrorism. That event made the lives of Ron and Penny hell for a long time. They were treated like criminals after reporting to their local authority many times that they thought 'something' was going on. Even though their worries reached the highest level, various people who should have known better ignored their concerns. Ron died earlier this year and I am so grateful to have met him and painted his and Penny's portrait. Ron also knew of my birth father from when he worked in the same area in the 1960s. I have never even seen a picture of my father, so when Ron described him and his brothers, I was thrilled.

I hear Lily tell a version of all this to Sparkle. Now she is the gallery curator informing the gallery visitor of the provenance of the painting. Not only is it moving to hear her tender account, I am amazed that she has actually retained all the information, because I think she never listens to a word I say.

Today is certainly an interesting day.

The girls carry on upstairs, continuing the grand tour of every single room and cupboard. I can't fault Lily's attention to detail.

Lloyd appears at the back door, laden with shopping bags. I dash out to give him a hand. We have a well-rehearsed moan about how heavy the tins of dog food are, and how expensive it is to feed the family pets. We sound like a pair of pensioners lamenting lost times, but although no doubt that day will come, we shouldn't be quite there yet. I continue the theme but change the subject to how expensive it is feeding the one vegetarian in the house who won't eat vegetables, fruit or pulses. Lily has, however, discovered that she does like homemade egg fried rice, so Lloyd has two large boxes of eggs sitting at the top of the shopping bag squashing the cakes and bread. I pull them out and carry them along with the box of dog food tins.

'Where's Sparkle? How's she settling in?'

I explain about the grand tour of every ornament and bath towel in the house, and how lovely it was to hear Lily talk about the painting of Ron and Penny.

Lloyd is as impressed as me. 'Sounds like Sparkle's arrival might be really good for Lily!'

VI

For the first week that Sparkle is with us, the boys generally stay away from Lily and Sparkle, who are quite the inseparable pair. To be honest, Lily is doing such a good job that even I feel surplus to requirements. Lily helps Sparkle to unpack, spends time sorting her room out, parts with some of her Yungblud posters to give to her new friend, and is on hand to explain everything about how our household runs. One evening is spent having a clothes swap which seems funny to me. From my perspective they have more or less the same clothes and appear to be exchanging like for like.

Lily has more items and they are certainly in better condition than Sparkle's, but I see similar themes. They swap their Nirvana T-shirts and have been up in each other's room listening to *Smells Like Teen Spirit* on repeat and trying out increasingly thick black eyeliner. It's fascinating the way that teenage identity seems to be constructed around looking as identical as possible to others in your tribe.

Meanwhile, I'm good only for lifts and getting supplies from the shop. We are yet to get beyond a ready-meal for dinner. Sparkle has quite a fondness for a particular brand of chicken tikka masala and has rejected most other things.

Lily wants Sparkle to be able to attend the same school she goes to in September, when Sparkle is old enough to move up to secondary school, but I don't know how feasible that is, or even if Sparkle will still be with us by then. I hope that Richard, the young, enthusiastic social worker, will arrange for a primary school transfer to happen soon.

Meanwhile, I do my best to entertain and amuse Sparkle during the day while the others are at school. I try not to think about the work piling up on my desk. There are books to write, illustrations to finish, and tasks for the new client I have just started to work for. Deadlines get closer as the stack of untouched jobs gets larger. It would be lovely if foster caring was the only job I did, but the ironic reality is that if I didn't work then we couldn't afford to foster.

On Friday I offer to take Sparkle shopping for some new clothes and bits and pieces, as I always try to do with our new arrivals. To my surprise she says a very polite, 'No thank you.'

How peculiar. I've never known a tweenager turn down the offer of new stuff. But then I twig. She would prefer to go with Lily.

'Shall we wait until tomorrow when Lily can come too?'

Sparkle's face breaks into a broad smile. So, we go on

Saturday instead. They buy exactly the same shirts and jewellery, and a new eyeliner each, since we seem to be going through that rapidly.

Richard does some magic and it's arranged that Sparkle will start school in a week's time. I'm surprised and impressed with how quickly that has been sorted out. Social services could have drawn it out, as could the school, I imagine, given the proximity to the summer holidays; but no, both sides have acted quickly and all has come good. I'm particularly pleased because it will help socially in the long run, giving Sparkle the opportunity to make some friends before she moves up to secondary school in the autumn.

That is, of course, assuming that she is still here living with us by that stage. At the moment all is looking good and I could not have wished for a better friend for Lily. They are thick as thieves, as the expression goes.

Richard is going up and up in my estimations, too. He comes to visit twice in the first week and makes an appointment to see her at the end of the second week, too, which he says will be a regular slot. This is good, and exactly how things should be.

He engages with her in a way that not all social workers seem able to do, and always seems ever so enthusiastic. I have discovered that he is actually a locum. He left university two years ago, and has decided that he prefers the freedom of locum life. I don't blame him for that. They get paid more than the council social workers, which I think must make for a difficult working relationship, but his determination to be professional and to take his responsibilities seriously is impressive. I hope he keeps it going.

Just imagine if someone like Sparkle could have the same social worker until she is 18. What a difference that might make to her life. I smile ruefully, knowing how very unlikely that scenario is within the current culture in social work. Work overload and stress are common which makes Richard's buoyant attitude a real breath of fresh air.

At the end of the first week, Lloyd and I sit down for a debrief. Though, instead of an agenda and minutes, there is wine.

'Cheers!'

We clink glasses and discuss the ease with which Sparkle seems to have settled into our home, and the efficiency of Richard in organising meetings and jumping on the educational aspect of her care.

'He's also arranged for Sparkle to have a visit with her siblings next week.' Again, I'm impressed because he has taken full responsibility for doing this, and managing the logistics with another social worker. It isn't me driving around the country to make the visit happen as it has so often been in the past.

'Could it be that the system is working?'

'I know. I can't believe how straightforward this has all been.'

I will remember those words later on.

VII

Richard is as good as his word. By the end of the first month, he has already been to visit Sparkle at home no less than five times. That might be something of a record in my book.

Alas, going to school for the last bit of term doesn't work quite as well as we might have hoped. Sparkle struggles with the transfer, doesn't seem to make a good impression with the teachers. Even though her uniform is new, she looks self-conscious and uncomfortable in it, unhappy to be away from the loose-fitting shirts she favours. She doesn't make friends quickly. Part of me is surprised by that, given how well she hit it off with Lily. She clearly has good interpersonal skills. But, in the final half term of primary school, I suppose that friendships have already been well-established over a number of years. And I remember Marcie's explanations about how Sparkle didn't get on with the other girls in the residential home. It's early days, and there will be a bigger pool of pupils to make friendships with when she arrives at secondary school in September, so I try not to be unduly worried.

The other thing that doesn't go terrifically well is the sibling time that Richard arranges.

Again though, he keeps his promise and handles the whole thing himself, picking her up from us and driving her to and from the contact.

And, when Sparkle comes back from the contact visit, she seems happy enough. But she is full of talk about where Cormac and Cahira live.

'They have this cool trampoline in the garden. It's massive. You should see it, Louise. And an amazing TV room in the basement of their foster home. It's like a den that they have all to themselves.' She looks pointedly in my direction. 'Imagine it. It's a great set-up.' Her tone is strange. It's more about seeing what her siblings have or do not have and comparing it with her lot. There's no talk of how it was to see them again, or how much she misses them. It sounds like a bizarre mixture of boasting and envy. Perhaps that's exactly what it is.

I feel a little bit inadequate. I can't tell if that's what she intends.

I obviously can't do anything about not having a basement, but it sets me off trying to remember exactly why it was that we decided to get rid of our trampoline, justifying the decision all over again in my head. I know that the children treated it like a cage fighting event. One time they hadn't zipped up the entrance properly and as I was gardening I saw Vincent fly out of it and land on his back with a thump. I decided that for all the therapeutic calm that we were told about in the trampoline marketing and by social workers, the health and safety aspect was not worth the risk.

There was no way Lloyd or I could be on hand to stand next to it the whole time while they bounced. It has to be said that my neighbours hated it, too. In fact, when we took it down they cheered. I get over myself, remind myself of all the reasons why removing it was a good idea, and remember that Sparkle has been neglected.

She finishes her account of all the great things that Cormac and Cahira have at their foster home, then heads off to find Lily. Richard follows me into the kitchen, evidently wanting to talk.

'That was quite strange. I think perhaps Sparkle must have found it very difficult.'

I remember how young he is, and how little experience he has. He won't have supervised many contact visits so far, I'm sure.

I try to reassure him. 'It's always a little bit awkward to begin with. They are unusual circumstances. I'm not surprised she found it difficult.'

'But she isn't sure if she wants to arrange another visit to see them.'

'Oh.' That does seem odd. 'I suppose she might come round in a few days when the dust has settled.'

But she doesn't come round. Her attitude towards her siblings is interesting. She seems quite ambivalent towards them. Richard was right. She doesn't really seem as if she wants to be with them.

'Suppose so. In a little while, maybe,' she says, when I press the matter further.

In spite of the air of maturity she possesses, she is often unsure of herself and sometimes seems very young indeed. Far younger than her years. Another thing I notice for example is that, almost like a toddler, she has trouble sharing. If she has sweets or crisps she won't offer them round. She is strangely possessive when she has just been given something. Perhaps it comes from not having, or having to go without before she came to us.

But the trickiest thing of all is that having Sparkle living with us has put paid to our summer holiday plans. At first we thought that her grandparents would look after her while we took our very much needed little family holiday, but they have now decided that they aren't 'fit enough' to look after her. Given Sparkle's age and self-sufficiency, this seems a strange thing to say, and Sparkle was saddened by the news. It seems to have sent her on a long-lasting downward spiral mood-wise. Because they left it to the last minute to cancel, Richard has not been able to find respite foster carers.

Not one to be easily put off, we looked into adding Sparkle onto the booking, thinking that she might just come away with us. I didn't get as far as looking at passports, because that didn't work as a solution either. She flatly refused to go on the trip.

We are beginning to see that Sparkle doesn't always sparkle.

In order not to deprive Lily, Vincent and Jackson, we do something that we have never done before. I plan to stay at home with Sparkle while the others go on holiday to Spain. There are lots of sacrifices you have to make as a foster carer, but this one seems particularly hard. I, like the others, had been looking forward to our family holiday. But, if we cancel the whole thing we'll lose all of our money. I'm not prepared to do that.

The children aren't pleased that I'm not going with them. My inner six-year-old wants to shout, 'it's not fair' and sulk for a while in the corner.

I have dark thoughts about Richard, in spite of all the good work he has done so far. I find myself wondering how hard he actually tried to source the respite care. It doesn't help much that we haven't currently got a supervising social worker. We have been told that it's taking a bit longer to recruit one than they expected. I've learnt that this is code for 'no one wants this job'. It must be a tough job actually. The role of a supervising social worker should be one that supervises, develops and supports foster carers. In reality it's listening to foster carers' frustrations and responding in an appropriate way. It can't be easy listening to people moan all day, every day. Still, I probably wouldn't be moaning about

Richard if I had a supervising social worker to speak to. I'm just unhappy about this holiday arrangement.

The atmosphere in the house changes.

Sparkle has been unsettled by seeing her siblings. It has definitely thrown her off course. The fact that her grandparents changed their minds about having her has dented her carapace. Her parents seem to be behaving as if they have no interest in her at all. It's not surprising she is on edge. But it all adds up to us having a rather challenging young woman in the house.

I am weary. Not just a bit tired, but what we call the 'foster carer's fatigue'. It's when our bones ache along with our heads, and our hearts hurt, too. Sometimes there is simply too much to absorb and, over the last few days, I have begun to feel that something is brewing in Sparkle. Nothing happens, but it feels like it might. Her reactions are less polite and more abrupt. The easy manner she displayed on that first car journey home and in that first week is gone. The honeymoon period of her arrival is definitely over.

I pack the children's suitcases. Usually it's a really exciting event when I'm packing for our holiday, but since I'm not going on it I can't seem to muster the same enthusiasm. I tell myself that this is all happening for the right reasons and that, actually, having this focused time with Sparkle when it is just the two of us might be exactly what she needs to feel like herself again. I'll find lots of things for us to do together, and try to let her know that someone is genuinely interested in her and wants to enjoy her company.

But putting on a brave face in these last few days before departure is very hard. Sometimes I worry that we put our birth children through a lot, and they do it for children that are only in our lives for a relatively short space of time. They may never meet again once the placement is over. But it's not just the children that I'm putting in a difficult place.

I can feel myself plummeting downhill.

My mood has deteriorated, like Sparkle's. I feel negative about nearly everything. Just very flat about life itself. But, as those who foster know, there is no time or room for that when you are caring for someone else. We are expected to behave like robots and not incur normal human emotions. We have to be 'copers' or face criticism.

I'm already missing the children and they haven't even gone yet. I love seeing them in the sea. It takes years off them. They play again. And the treat of going out to restaurants. All the laughing and chatting. As I fold laundry, which I usually find therapeutic, I have tears in my eyes as I think about what I'm missing out on. I know that I'm doing a 'good thing', but I'm not sure that this level of selflessness can be healthy. I start feeling a little resentful. I love them so much. How is it fair not to be with my children on holiday? To miss out and lose our hard-earned money for someone else's child who I have only known for six weeks?

My thoughts spiral round and round.

I feel the need to talk to someone, but I'm not sure who I can confide in. If I start saying too much to Lloyd then I know he'll get upset and pull the plug on the holiday, and I definitely don't want that. I want them to have some fun. Even if that has to be without me. I decide that I must swallow my pride and call my fellow foster carer, Kristina.

'You are joking? You are going to let your family go on holiday without you? Louise, what are you doing? No, scrub that. What are they doing? This is outrageous!'

She is crystal clear that this should not be happening and that 'they', the social workers should never have let this happen.

'I'll tell you what you should do. You should give the NUPFC a call. See what they have to say about this.'

She means the National Union of Professional Foster Carers.

'I don't know if I can do that, Kristina. I mean, it all feels a bit pathetic.'

Kristina knows about my background, and that having grown up in care myself I know that actually going on holiday is a privilege. 'If I complain I'll sound spoilt.'

'Oh, Louise. You know that is the care-kid inside you speaking. Everyone is entitled to a break. That's what unions fought for in the 1930s. *Especially* foster carers!'

'But they're not actually going to be able to do anything, are they?'

'Just make the call.'

I hang up, agreeing that I will, indeed, contact the NUPFC. I feel uncomfortable about it nevertheless and, although they are sympathetic, as predicted, the union can't actually do anything either. With a little more notice they may have been able to help organise some respite care, but this is all so last minute.

I can't help myself but look for someone to blame. None of this is Sparkle's fault. I decide that I'm rather cross with Sparkle's grandparents; they've let us all down. And the manner in which they did it, so last minute, was unfair. They knew what was at stake for us.

Perhaps I should meet with them and try to understand what's going on. It might help me to understand more about Sparkle, too. Emotionally, she's all over the place. We both are. I struggle until Lloyd and the kids leave and actually, when we finally wave them off, I start to feel better knowing that they will all have a good time. I resign myself to being at home and try to make the best of it. In my head I rebrand it not as missing out, but as an opportunity to really be with Sparkle. Perhaps I can use this focused time to help soothe some of her pain away.

The weather in Spain is perfect. In the UK it is a little more erratic but we do manage to go for some lovely days out together.

The first is a day out in London. Sparkle, like so many children who come into care, has never been to the capital city. That means we can embrace full-on tourist mode. We begin with a Thames boat cruise. The tour guide is hilarious as he points out the London landmarks and tells stories to go with all the buildings that we see. He could be a stand-up comedian. He includes all the passengers in his spiel, and gets a great atmosphere going on the boat. Sparkle is speechless, but clearly enjoying herself. After the tour, we take a walk through the West End. I show her Carnaby Street and, while I can't do as good a job as the cruise guy, I explain that in the 1960s it was the most happening place to be. Mary Quant and the mini skirt and the Beatles make it into my talk. Post our packed lunch, we dash to the V&A museum where I am able to show Sparkle actual miniskirts along with all the other amazing clothes. I think these bits of the day might be for me, but I can tell that Sparkle genuinely loves the whole experience. Before catching the train home we have dinner in the Giraffe restaurant on the South Bank, and I realise that I'm enjoying Sparkle's company.

She is tired on the way home, and wants to sit quietly. The clothes I bought her from Oxford Street and the lip gloss from Benefit Cosmetics in Carnaby Street are held tightly on her lap. She gets the lip gloss out of its box several times to look at it.

We've had a great day, and I've learnt a few things about her. Beneath that moody façade is a fragile soul. The posturing is a front, as it so often is.

Lloyd and the children FaceTime us towards the end of the journey, much to the annoyance of the other passengers,

I'm sure. They have been out for dinner and are paddling in the sea before it gets too dark.

'Then we're going back to the villa to watch whatever strange DVDs are in the collection,' Jackson explains.

I'm excited to speak to them all, and wave frantically at everyone through the screen. I find that tears have sprung to my eyes.

'Give them a wave, Sparkle!'

She politely waves her hand, managing to look rather sulky at the same time, but I'm pretty sure now that it's shyness and awkwardness.

I have parked at the station, and when we head round to the car I notice that Sparkle is clutching her stomach.

'Is everything okay, Sparkle? You look as if you're in pain.'

She groans. 'My tummy hurts.'

That could be a few things, I think, trying to recall what we have eaten on our trip. I tried to save money by bringing snacks and lunch with us, but it hasn't all been healthy, and our meal at the end was chip-heavy, accompanying loaded burgers. Perhaps she has over-eaten.

Although she wears baggy T-shirts and sweatshirts that cover up most of her body, she does have quite a strange body shape. Skinny arms and legs but a very rounded, almost distended middle. It's most likely related to a poor diet, but I haven't yet done as much as I must to rectify that. I need to do more to wean her away from the ready-meals she still favours. But she's also developed enough to be hitting puberty, so my mind goes towards periods and period pain.

It's difficult to know where to start, so I plunge straight in.

'Have you started your periods, Sparkle?'

There is a fierce shake of the head. She looks mortified. Her hands drop to her sides, away from her body.

'Probably nothing to do with that,' I say, to reassure her. 'More likely you need the loo, after all that food we've eaten today!'

She nods, as if she is far happier with that suggestion.

'Do you know about periods?' I press.

She casts her eyes down, and nods again. 'Another thing that's horrible for women.'

It's one of those moments when she sounds mature beyond her years. A strange thing for an 11-year-old to say.

'Too true,' I agree, leading her back in the direction of the toilets on the station platform.

She is a while inside.

'Better?' I ask.

'Better,' she repeats, but I notice that she is still touching that tummy area.

On the drive home I bring the conversation around to Sparkle's grandparents.

'Would you like to see them?'

'Sure,' she says, but the accompanying shrug suggests that perhaps she isn't so sure.

'What about your other grandparents?' I ask. 'Do you have much to do with them?'

I learn that Sparkle hardly sees them.

'Granny, that's mum's mum, is always angry with her. Angry with Lois, I mean.'

'Oh?'

'She thinks that Mum should leave Dad.'

Woah, that is a loud idea. As ever, I don't want to push it, but the first rule of talking to children from trauma is not to look at them while it's happening. The car is a good place for this to be able to happen. The car at night is even better. Somehow it helps to release words without the pressure of having to make eye contact.

'Dad can be a dick and mum is off her face most of the time.'

Aaah. Here it comes. I wonder what else she could do with getting off her chest.

Instead of the usual route home from the station I drive to another town, then another one, clocking up a further forty miles. Sparkle holds her hands together around her shopping bags while she opens up about her father.

I keep driving, mostly making 'mmh' and 'aaah' sounds whenever there's a gap.

'Is he kind?' I ask.

'Sometimes,' she says, with a sigh.

I stay quiet.

'He is when he wants me to do *things* for him'.

Uh oh. I've been here before with sexually abused children. I brace myself for the worst. What Sparkle shares next shocks me. She is certainly a victim, but not quite in the way I imagined. Instead she goes on to tell me about how she had to look after her brother and sister and mum.

'I used to have to get Cormac and Cahira up for school because mum and dad were asleep. I had to take the dog for a walk because no one else did. The garden was full of dog poo so the kids couldn't play out there.'

My heart goes out to her when she describes her younger siblings as 'the kids'. She is nothing but a kid herself.

'Grandpops was angry with Dad and Mum for not looking after the dog properly. There were lots of rows about that.'

'Dad deliberately makes Mum drunk all the time. I think he drugs her, too. He puts stuff in her drinks that she doesn't know about.'

I don't like the sound of that.

'She does nothing to stop him, though,' she continues, and her tone is disparaging.

She doesn't seem to like her father, but she's disparaging about her mother. Perhaps she is disappointed in her. That's a heart-breaking realisation to have when you are young.

'There's never any money in the house because Dad spends it all. He buys skateboard stuff. That's really expensive.'

She's not wrong. Vincent went through a brief

skateboarding thing. I was horrified at what a board could cost when I found out. But I suppose it could be good core muscle exercise for a slightly older person.

'Do you ever go skateboarding with him.'

'No. Of course not.'

She pauses. I insert an 'mmm.'

In my head I'm picturing a 40-year-old man in a baseball cap at the skatepark, behaving like the oldest teenager in town. But another key to successful fostering is avoiding being too judgemental. You have to kind of train yourself not to be biased against things you find out. It's too easy to think that our way is the only way.

'But he also spends money on online games. He games against some of my friends from school. That's just freaky. They warn teenagers about too much gaming. He should be setting an example.'

Another 'mmm' from me. I wonder if their parents knew who their children were gaming with. It sounds unsavoury at best and inappropriate whatever. I'm struggling more and more with the non-judgemental thing as she talks. The idea of Luke is beginning to grate my gears.

'And they would do weird sex things. Dressing up. He was into porn.'

She says it so casually, as if porn is everyday currency for an 11-year-old.

'In fact, that's why I'm called Sparkle. I was conceived on bonfire night during the fireworks.' She spits the words out.

I do a quick calculation. That would just about work given that she shares a June birthday with me, especially if she had been born a few weeks early. No wonder she is so ambivalent about her name. Who would want to be called after the sordid sex games of their parents? And why on earth would you tell your child that? I'm glad that I'm not hearing another tale of a physical abuse, but actually, the exposure to porn and the knowledge she has about her parents' sex life is a form of sexual abuse in itself.

Sparkle goes quiet. Perhaps she's said enough for today. She has certainly given me a lot of information. It explains why she has that strange mix of being old for her years but also bizarrely childish. She has had to grow up too fast, that's for sure. And essential bits of childhood are missed when that happens.

'How's your tummy now?' I ask, changing the subject.

'All good.'

I go all the way round the next roundabout so that we are pointing in the right direction for home.

'Nearly there,' I say. But the irony of the words isn't lost on me. It sounds as if this young woman has a long way to go yet.

VIII

In spite of all my feelings about missing out on the holiday, it feels like the family are back home again in no time at all, complete with their washing and their tans. Well, the boys are tanned. Vincent and Jackson both look very healthy indeed. Jackson has inherited my olive skin so he looks brown as a berry, as if he has been in the sun for a month, not a week. I do a double-take with Lily. She actually doesn't look any different from when I waved her off a week ago. Lloyd tells me she sat on the beach in her oversized hoodie with a towel across her legs. Lloyd looks well. Not as sun-kissed as the boys but sporting a nice summer glow.

We did have three sunnyish days while they were away, and I thought I was developing a healthy colour, but seeing them makes me feel pale and pasty again. 'I need to buy some fake tan. I feel left out,' I joke. I'm still sad that I haven't been with them, but I am so happy to have them home safely and my home full again, washing and all.

Sparkle is pleased to be reunited with Lily. I'm sure she is grateful for the young company once again. They are a little awkward around each for a few minutes but that soon disappears and they fly off upstairs to do whatever pre-teenage girls do. I soon hear Yungblud playing very loudly.

Summer rolls on and somehow before I know it there are only two weeks left until they all return to school. I will have four children at the same school, which is a rarity. The other good news is that I do not have to walk any of them there or collect them now that they will all be at secondary school. Imagine their reaction if I did that. It would almost be worth it. We still have quite a bit of preparation to do. I have learnt not to buy new uniform until the last two weeks of the summer holidays. They have this tendency to grow in all the sunshine, even when that's pretty hit-and-miss as it has been this summer. But since we are nearly at the start of term again, the time has come.

I decide to take the girls into town to do their school shoe shopping. Buying online is perfectly okay for some things, but I find that I need them in front of me to buy shoes and trousers.

Even though it's still their summer holiday, apart from those few days out with Sparkle, I haven't really noticed any holiday myself because I've still been working through it. I can manage my time flexibly as a freelance writer and artist, but I can't *not* work for the duration of the summer.

I'm still catching up. I am in the middle of setting up a

national charity for girls leaving care. There is a lot of work to do and when they go back to school I need to get out and about and get networking. Currently my hands feel tied and it's a frustrating time workwise.

There is no doubt that Lily is excited about moving up to year eight. She has done well and continues to be a joy to be around. She is very entertaining, and sometimes she strikes me as eccentric, in a good way. She has a flair for both science and the arts, confirming my belief that a school student can do both, contrary to the opinion of some.

There is still a strange attitude towards learning, I have found. That you are either one or the other. That we are binary thinkers and learners, rather than able to learn across a spectrum of disciplines. I remember finding some aspects of science amazing and exciting as a child, but since I was already labelled 'arty', I was encouraged to drop the science and geography that I loved. I wonder how much better science would be if the scientist made art or music, and vice versa. I will keep reminding Lily that she can exist in both worlds and that both science and the arts can work together and complement each other. Neither has a greater value – in spite of that other popular stereotype, that studying the 'arts' is easy. Oh, I wish anyone who thought it was easy actually did it for a career. They would find out that there's nothing easy about it at all and that it requires as much skill, experience and qualification as the sciences.

Sparkle, on the other hand, I am not so sure about.

When Richard makes his next social work visit, I tell him some of my concerns.

'I'm worried about the transition to secondary school. I'm a bit sad for Sparkle, too. She doesn't seem to have made any friends that will be allies for her in Year 7.'

Unbeknownst to me, Lily is outside the door when this conversation takes place, and overhears it all. I glance up and see the shadow of her feet beneath the bottom of the door.

'Lily? Is that you?'

She has a kind soul but a nosy one, and I've no idea how long she has been there or how much she has heard. Quite a lot, it transpires.

'I've got a good idea,' she says to both of us, as if she had been part of the conversation all along. She suggests that her friend Maria comes round to meet Sparkle. 'I know they won't be in the same year,' she explains earnestly (Maria, like Lily herself, will be moving into Year 8), 'but if she knows two of us then she will have at least two allies at break time to help and protect her.'

It's quite touching really. A lovely idea. 'Yes, why not? Let's see if she's free this afternoon.'

When Maria comes round, Lily does her best to ensure that Sparkle is included. I *think* Sparkle enjoys meeting Maria. It's hard to tell with Sparkle as she is so deadpan about nearly everything. She keeps her emotions very much under control and gives nothing away.

Sparkle announces that she is going to become a vegetarian.

I learnt, long ago, never to comment on such important issues to our young people. The only way forward is to offer support. My response is to simply say, 'That's great.'

'So, I'll start from now.' she says, just as I am hovering with a serving-spoonful of (exceedingly meaty) lasagne just above her plate.

I look at the laden spoon and compare its contents with what I have prepared separately for Lily. Lily being the only vegetarian I know who hates fruit, vegetables and pulses. The spoon returns to the serving dish. I decide that I will split Lily's meal of Quorn chicken bites with Sparkle and open a tin of beans to fill up their plates. A side offering of white sliced bread will fill any further gap. (Neither girl will eat brown bread.)

Vincent turns up his nose at their white sliced bread.

'It's too processed,' he complains, before supplying a potted history of the industrialisation of grain and why we should not eat bread that does not naturally go mouldy for two weeks. Vincent has clearly been paying attention at school, with that new insight. I'm very pleased. His last parents' evening reports suggested that he had some difficulty staying focused, so this is good news.

I thank him as though we are in an HR meeting and get back to dishing up. I keep Lloyd up to speed by sending him a memo before he sits down for dinner; the memo being Vincent.

Something is lost in translation when he flies into Lloyd's study, shouting, 'Sparkle's a vegetarian. We've got another loser in the house,' before running back into the kitchen and performing some weird version of a rap dance, at the end of which he bursts out laughing.

Sparkle and Lily are decidedly unimpressed. They both have tightened lips and rolling eyes.

The mood is changed once more. This time by Jackson coming into the kitchen wanting to know what's for dinner.

'Lasagne,' I say, in my best Italian accent, elongating all the vowels. Jackson takes one of the large knives from the knife rack. Note to self: put that away, out of reach. He stabs the melon sitting innocently on the side. It was destined to become part of the pudding.

'I hate lasagne,' he fumes.

'Since when?' Lloyd and I both call out in unison, incredulous.

Just a normal dinner time in the Allen household.

I sigh. Still, at least Sparkle's vegetarianism will mean an end to the chicken tikka masala ready-meals, and that can only be a good thing. It will soon be bedtime. Of course, bedtimes have got later and later over the summer, and I have become increasingly lax about supervising that sort of thing, but as we head closer to the beginning of the autumn term I begin to wean the children off their summer holiday bedtimes by sending them up half an hour earlier each night. If I'm honest, I know that they are faffing about in their rooms until it is their old summer bedtime but at least it's a move in the right direction. Rome wasn't built in a day and nor were children's changes in bedtimes or requests to tidy their rooms.

I also start to get them up earlier in the final week so that it won't be such a shock to the system when the school run begins again. Vincent and Sparkle are the early birds. Vincent has always been like that and Sparkle is used to having to get her younger siblings up and to school, as well as 'sorting out her parents', whatever that means.

All the things she told me on our London trip stay with me and my response percolates over time. I haven't given up on the idea of meeting the grandparents, and I'm not usually averse to a trip to Wilbury Antiques for a nose around. But, if I go there now without arranging it properly, I'll feel like a stalker. And anyway, who's to say they'll be there? It could be a wasted trip. Sparkle has talked about the fact that they are retired. Perhaps that means retired from the business, too. I resolve to check with Richard whether he thinks contact with Sparkle's grandparents would be a good idea. The more I think about it, the more I think I can justify it in terms of Sparkle's wellbeing. Given that her sibling contact didn't go well, and she has had no contact whatsoever with her mum and dad, she needs some kind of family acknowledgement to avoid feeling rejected.

The whole thing has been very hard on her, I know.

Every time Vincent or Jackson say the words 'mum' or

'dad' it resonates with a kind of sadness for Sparkle and for Lily. Inadvertent reminders of what they've lost in their lives. Lily does slip up and call me 'Mum' occasionally, but she doesn't mean to. As soon as she catches herself doing it she corrects herself back to 'Louise', and manages to make it sound as if it's my fault.

There is always a loyalty to birth parents. Even birth parents who have damaged and hurt their offspring. Loyalty goes very deep indeed. Sometimes it seems unfathomable to an outsider, but much is bound up in attachment. I totally understand because I experienced it myself. I have distinct memories of being in my adoptive home and calling my adoptive mother 'mum'. But, at some point she must have decided that she'd had enough of looking after me and my adopted brother William. My file says that she invited my birth mother to stay 'in a bid for us to bond'. Those are her own words. And so, while I was in my adoptive family home, the only home I had really known, I suddenly found myself with two mothers. I didn't know how to refer to either of them. Names seemed rude, and it was all too confusing. So, I reacted by pulling out my eyelashes and my eyebrows. I had a good go at my arm hair too. I began to resemble a frog. Perhaps the most frustrating outcome of that awful experience was that both mothers decided that I was a 'disturbed' child. And neither connected my self-harming with themselves.

So, I have a personal insight as well as a professional view about attachment. And I know that it needs gentle handling. The scientists and the experts theorise about 'four types' of attachment and give them names like 'secure', 'avoidant', 'anxious' and 'disorganised'. I'm convinced that they aren't as separate and distinct as all that. Children and adults can journey through all four of these on any day, depending on how they feel, or on how others make them feel. Like all things to do with humans, it's not an exact science in my book. Children are far more astute than we often give them credit for. Often more astute than adults. They are certainly much better judges of character than most adults. It's just that our hierarchies enable adults to dominate and control children's decisions. It's a conundrum.

What I notice, as we move daily closer and closer to school, is that Sparkle seems to be becoming increasingly reluctant to engage in the whole idea. She doesn't share Lily's excitement about the start of term, but she also doesn't leave Lily alone. She has become Lily's shadow, and I detect signs that Lily would like a bit of space. Actually, those signs aren't that subtle. At one point, Lily shouts at her.

'Get lost, would you? It's like having a fucking puppy following me.'

Ah, the swearing. I've almost missed it. But I know that once they are back at school their swearing vocabularies will only expand further. Though I'm perfectly fluent in 'dockyard' myself, my own language sounds like syrup compared to what I hear when they don't know I'm listening.

They must be warming up. Doing their swearing homework in preparation for the first day. My absolute sympathy goes out to the poor teachers who need to handle it all in a professional context.

It's only a little outburst. Sparkle and Lily are friends a lot of the time, and I guess it could be argued that Lily's behaviour towards Sparkle is typical of any sibling, even within synthetic realities like our fostering family. Our beautiful blended family, that's what I tell everyone.

But, as each day goes by, Sparkle, my early riser, is lying in later and later. I am pretty sure that she is pretending to be asleep. In spite of my efforts to intervene, her room is becoming quite squalid and her mood is darkening daily. I imagine that she is setting out her stall to creep, as Shakespeare's schoolchild, like a snail unwillingly to school. But I'm beginning to feel a few concerns about her attitude.

I see trouble ahead with Sparkle.

IX

It's September 3rd. First day of the new term. First day of secondary school for Sparkle. An important time.

I can't get Sparkle out of bed.

The others are all up and dressed and, if not quite raring to go, at least looking the part. Not Sparkle. She's sparked out still. Or at least she's doing a very good job of giving that impression. I am pretty sure she's bluffing, though. Her long blonde hair hides her face. I lean into her and put my hand on her forehead. She snatches her face away and says something that sounds a bit like 'hggnnnngh'.

'Darling Sweet Pea, it's time to get up. It's a fresh start, and it's a beautiful day,' I say, unperturbed by the approximation of a growl that has just come from her. 'Lily will walk you in.'

Not a sound.

I walk over to the window and pull back the curtains, pushing open the small middle window to its full extension. It's a bit on the whiffy side in here. I guess Sparkle's body is adjusting to the new, mainly vegetable diet. I cooked the girls vegetarian chilli last night. Maybe that wasn't the best choice the day before school. Sparkle is, surprisingly, much better at being a vegetarian than Lily.

After rejecting the whole ready-meal thing, she enjoys trying out new food. Lily is her main influencer, but I'm hoping that in the realm of vegetarianism, Lily will actually be influenced by Sparkle and eat a more varied diet. I've already thought about this evening's meal: bean burgers. This is a good one because everyone loves them, even the non-vegetarians. I must add nice bread rolls onto the shopping list in the kitchen. My interior monologue races in all directions, but there's still not a thing coming from Sparkle.

Time to get the Cavalry in.

I go to the hall and call out, 'Doug! Dotty!'

The licking, kissing machines respond immediately. They know that they are not usually allowed on beds, so when I give them full permission to jump on Sparkle they can't believe their luck. Doug shoots under the duvet and starts wriggling around in the warm, farty bed as if it's heaven on earth.

'Blimey, Sparkle. You'll gas them,' I joke.

She actually laughs. She's still young enough to giggle at fart and toilet jokes. I generally only resort to this level of humour in emergency situations. I'm not one for 'potty humour' under ordinary circumstances, but the stink of Sparkle's farts has driven her out of her own bed.

I put her reluctance down to fear. It's scary starting a new school, and Sparkle struggled at primary. This is a big deal.

I remind her how wonderful and amazing she is for getting up and getting dressed.

Perhaps my positive praise goes a little over the top this morning. The other children look at me as if I have gone mad. After all, they got up and got dressed all by themselves and I didn't say a word about their achievements.

I shrug. Such is the way of a slightly-stressed foster carer who needs to get this child to her new school on day one. It would be a disaster if she didn't go in with everyone today. Tomorrow would be even harder.

'And you look great in the uniform. Suits you.'

Sparkle checks herself in the mirror, but steps away again quickly, as if she doesn't like what she sees. 'No, it doesn't.'

Lily is lovely. She helps make a big fuss of Sparkle, and checks that she has everything she needs. There is a slight hiccup as we hunt high and low for the newly-listed requirement for a 'purple biro' that is part of the school's self-assessment process. I add a few snacks for breaktime, as we have discovered in the past that in the first week back the lunch 'thumbprint technology' that enables them to purchase food isn't always working. I encourage them all to have a bigger breakfast just in case.

Even though they will all leave via the same front door and enter through the same door at school, they tend to all walk separately. Today, though, the girls walk together. Good old Lily. She understands. Oh, I so want today to go well for Sparkle. I really do.

I stand on the doorstep watching, even though they can't see me.

My heart always beats louder and harder on their first day. Inevitably, there are complex emotions attached to this time of year. They all have changes to negotiate. It's a reminder of how old they are becoming. At the same time all the vulnerability is on display. It shows how young they still are. I watch each of them until they go out of sight.

Then I leap into action. First things first, I dash up to all their rooms and take full advantage of them not being there to remove any offending objects. Access isn't so easy over the summer.

Plates, cutlery, dirty underwear, dead mice.

Yes, dead things too. Mabel, Lily's adorable little cat, is a very good hunter. Over the summer she has taken to bringing in mice, voles, pigeons and rats. At the weekend, she even progressed to a squirrel. The vegetarian girls are not impressed with Mabel's hunting skills and don't appreciate these 'gifts'. The boys, on the other hand, seem to think it is amazing and spend ages photographing the bodies to send to their friends. I'm not sure either attitude is entirely healthy.

Once the bedrooms have been made safe, I head to my studio to attend to the business of setting up my new charity. There is a lot of admin to plough through for Spark Sisterhood. Spark and Sparkle. Another little coincidence, like our shared birthdays. And actually, it's the kind of charity that Sparkle might benefit from when she's a bit older. The aim is to break negative cycles of struggle associated with the start of independent living for girls who leave the care system. They are at far greater risk of unemployment or involvement in crime than their 'sisters' who haven't been through the care system.

There is also the risk, for girls leaving care, of being groomed or exploited, as well as the increased likelihood of becoming pregnant compared to other teenage girls. So the charity is about offering friendship, guidance, mentoring and support to these girls as they leave the care system and are at their most vulnerable by finding apprenticeships, funds, life skills support, job opportunities, business start-up opportunities, education and training. All very worthwhile. But all for the long term. I have a vulnerable girl in my care right now, too.

I remind myself that I need to talk to Sparkle's social worker about contact. He's continued to maintain his regular programme of visits. I wonder if a second sibling visit should be arranged. I do worry about how little Sparkle has seen of her family. I wonder if, on this significant day of starting secondary school, some telephone chats to her parents might be in order. What parent wouldn't want to hear how her first day has gone? These things are so important. Sparkle could grow up resenting her parents if things like this are missed. We never know if a child will return home. Foster carers have always got half an eye on that as a possibility. The tenet to 'treat them as one of your own' is a bit difficult when you take that into account. I send Richard an email outlining my suggestions.

Despite the freedom of being able to work without interruption from the young people after so long, I find that I do miss them. I have to get used to school days again, too. I can tell that Lloyd is also a little unsettled. We've got the 'ants in the pants' syndrome and don't quite know what to do with ourselves. I decide to pop out to the shops to get a bag of doughnuts for when they all return, and bake some shortbread just in case they're hungry. When I'm back at my desk I see an email from Richard giving me Lois's number to give her a call later after tea. He's very efficient. When Sparkle comes home I can give her the exciting news. I'm thrilled to have this up my sleeve.

Eventually, the clock rolls around past the end of the school day. When they start to dribble back home, I can't help smiling. Not just because they are back, but because they all moan like crazy about school, even though they have clearly enjoyed themselves. This was chaos; that wasn't right; this person is annoying; that teacher hates me; all the usual joys of school.

'What did you do today?' I ask Vincent, in classic mum-fashion.

He can't remember.

I'm not convinced by any of their complaints or

nonchalance. I see nothing but happiness in all of them, including Sparkle. I'm so pleased. Things must have gone well.

I take her to one side to let her know that she can talk to her mum this evening. 'You can tell her all about your first day!'

Sparkle looks so happy. Like the child she is. Her face is still so young when she smiles, even though sometimes her demeanour can make her appear far older. I have noticed recently that her nose is becoming a bit spotty. Signs of puberty ahead. Lily has a few, too. Jackson has not had one spot appear on his face and Vincent is still clear but the girls are developing fast. I know it's a cliché but the days of childhood are so short, even though it doesn't feel like it when you're in the thick of it.

When it gets to 6.30pm, I text Lois from my phone on 'withheld number' just to let her know that we will be calling in five minutes. I want to make sure that she is ready for the conversation. I want this experience to be good for Sparkle and for her to feel safer, happier and reassured as a result of it. Regardless of what her mother may or may not have done (and I suspect the 'not have' is most appropriate in this case), she is still her mum. I don't know whether her dad will be on the call, too. Richard didn't say anything in his message, but there's no reason to think that he won't be. I assume that they are still together, and I haven't heard that there are any other plans or court cases to state that Luke isn't allowed to talk to Sparkle.

I dial the number with Sparkle sitting next to me. Her face is eager beneath the messy blonde hair. I wonder if she has put a comb through it lately, but I know it's a cultivated look. That's her style. What can I say? Sparkle is quite sensitive about her appearance, so I only say positive things.

The phone is answered within a couple of rings. 'Hello, it's Lois.' Before I have a chance to introduce myself she asks, 'Is Sparkle there?'

'Hi, Lois. Yes, she is. I'll just hand you over to her. I'm sorry, but it's a condition of the call that I have to put this on speaker. Is that OK?'

I hate sitting down and listening. It just feels invasive, but I understand why it has to be this way. On this occasion, I'm also keen to hear Sparkle's perspective on her first day.

'Yeah, no problem. Richard told me that would happen.'

I signal to Sparkle that I'm making tea and would she like one?

She nods enthusiastically and settles into the sofa with her legs under her, smiling.

'Hi, baby, you okay?' I can hear the conversation start as I go into the kitchen. Lois asks Sparkle about her day at school. 'Did you make new friends?'

'Yes, Eleanor and Alina.'

Good. That's the first time I've heard her mention anyone but Lily by name. By the time I get back, I hear her mother say, 'No, I'm not at home. I'm with Nan. I'm not well enough to go back with your dad.'

That's an interesting turn of phrase. Will she ever be well enough? How well does Lois have to be to go back to her partner? I loiter a bit by the door, so that Sparkle doesn't feel inhibited.

'How's Dad? Is he at home? Why doesn't he phone me?' Sparkle's tone is petulant.

'Well, love, since I came out of hospital I've been staying at Nan's. Your dad and I haven't seen much of each other.'

'Oh.' There is a pause. Then, with the directness of the child that she is, Sparkle asks, 'Are you splitting up, then?'

Lois sighs. 'I've met someone else.'

I feel the words like a punch. This is not what I'd expected. Why didn't Richard warn me? This has come out of the blue and won't help Sparkle at all. If I have such a visceral reaction on her behalf, how must she feel? I carry on listening.

Lois tells Sparkle about the man she has met online. He lives in America.

'Sparkle, he's all I could hope for. I really feel love for the first time.'

I instantly feel the sting of those words on Sparkle's behalf. As if Lois has not loved Sparkle or her siblings. I know it's a different kind of love, but still my hackles rise. I want to hurry this call to its conclusion and do something nice with Sparkle.

Then Lois pulls another punch.

'Dad is with someone else too. Which is why he hasn't contacted you. He's been busy with her and he's got people living in your bedroom to help pay for things because granny cut off his money.'

Wow. That's a lot for Sparkle to hear. I am furious. I turn

my back on Sparkle in the doorway and clench my teeth while counting to ten and walking towards the kitchen. I return with a great big smile on my face, holding a tub of Ben and Jerry's ice cream.

'Time to finish up now, Sparkle,' I say, with as much cheerfulness as I can muster. Though my sing-song voice sounds lame, even to me. 'Ta da! Ice cream awaits.'

Sparkle, without any preamble, cuts off her mother. 'I've got to go now, bye.' She ends the call without waiting for a reply.

My heart aches for this child. On her first day of secondary school she has had her world turned upside down. Rejection, chaos and fear. This kaleidoscope of emotions will be zooming around her head and heart. I will see that she's okay by talking her back through the call, as if I hadn't listened, in order to gauge how she heard all that awful, thoughtless, selfishly-delivered news. I know that the fallout will manifest in many different ways. These self-centred and stupid comments have been delivered without any consideration of their impact on Sparkle. A child can be hurt on levels that these stupid adults, it seems, could never imagine. Don't they care? Sometimes the parents of the children that I foster absolutely astound me. It's things like this that, for me, serve as the barometer for whether or not the parent is emotionally mature enough to look after their child.

God knows how Sparkle feels right now. I am absolutely smarting. How dare they?

X

Sparkle's mood is flat as she moves about the house for the rest of the evening, and I'm not surprised. Ben and Jerry's is no balm for what she is dealing with right now.

I pop my head into Lily's room and whisper to Lily. 'Sparkle needs cheering up. She just got off the phone to her mother and has had some unpleasant news.'

To my surprise, Lily's reaction is dismissive. 'Her mum? Oh, that old cow. She's an arsehole.'

I knew that one day back at school would be enough to turn on the swearing button. While it isn't quite the response I was expecting, it does at least tell me that the girls have been talking. Of course they have. I'm glad. It means that Sparkle isn't bottling everything up. I'm very happy that she's able to confide in Lily. That must be a positive.

She slides off the bed. 'I'll go down and talk to her.'

They go upstairs to Lily's room, and within a few minutes Nirvana is blasting *Smells Like Teen Spirit*, and the two of them can be heard screaming the lyrics at the top of their lungs.

This I can relate to. As a teenager I would often play air guitar and screech my way through rock songs in order to feel better.

Lloyd walks into the kitchen. His face is a picture. 'What's that awful noise? Shouldn't we tell them to calm it down a bit?'

I remind him that us parent folk must remember our younger selves. I have a sudden flashback to Lloyd at art school, all dressed up in his punk attire, ready to rebel against the world.

I make a face at him. 'It's therapy.' I go on to explain the contents of the phone call. He, like me, is furious.

'Email Richard straight away, and copy in our supervising social worker. Who is that at the moment?'

'We haven't got one, remember?'

'Right.'

I'll cc Lloyd in.

The next morning, Sparkle is slow to get up for day two of secondary school.

I had innocently set up yesterday's call with her mother, hoping that it would have been exactly what she needed to feel happier and help her settle in. But no, it has done the exact opposite.

'I can't be late today,' Lily says. 'I promised to meet Maria before school.'

She heads off without Sparkle.

'Okay, Sparkle, not to worry. Concentrate on getting yourself ready and I'll drop you down to school in the car today.'

If she gets herself together she still might just make it in time. I can tell, though, that she hasn't washed. There is a whiff of body odour. The poor child is going through it all right now. I wonder again if she has started her periods since the last time we spoke about it. Would she have told me? Now is not the right moment to bring that up. It's obviously not something she is keen to talk about. Somehow, I manage to coax her into her uniform and out of the house. I put my foot down and get her to the school gates, just as the last of the stragglers are going through. Phew. Mission accomplished. I don't blame Lily for heading off by herself, not wanting to be late, but I don't want mornings to be as hard as this.

I decide to head into town straight after dropping Sparkle off and do a spree in Superdrug. I get one of their black plastic baskets and load it up with sanitary towels, a nice wash bag to put them in, shampoo, conditioner, a new tangle teezer hairbrush, face wipes, deodorant, new-every-personal-hygiene-product I can think of. I throw in some Lynx for the boys and a perfume for Lily. Before they get home I put Sparkle's new items on her bed. I take a look around the room, and wonder where she keeps the other stuff that I have previously bought her. I think back to when she first arrived. I remember buying her a little welcome pack of toiletries and bits and bobs. I wonder if she has ever used them. Maybe not. I add it to my list of things to talk to her about.

I leave the Lynx on the kitchen table for the boys to take to their rooms later. Lily arrives home first and is hot and red-faced from the walk home. It is blazingly hot. Early September has mistaken itself for the height of summer.

'You could take your blazer off?' I dare to propose.

She looks at me as if I have suggested that she could take her own head off.

A couple of minutes later there is a knock at the door. It's Sparkle, also red-faced and, if I'm honest, more than a little bit stinky.

'Why don't you all have a quick shower before you change into civvies,' I say, not wishing to single her out.

Sparkle comes straight down in a thick black hoodie and black jeans, as if in defiance of the temperature. Lily jumps in the shower, and when she comes down she is looking much fresher in shorts and T-shirt, albeit also black. The boys take showers and head off to their rooms to game. An essential to take the edge off after a day's education, it seems.

The girls take a blanket and spread it out on the grass outside to lie down on. I bring them ice creams. I sit on the wooden garden bench nearby with a cold drink and take the opportunity to ask them about their day.

'I liked Textiles and History,' says Lily, 'but not Science. I hate Science.'

'Oh, really?' I joke. 'That's such a stereotypical thing for a girl to say.'

Lily sees the humour and goes on to tell me that she wants to be an engineer.

'Cool. Science would probably be useful in engineering, though.'

She frowns.

'What would you like to do, Sparkle?'

Sparkle gives what seems to me to be an unlikely answer. 'I'd like to be a hairdresser.'

I don't know what I was expecting her to say, but it wasn't 'hairdresser.' I don't know why. She doesn't seem to care that much about her appearance. She isn't one of those girls who like playing with hair and experimenting. Or if she is, perhaps I haven't noticed.

'How are those new friends of yours, Sparkle?'

'Good.' She nods, in what is an uncharacteristically enthusiastic way for Sparkle.

Later, Lily asks if Maria can come round after dinner for a few hours.

'Yes, of course.'

'And she wants to bring Groove,' she says.

I smile. 'Groove? Who's Groove?'

'Groove. She wants to bring them.'

'What?' Is that a school band? I think.

Lily rolls her eyes and repeats, 'She wants to bring them.'

'Groove? Help me out here.' I expect her to reel off a list of friends.

She sighs. 'Last year Groove was Alina but now Alina identifies as Groove and as 'them'.

'Alina? Is that Maria's older sister?'

Lily gives another sigh. A slightly less patient, huffier one this time. 'She used to be a sister but now is them. She's non-binary.'

'Oh, okay. Is her legal name still Alina?'

'Yes. For the moment. But it's a technicality. We no longer use that name. She's rejected it.' She explains it to me as if I'm the child and she is a weary adult, though I notice that Lily uses 'she' rather than 'they' in her explanation. It's going to take some getting used to for all of us.

'So her mum and dad don't know that her name has changed?'

'No, they don't. At home she is called Alina. You've met her parents. They're Catholic and wouldn't understand her new identity,' she says, adding, 'her dad would freak, actually. So would her mum, probably.'

I'm not sure of the logic here. Faith gets you some kind of pass card so that you don't have to respect someone's identity. But not being religious means that I will support the trans community?

I check again, 'So, I am to call Alina Groove?'

Lily nods.

Then I say something that sends the girls into a frenzy.

I say 'But if Groove can't tell her, sorry them, I mean, no, sorry, their parents, because of their religious beliefs, then why do I have to call her Groove?' I correct myself again. 'Sorry, call them Groove?'

Sparkle replies now. 'Because you just have to, or you're transphobic. Simple as.'

Bloody hell, this is confusing. It is anything but simple.

'Can't just Maria come round?' I joke. 'By herself? I'm much less likely to tie myself into knots.'

'That won't help you. Maria is thinking about changing her name to *Taupe*. She hasn't decided yet.'

My head is hurting. 'Taupe? Isn't that a colour?'

'Names can be colours.'

'They can, indeed,' I say. Though I can't think of any off the top of my head. Violet, Ruby, perhaps, but they're a flower and a gemstone as well. Taupe doesn't even sound 'namey' to me. 'So, is that because Maria wants to become non-binary too?'

Lily rolls her eyes again, as if I'm the stupidest person on the planet, but it's also clear that she's quite enjoying her role as fount of all non-binary knowledge. 'Not *become*, she already *is*.'

I am genuinely confused. 'If she already is, then why isn't she identifying as them rather than she?'

I'm not trying to be difficult. I want to understand.

'You can be non-binary and still use she/her pronouns.' Sparkle pretends not to be as confused as me and rolls her eyes. But I don't believe that these two quite have all the answers they think they do. All of this takes some getting used to, a few days ago, Maria was Maria. Lily was dashing off in the morning to meet Maria. Maria whom she's known since primary school as Maria. I wonder if her sister is the Alina that Sparkle has made friends with at school – although she's older than Maria, so that would be unlikely.

'Will Maria and Alina's parents have two sons instead of two daughters?'

Sparkle says 'yes' at exactly the same moment that Lily says 'no'.

Lily overrides her with a slightly warning look. '*No*. Because they are *non-binary*. And anyway, Alina is pansexual and Maria is polysexual.' She looks very pleased with herself about these additional details.

I didn't think sexuality and gender identity were linked, but Lily seems to be putting them together. Feeling somewhat like Manuel from *Fawlty Towers*, I want to say 'Que?' but stop myself. Instead I say, 'I'm going to put dinner on. I'll leave you to it.'

But I don't put dinner on straight away. I take a quick detour to my studio and google 'pansexual' and 'polysexual'.

Google tells me that: *A polysexual person is someone who is sexually and/or romantically attracted to multiple genders. It is not the same as being bisexual or pansexual, although all of these sexualities involve being attracted to more than one gender. It also is not the same as being polyamorous.*

What the hell is 'polyamorous'? My vocabulary is expanding by the second. I google and find: *Polyamorous people have multiple loving, intentional, and intimate relationships at the same time. Polyamory is a type of open or non-monogamous relationship that follows certain guidelines. Polyamory specifically refers to people who have multiple romantic relationships at the same time.*

Multiple intimate relationships? Gulp. These kids are 11 and 12. There was another word I needed to look up. What was it? I remember I said I was going to put dinner on. Pots and pans. Yes! Pansexual. Wikipedia tells me that: *Pansexuality is sexual, romantic, or emotional attraction towards people regardless of their sex or gender identity. Pansexual people may refer to themselves as gender-blind, asserting that gender and sex are not determining factors in their romantic or sexual attraction to others.*

I *think* I understand that. But it goes on: *Pansexuality may be considered a sexual orientation in its own right or a branch of bisexuality, to indicate an alternative sexual identity. Because pansexual people are open to relationships with people who do not identify as strictly men or women, and pansexuality therefore rejects the gender binary, it is considered by some to be a more inclusive term than 'bisexual'. The extent to which the term 'bisexual' is inclusive when compared with the term 'pansexual' is debated within the LGBT community, especially the bisexual community.*

Right. So now I'm confused. Are they the same with slight differences? I am in a whole new world and it's a bloody labyrinth. Research. It starts to fry my brain. I know I'm not homophobic, but when I look up 'transphobia' – that I was almost just accused of — I come across other words I haven't heard of like biphobia and acephobia. I have to be honest with myself.

My first thoughts were that these children are too young, and it's probably just a phase that they're going through because it's cool at school. But then I read about how believing this to be just a phase is dismissive and undermines someone's experiences and feelings about their own sexuality and identity. Having your feelings dismissed is upsetting. I definitely don't want to be responsible for undermining. I think I'm probably at the start of a big journey here.

After dinner, the door goes and I leave the girls to go and let in their guests. Maria and her older sister — which I mentally correct to 'Maria, possibly Taupe, and their older sibling' (I am trying), come into the kitchen. I'm so confused and scared of offending anyone that I avoid names altogether.

'Hello, nice to see you both. How are you?' I say brightly, and hope they go upstairs very quickly.

Once they have disappeared up to the bedrooms, I look at Lloyd.

'We've got a lot of research to do…'

It's Lloyd's turn to look confused. 'We?'

'Yes. *We*. Lloyd, we really need to gen up on what we can and can't say.'

'What do you mean, *can and can't say?* This is my home. I can say what I like.'

'No, you can't.' I make sure he holds my gaze. 'Not any more. You have to show respect and understanding to our trans community.'

He's not impressed. 'I'm not homophobic or anti-gay. I've never had a problem with people's sexuality. So why am I having to *gen up*, as you put it?'

I sigh. 'Lloyd, we are now in a new world. Children are choosing their sexuality and 'non-binary' and 'gender-neutral' is how we need to think.

XI

I sit in the kitchen all evening with my laptop open and printouts spread across the table. I have the Stonewall list of LGBTQ+ terms. There are fifty-two of them. I also have a big glass of wine. I'm not sure if this is helping or hindering. Lloyd is in the sitting room watching some sci-fi series, though I suspect he is actually asleep. When I look in on him and catch a glimpse of the screen, I vaguely recognise the actors in spite of their funny, latex faces. They look a bit daft to me, but Lloyd loves sci-fi. Each to his own. Actually to 'their' own. See, it is going in.

The weeks go by and I have been learning about pronouns. What different pronouns mean. It's like unlearning everything you know and starting again. Language is very powerful, so a community trying to alter language is both remarkably ambitious and brave. I shall be as supportive as I can be. But I still wonder if children should even be thinking about their sexuality at 11 years old. One mum I know told me that her eight-year-old son announced that he was bisexual. Does he know what this means? Really? And if eight years old isn't old enough to know, then when is? Children are not taught sex education until they are in Year 6. Should it be earlier? I don't know. And I'm starting to discover quite how much I don't know. I will keep researching. I'm big enough and old enough not to just jump on a bandwagon in case I look uncool. I've also learnt that if you suggest that young people are just children and that the LGBTQ+ ideology might be a bit beyond a child's remit, then you very quickly get called a 'Boomer'.

Though technically, I am Generation X. Lloyd, however, is a bona fide Boomer and when I tell him these details he rolls his eyes. In a similar way to Lily and Sparkle, now that I come to think of it. Funny, that.

A new day dawns.

It takes a good while to get Sparkle going once again. I'm finding mornings extremely hard work.

When the children come home from school, Alina-Groove (it's progress), arrives home too. No Maria, just Groove – who is up in Lily's room with Sparkle. I feel a little odd about this and I try to keep myself in check. It's the age difference, rather than Groove's non-binary status that's bothering me. In terms of looks, they have changed a great deal of late, and they are now fairly androgynous. I do remember Maria and Alina from primary school days. They looked like 'regular' girls back then. I remember too, how Lily refused to wear the green gingham summer dresses that the sisters wore. I recall Lily's red, sweaty face on a hot summer's day, and remember remarking to her how cool and fresh the sisters looked because they were wearing their dresses.

I have no bad memories of them at all. But it was Maria I knew better because she was the same age as Lily. And now I feel ill at ease. Sparkle is younger and Groove is older. I don't know the physical details, but in some way, Groove is a little more male now – at least according to Lily and Sparkle. But perhaps I have that wrong. It's very confusing indeed. But I am bothered that Groove is two years above Lily, and three years above Sparkle. It doesn't seem right somehow. And is this friendship, or has their friendship been sexualised. I'm not comfortable with any of it. It feels inappropriate.

This is ridiculous.

They are just kids, I tell myself. And I'm being old-fashioned. Or am I? The over-sexualisation through references to genitalia that they have put in my mind, and have been so keen to put forward as part of the message they are sending, has tainted this new little friendship group. Would I be happy if this was a teenage boy, upstairs in the bedroom with much younger 'girl' friends? No, I wouldn't. I would consider that odd. More than odd. I would be worried about coercion. And influences that the younger child isn't ready for. So, in spite of all my research and determination to support, I'm concerned.

I head upstairs to see what they're all up to. I need to

know before I start cooking if anyone is staying for dinner, and where the boys are. To my disapproval, Lily's bedroom door is closed. This is an absolute fostering no-no, and she knows it. If there are other people in her bedroom she knows that the door must be open, even if it is only a little. Sparkle knows this, too. We have been very clear about it. It's non-negotiable. When they are together they leave the door slightly open, and it doesn't matter which room they are in, the rule applies. I'm trying very hard to be patient, but all of this is unsettling me.

Is it Groove? Why have the girls shut the bedroom door despite knowing the rules? They wouldn't do that normally. Is Groove somehow controlling them? After all, he-she is older. And, being older, Groove carries greater influence.

I know that I am not allowed to say 'he-she'; that's just my own personal confusion. When I think about the sentence in my head, I don't know whether to say they 'is' older, or they 'are' older? I settle for he-she to make a kind of private sense of the non-binary. According to what I've been reading, I know that I am in breach of the (new) rules, and misgendering Groove.

It's weird, but after looking at Stonewall I feel that I somehow am not allowed to have any personal opinions or emotions about this. I just have to accept their rules. I'm not sure at all. I'm very up on the legal side of things from a fostering perspective. I know that following the passing of the Children and Social Work Act 2017, all secondary schools in England were required to teach Relationships and Sex Education. Primary schools, too, were required to teach relationships education as of September 2020. This is most certainly good news, and all the older children have benefitted from this. As a result of it, we managed to carry on the school conversations at home, and I love that the boys, especially, feel comfortable enough to talk about sex and relationships.

I have raised my sons as feminists to respect girls and women in all aspects of their lives. They know the statistics. They know that one in four women experience domestic abuse and that one in nine girls under the age of consent experience sexual abuse. The boys know that it isn't appropriate to be sexual around girls and that they must never touch a girl without consent. I was thrilled that they were teaching the meaning of consent in Year 6. I remember taking Lily out for lunch and talking to her about ownership of her own body and how consent works. I showed them that wonderful animation *Tea and Consent* that instead of talking about sex uses a cup of tea. It's brilliant, and the children get it immediately.

I must show it to Sparkle and make sure that she is up to speed on this, too. With the interruptions to her schooling she may have missed out on some of this stuff and, as a child in care, is particularly vulnerable.

I decide to go back upstairs and take control. I shall knock on the door and go in. This is my house, after all, and I am responsible for Sparkle and Lily.

I knock first, and as I start to open the door I meet with unexpected resistance. The door won't open. One of them is sitting on the floor with their back against it. My hackles are rising, but I remain outwardly calm.

'Hello,' I say, feeling a little foolish. 'It's dinner time soon. Is Groove wanting some dinner?' I ask.

The door is pushed shut and I hear Sparkle's voice, 'No.'

This is quickly followed up by Groove, 'No, thanks.'

'Right.'

Why is this so tricky? I feel uncomfortable. Why do I feel so uncomfortable? I am an experienced foster carer. That experience has taught me two things (well, a few more than two, but two important things that outdo all the others): the first is, 'don't panic' and the second is, 'plan for the worst, then whatever happens will seem better'.

So, I will not panic or get cross. If I plan for the worst, I imagine that some form of sexual impropriety is going on in this house. At the same time I know that I'm being weirdly biased, and my reaction is inappropriate. As I keep reminding myself, they're just kids!

Shortly after, Groove slips out of the house without me seeing. A few minutes later the girls are back in Sparkle's room. The door is open, and they are smiling sweetly, as if everything is perfectly normal. They both try to look like butter wouldn't melt in their mouths, but I know that they're up to something.

Throughout the whole of our evening meal the girls appear to be in solidarity on just about everything from passing the ketchup to views on meat eaters. Of course, this includes the boys, who are total carnivores, but Sparkle and Lily decide that their food choices make them 'murderers' and 'misogynists'. I'm not sure how the latter connects to meat eating, nor am I entirely convinced that either of the girls are fully aware of what the term means.

Nevertheless, Sparkle in particular seems to be carrying an inordinate amount of anger for the boys and Lloyd.

'It's Boomer-men who are basically to blame for everything that's wrong in the world,' Sparkle explains. 'Especially the white male supremacists, like you,' she says, directing her charge against Lloyd.

Again, I am not convinced that the girls really know what all these words actually mean, but even so, both are quite aggressive in the pronouncement of this new ideology.

I attempt to calm things down a few times by saying things like, 'that will do' and, 'not at the table, thank you'.

The third time I try to intervene, to my horror, Lily cries out, 'You're even worse. You're so weak!'

Well, that's a new one on me. I have been called many things in my time, but I don't think I've ever been described as weak before. Usually, I'm accused of being strong, sometimes of being 'too strong' and regularly criticised for 'saying it as it is.' She's not entirely wrong, though. I felt weak upstairs just now.

Jackson, who so far has not engaged, says, 'Chill, Sister.'

With that, Sparkle stands up and walks out of the kitchen leaving the food on her plate half-eaten.

There is a moment's pause and then we all look at each other as if our home has been invaded by aliens. Which is actually not far away from how this feels.

I try to read Lily's face. Something is not right. I don't know where all this is coming from. Lily is more than capable of getting worked up about things and she can certainly have her moments, but this doesn't feel like her.

She catches me observing her and blushes, then stands up, pushes her plate away and walks out too. I follow after her and call up the stairs, 'Stay in your own room, please. That's enough for tonight.'

In reply, both their bedroom doors slam in unison.

Back in the kitchen I look at Jackson and Vincent and try to play down what's just happened.

'Hormones, eh?' I say. 'They're at that age.'

'I don't think so, Mum,' says Vincent.

Jackson also shakes his head.

'It's not hormones,' Vincent continues. 'They're hanging out with the LGBT lot. Both of them.'

'What do you mean?'

'They're not the nice LGBT ones. They're mostly Emos.' Vincent seems quite upset. 'It's a load of kids that don't fit in and they bully others.'

Wow. Normally it's the 'popular' kids, or their hanging-on wannabes accused of bullying, not the sensitive ones.

Jackson names a few children that I knew from primary school who are in the LGBT 'gang'. I am surprised by a few and not by others.

'Yes, I knew they were gay years ago. Using my ex-fashion industry gaydar,' I nod.

'You can't say any of that, Mum,' Vincent says.

And he's right. Oh, my. I'm feeling like I've transformed into some sort of Alf Garnett figure. They'll be accusing me of being racist next. Life has become very complicated and all that we are and identify as is spread across a spectrum, as if it can be measured. I feel very old right now. Very out of touch.

'The school has set up an organised LGBTQ+ lunchtime group for students in all year groups,' Jackson explains.

'Well, that's great that the school is supporting and recognising students who identify as LGBTQ+.'

'Yeah, but some of the kids are trying to set up an alternative group.'

'An alternative alternative group?'

'Yeah. I dunno.'

The conversation moves on. Jackson tells me about two of his childhood friends, two boys. 'Archie and Daniel started going out with each other.'

'What does that look like for two school boys?'

'They walked around the field at lunchtime and held hands for a few minutes.' He pauses. 'Then they decided that they weren't gay and went back to being friends.'

Lloyd gives a dismissive shake of the head. I shoot him a warning look.

'And have you tried any LGBTQ+ identities?' I ask Jackson.

He laughs. 'No, not yet, Mum. I'm still trying to work out who I am.'

Good for you, my wise boy, I think.

I'm well aware of the importance of sex education and its role in promoting healthy, respectful relationships, as well as championing consent. I'm all for teaching about contraception and reducing teenage pregnancy. I'm also committed to an approach that includes understanding and accepting orientation and gender and I know that it's quite healthy to explore sexual identities, but I can't help feeling that it's too early for Sparkle and Lily to be expected to investigate their own sexual orientation so closely, in what I hope will be several years before they start having sex. Childhood is a right, a human right. To be burdened with sexualised thoughts so young feels too much. Especially when I look after children who have been sexually abused. Too often that happens because in our society some adults, or older children as it was in my case, exploit their power over children's innocence. It's an abuse of power. That's what abuse is.

I don't know where to stand, or what to think. The dominance of LGBTQ+ in children's lives is starting to feel invasive. In this household, anyway. I'm sure this can't be what the school intends.

XII

At breakfast, and after even more reading online, I attempt to start up another conversation.

'I'm so pleased that the school has set up the LGBTQ+ group. Vincent and Jackson were telling me about it last night. It sounds like just what is needed at school.'

Lily smiles, 'Maria really likes it.'

I note that Maria is still being called Maria, and not Taupe, but choose not to ask further. No doubt these things take time to fully consider and establish.

Sparkle, on the other hand, only has negative things to say about the school group.

'Bunch of losers. It's being run by Mr Simmons, who is so straight it hurts, and Miss Everett who is also straight. Maybe we could turn them?'

Yet again, I find the whole conversation mind-boggling. Why would a teacher need to declare if he or she, or 'they' were gay? Why should their sexuality be a topic of discussion for Key Stage 3 students like Lily and Sparkle. Maybe we could turn them? She's 11!

'None of them are non-binary or gender-neutral.' Sparkle is positively acidic about it all.

'So does that mean you won't go along?' I ask.

She ignores my question.

'By the way, I would now like my pronouns to be 'they/them,' she announces.

'Me too,' says Lily, through a mouthful of cereal.

Lily goes on to explain that she now identifies as 'questioning' but is probably pangender, whereas Sparkle is pansexual but feels more MASC.

Okay, my head is spinning once more. Too many unfamiliar terms. I need the aid of Google once again, and it's far too early for all this. More coffee needs to be consumed before I can get my head around it all.

For now, I say, 'Okay, that's lovely. I am thrilled for you both,' which even to my ears sounds sarcastic, but the day is already running away with me and I need to catch up with everything that's just been said.

The truth is, I'm not sure what to make of any of this. I'm concerned by some of the language that Sparkle has just used in relation to the teachers. And by the rejection of a group that has evidently been set up by the school and intended to be supportive of students who might be 'questioning'.

My overriding feeling is that somehow I've been

manoeuvred into a position where as a woman, and as an adult, I can't say anything. I have to go along with it.

When the girls – no sorry, make that when the thems – wait a minute, that doesn't work either. When the theys – no. I can't even construct sentences now. This is messing with all that I know of the English language. Is it when them? Does that work? But I call a singular them now too - how do I differentiate?

My head is fried before I've got to the end of my thought. I shoo them out of the door to school and go into Lloyd's studio. I deposit a cup of coffee on his desk.

'Trust me, you're going to need that.'

I use his computer to search up the new words 'MASC' and 'questioning', and to remind myself of the difference between 'pansexual' and 'pangender'.

I type the words into Google and explain what I'm doing to a still-bemused Lloyd.

He raises his eyebrow. 'Why can't they just be them?'

I laugh, partly because I've just been grappling with they and them, but also because I know what he is really trying to say: 'Why can't they be themselves?'

I laugh and say, 'They want to be them?'

I sound like I'm in a farce on stage. The pronoun war has changed how we think about all of this.

'So, Pangender. Exhibiting characteristics of multiple genders; deliberately refuting the concept of only two genders,' I read from the screen. 'And you need to understand this because, according to Sparkle, this is now what Lily identifies as.'

Lloyd is open-mouthed in astonishment.

'Wait though. Lily is also currently identifying as questioning.' I read out the definition. 'Questioning refers to individuals who are in the process of examining their sexual orientation and/or gender identity.'

Lloyd looks as though he is in a state of shock.

'There's more.'

Lloyd's expression suggests that he isn't capable of taking much more, but I plough on. 'Sparkle is identifying as Pansexual in terms of her – their – sexual orientation. Which means A person who is emotionally, romantically, sexually, affectionately, or relationally attracted to people regardless of their gender identity or sex assigned at birth. Use of the term often signals a repudiation of the concept of binary sexes.'

Lloyd is still saying nothing at all; he just looks confused.

'So, it turns out that Sparkle also feels that she is actually a MASC. This is-' I pause to tap the letters into the search bar. 'A term referring to the broad, dynamic representations of masculinity or masculine characteristics regardless of gender. MASCS claim a relationship to masculinity without, necessarily, claiming a relationship to manhood.'

Lloyd creases his brow, a sure sign that he is concentrating. 'So, a butch lesbian in old money, then?'

'I don't know. But I'm guessing that you're probably not allowed to say butch lesbian these days.'

'What would Nik and Lou make of that?'

We used to hang out with two 'butch lesbian' punks when we were at art school. They introduced us to a nightclub in town called Martha's. I loved going to Martha's. Everyone would dance and have a complete laugh, regardless of sexuality. Gay, lesbian and bi-sexual, and people like me and Lloyd who are, I suppose, heterosexual. We all just had fun together. Nothing untoward. Well, not really. And I don't remember being that concerned about everyone's sexuality.

This generation describes their sexuality like trainspotters. I hear the word 'fluid' and yet it seems to me so rigid and labelled.

Lloyd is the sort of person who is so laid back he has never expressed a negative thought to anyone or group. But now he is totally stumped. The burden of having to know the 'correct' response, rather than taking people for who they are, is weighing heavily.

He goes so long without speaking that I feel I have to change the subject. 'Is it lunchtime yet?' I know that it isn't, but I feel like it will be far easier to talk about food. We're on safer ground with that.

Lloyd ignores the question. 'So, Louise. Ummm. I've been waiting for the right moment. I don't quite know how to say this, but I think it's important that you know I now identify as questioning.'

I throw him a look and say, 'In that case you'll have what you're given!'

I head to my own studio, but don't have a productive day. Thoughts go round in circles. I can't lose myself in anything artistic, or even anything mundane and administrative, because I'm wrestling with all the billions of questions, and worries, that I have.

There are no visitors after school, but I'm still too distracted to cook. Takeaway fish and chips it is. I call the boys and the 'thems' down for dinner. I open the chip paper and identify each meal, 'Sparkle this is yours: pea fritter and chips; Lily this is you: fish bites and chips with curry sauce.' As I say it I think how weird life has become. I could be saying, 'Sparkle this is yours: pansexual with MASC; Lily you are questioning with pangender and curry sauce.' The trouble is, I'm not sure gender and sexuality are quite the pick-and-choose menu that Sparkle seems to think they are.

The boys are still straightforward 'Fish'n'Chips'. For now.

To start with, the meal seems quite civilised. Lloyd and I are very hungry. In spite of my earlier question about lunch, I don't remember stopping for a break. Lloyd has been working on designing my new website, and I've done my best to supply some content for the website, in spite of my preoccupations. Then, at some point, I notice that Sparkle has cut one side of her hair off. Actually, it's Vincent who spots it first.

'Aah ha! What have you done to your hair? You look like you've got a mullet.'

Sparkle is straight back with a litany of personal attacks on Vincent. He looks gay. He is repressed. He's ugly. He's this, he's that.

I'm all for 'them' standing 'their' ground but this is a nasty attack that is full of expletives. Also, should she be challenging his sexuality in calling him 'gay'?

Vincent begins to defend himself, calling Sparkle a 'Femm Nazi'.

Jackson joins in. 'You're trying to be cool but you're not. You're a saddo.'

Sparkle retaliates. 'You're all fucking racists.'

Delightful. The chair is scraped across the floor and slammed against the table. Sparkle storms out of the kitchen. Lily takes a small handful of chips and scurries out too.

'Sparkle was hanging out with Alina and her loser crew at school again,' Vincent says, by way of explanation.

The boys are fuming. Though not enough to stop them from eating their leftover chips.

Lloyd looks up and says. 'I'm a racist now, am I?' He is not happy at all.

I tiptoe around them all through the evening. I encourage them to occupy themselves in their own rooms after dinner. The thing is, if you have to tiptoe around people, then you're with the wrong people. This is my home. I'm not very good at tiptoeing around in it.

I feel very stressed and edgy. Each mealtime turns into a war zone. Sparkle troubles me more and more. She seems to be heavily influenced and, according to the boys, it's by some older students at school. I recall how quickly Sparkle switched to becoming vegetarian under the influence of Lily. She seems to have that easily-persuaded kind of personality. The boys also explain to me that these older ones aren't part of the official school LGBTQ+ group; it's a little breakaway faction who are critical of the school group and do their own thing. Their own thing, the way it is being described, seems subversive: being critical of the teachers and perhaps picking out vulnerable individuals like Sparkle.

I am beginning to feel like Sparkle is not the kind of 'them' I really want around Lily. This is not really Lily. I had not noticed that she was 'questioning' or 'pangender' previously. Certainly, there were no obvious signs. In fact the way she would make herself noticeable when the boys' friends came round was by screaming and engaging in what I can only describe as 'awkward flirting'. That's a point, now that I think about it. None of the boys' friends have been around for ages. That isn't normal behaviour, especially not at the start of term. Perhaps they're too scared. As ever, I have to think about balancing the needs of all family members. Time to talk to Richard, and to Lily's social worker.

Something is going to have to give here.

XIII

I log my observations with Lily's social worker. She emails back with a comment: *interesting times*. Aren't they just? I feel a little reassured.

Richard is helpful too, in a more practical way, when I call him.

'How about I take Sparkle out for a coffee or caramel latte in that new coffee shop?'

I think that it would be good for her to speak to someone else properly about all this. The way things are at home, it's actually difficult to talk. Lily and Sparkle aren't interested in conversation, only in getting their side across in an aggressive and sneering way, dismissing everyone else's feelings. External influence will be valuable here.

Richard also suggests that I educate the family on what being in the LGBTQ+ community means to the girls. Those are his words, not mine, so I have great pleasure in pointing out that he can't really say girls. He agrees and revises his description to them. I hear him struggle which confirms that it isn't just me. It isn't as easy as one might think to make the instant switch. Our brains are hardwired to use language in a certain way.

'By the way, I haven't kept you up to date. I meant to tell you a while ago that the siblings, Cormac and Cahira, have gone to another placement and are doing very well.'

I wonder why they moved? The way Sparkle told it, their placement was perfect.

Richard explains, 'The other foster carers struggled with some of their behaviours. Because there were three other foster children in placement it became a bit unmanageable.'

You don't say! That's hardly rocket science is it? Five looked-after children, all with differing needs and experiences, pulling in all directions. I'm finding it hard with *just* the two foster children and two birth children. I don't say all this out loud though, just, 'I see.'

He goes on, offering more surprising detail. 'It was a second marriage for both the foster parents and between them they had another five older children, which was also complicating things.'

I puff out a deep breath just at the thought of it.

What a household. How was it even allowed?

But I know the answer to my own question without Richard having to explain it. Matching isn't so easy when the country is in the midst of extreme shortages of foster carers. Roughly 10,000 short, in fact. So, blind eyes and all that.

You can see how it happens. The foster family were probably bringing home about £2,500 a week in allowances. And the independent fostering agency, before paying their carers, would have been netting approximately £12,000 per week. If only this sort of money was rolling around in the state system. The local authorities struggle to recruit and retain foster carers because they are so stretched with resources and money. Their social workers can have caseloads of 30+ children.

Knowing the complexity of the individuals who are likely to be in care, this caseload figure seems insane. No wonder so many social workers and associated staff are off on sick leave. And, as with most private sector initiatives, the independent fostering agencies tend to look after their staff more, being better placed financially to do so. Most social workers I know who work for the independents have case loads of 12 children.

'The siblings have now been placed with a couple called Tristan and Bart who live in another county, so they have a new social worker, but as they have no other children to look after they can better concentrate on the two.'

I think about this for a minute, knowing only too well how busy Richard is.

'What is the possibility of me going to them directly and arranging contact for Sparkle with her younger brother and sister?'

He pauses long enough for me to suspect that he might say no.

I jump in with some persuasive arguments. 'You know

it's well overdue. She hasn't seen them since shortly after she first arrived with us, and that's-' I do a quick calculation. 'That's four months ago.'

'I do know that-'

'Right. And Sparkle, after a brilliant start here, is spiralling out of control. Or at least that's what it feels like. Maybe part of that is because she hasn't got the anchor of her family any more.'

Whatever anchor that family actually provided. The last time she spoke to her mother was on the first day of school, more than two weeks ago. I remind Richard about how badly that went. 'What do you think that must have felt like for Sparkle?'

'Um, yes-'

I like Richard a great deal, but I know a distracted person when I hear one, and I can hear other texts buzzing on his phone while he's talking to me.

'Look. How many children have you got on your caseload?'

He lets out a short, rueful laugh. 'Thirty six.' He also shares with me that his managers are having to take on case work directly, despite them previously being protected from it so that they could do the job they are paid to do and be managers.

I sense the patterns and echoes with Sparkle herself here. The local authority also has spiralling needs and requires an anchor.

'I'm not being critical and I'm not trying to do your job

for you. I'm not questioning your professionalism, or trying to take over. I'm trying to work with you in the best interests of Sparkle.'

Richard gives me Tristan and Bart's number.

I head back to the kitchen to make a cup of tea, only just remembering to call out to Lloyd as I fill my cup with water. Sometimes I forget he's in his office if he's quiet. I hear a preoccupied, 'Yes please' from down the hallway. As I deliver his brew and tell him of my plans, he's in agreement that it could help Sparkle. 'Something needs to help her. I'm getting pretty fed-up with meal time war zones of conflicting gender identities. Why can't children just be left alone to be children without all this stuff!'

I give him an exasperated look and remind him that attitude isn't helpful.

Back in my office I reach for my phone, feeling rather grumpy. Lloyd has spoken to me as if somehow this is all my fault. He needs to share some of the responsibility. He can't just be the ostrich with his head in the sand. Though that option is pretty appealing to me, too.

I dial the number that Richard gave me, my fingers tapping with some ferocity. Within a split second, however, I'm smiling because of the warm friendly voice that greets me on the other end when I introduce myself and explain why I'm contacting them.

'Louise! So good of you to call! Bart's right here. I'll put you on loudspeaker.'

I quickly sense that I'm going to rather like Tristan and Bart. They are my favourite kind of people: fun, open, friendly and so kind. They offer to drive here and bring a picnic with them so that I don't have to cater. It's a generous offer, but I insist that I bring Sparkle to them. Partly because I really need a day away from the ferocity of gender identity war, but I also want some alone time with Sparkle to gauge where she's at right now. We haven't spent time alone together since the others came back from their holiday.

I'm on an information-gathering mission too. I want to tease out more detail about her LGBTQ+ friends. If my hunch is right, that some of this militancy is posturing and parroting things she's heard said by older children, we might be able to unpick more about how she is actually feeling. I will save all the difficult stuff for the way home. I don't want to overburden her before the visit.

It's a two and a half hour drive to Tristan and Bart's house and, my word, what a house it is. It's beautiful. We park the car on the street, then realise, as we walk towards the front door, that we could have parked in their massive car park just to the side of their majestic mansion.

I knock at the front door, admiring the pale teal shade they have chosen to paint it. It looks great next to the pink sedums growing alongside.

Within a few seconds I hear the barking of little dogs. A familiar sound that is a kind of music to my ears. The door is opened by a golden-tanned, handsome man. I think I detect a residue of a Scandinavian accent when he welcomes us in.

'It's so lovely to meet you, Sparkle,' he says, greeting her first, before me. 'Come on in. You must be Louise. I'm Bart.'

He gestures for us to come inside, with Sparkle to lead the way.

'Your brother and sister never stop talking about you.'

I note the insecurity and anxiety fixed into her stern face almost melt away at his words. We walk along a beautiful stone hallway. The house looks like a Farrow & Ball paint catalogue. It's stunning. I smell good coffee and something baking. From the kitchen steps another very handsome man. He wears a green and cream striped apron with leather straps. I've seen these in my mother-in-law's gardening magazines. He wipes flour from his hand onto the apron before he holds it out to shake mine.

'I'm Tristan. How lovely to meet you! Hello Sparkle. We hear nothing but *Sparkle, Sparkle, Sparkle* from your brother and sister.'

Again, I feel her transform, carrying herself a little straighter, as though his words are lifting her up.

The kitchen is painted black. Big copper lights hang from the ceiling and there are plants everywhere. I'm also pleased to see art on the walls. There is a large, old table, not dissimilar to mine, with six chairs around it, but the space is dominated by a kitchen island that looks like it's made from smooth concrete. The massive bi-fold doors are open, and look out onto the most spectacular garden.

I can't resist. I edge towards the garden. 'Wow!'

Bart follows me outside while Tristan chats to Sparkle. I hear the sound of excited children running into the kitchen from inside the house.

I take in as much as I can of the garden and then look towards the children. I watch Sparkle carefully. She bends down and Cormac and Cahira throw their arms around her so that all three have a massive hug.

Tristan gives me a wink and attempts to fit far too many homemade muffins onto a plate. He places them onto the big table. The sun pours into the huge kitchen and the black walls look sparkly and magical. I wonder to myself if I could persuade Lloyd to paint our kitchen black. It's at the back of our house so may be too dark.

I sit down and enjoy an excellent cup of coffee with my muffin while I learn about Bart and Tristan.

Bart is a landscape gardener. I knew that one of them must be. Oh, we have much to discuss! Tristan used to be a banker. They gave up city life in London and moved to this amazing house eight years ago. Tristan makes handmade soap.

That's why the house smells so good! Oh my word, I think I want them to foster me, too.

Cormac and Cahira are desperate to show Sparkle their rooms and give them a tour of their home. The children are followed by two Yorkshire Terriers called Dib and Dob. They are a hilarious pair.

Bart sits at the table and pours more coffee. I find myself unable to refuse another muffin. Tristan gently closes the kitchen door. He tells me a bit about the children and about their new social worker. We talk about how crazy the caseloads are for social workers. Tristan's youngest sister is a social worker in Croydon, and one of the reasons that Bart and Tristan became interested in fostering.

'But sadly, she's now on long term sick leave,' Bart explains, putting a consoling arm around Tristan.

'I doubt she'll go back,' Tristan says. 'She's burnt out and is back home with our mum.'

An all-too-familiar tale.

The new social worker, Penny, is from Eastern Europe.

'She has a much more direct approach,' Bart says. 'She tells us things and we are grateful because it helps explain the children's behaviour, which can be rather challenging and a bit odd at times.'

I nod.

'Very sexualised behaviour. Which is hardly surprising under the circumstances.'

'But we feel that they are making progress. And it helps that we know what we are dealing with,' Bart adds.

I am desperate to hear more, but the children choose this moment to burst in, making quite the posse with the dogs in tow. My natural curiosity can't bear to wait politely. I need to know what 'the circumstances' are. Bart and Tristan, though, are clearly my kind of people.

'Now, Cormac. Why don't you show your big sister the playhouse? And then onto the meadow. I bet she'd like to see the big swing.'

Sparkle nods and Cormac takes her hand, proudly leading them off away from the house. Cahira grabs Sparkle's other hand.

The coast is clear and we carry on talking. Tristan tells me about the sex parties, and that Luke likes 'unusual sex'.

Bart does a cringe face and shoulder movement that makes me smile.

'Have you met him?' I ask.

They have, and talk me through a difficult contact visit.

'He turned up with this young girl who looked just like the mother, Lois, but a younger version.'

Tristan is definitely the bigger gossip of the two.

'Luke has a *big* drug problem.' He mimes snorting a line of cocaine.

'Now Tristan, you don't know that for sure,' Bart admonishes him.

'Well, that's reading between the lines,' Tristan concedes, emphasising the word 'lines' and touching his nose again. 'Lois was subservient to him. Completely controlled by him, or at least she was until she went to the hospital. Now apparently, her care plan is to have nothing to do with him.'

'Well that's the best approach to any abuser, narcissist and bully,' I say. 'To keep away from them.'

I share with them some of what's been happening at my house. 'If I'm honest, I don't mind admitting that I'm struggling to understand and keep up with it all.'

They nod in agreement. 'Of course we always want to support the LGBT movement, but it can be a little hostile,' Tristan says.

'My family lived in Paris for a while, so I grew up speaking some French. It wasn't until I left to come to England to study that I felt liberated,' Bart says.

I make a rather crass assumption that perhaps his family may not have been supportive of his being gay, but no.

Bart explains, 'I was finally free from describing furniture: chairs and tables as male or female.'

He laughs. 'Pronouns have made a muddle in our lives too.'

I find this interesting.

'Look, being gay is *our* business,' Tristan says. 'Nobody else's.'

'As gay men, declaring our gender pronouns feels somewhat-' Bart gropes for the right word, 'invasive.'

'We want privacy and choice. The choice to be ourselves.'

'Take our supervising social worker, for example,' Bart says.

'Show off!' I joke, and explain that I don't even *have* a supervising social worker at the moment.

'Well, think yourself lucky,' says Tristan. 'Ours is an agency supervising social worker who specialises in being a judgy religious sort.'

'Her name's Judy,' Bart adds.

'And frankly, as far as we're concerned, Judy is homophobic. The woman can't get out of here fast enough when she visits. We didn't realise when we joined this agency that it was a devout Christian organisation.'

'We certainly haven't met any other gay foster carers on their books,' says Bart.

'I suspect that we're only tolerated because we take challenging children and have money.'

'We feel trapped, actually, and we're looking elsewhere.'

'Aren't we all?' I smile.

I'm so glad that we are able to talk about all of this. I feel as if I've found some allies. 'So, is it okay if I bounce a few ideas and thoughts off you as we move forward?' I ask.

'Oh yes. We're more than happy to work with you. Always happy to share ideas,' Bart says.

'Shall we keep the social workers on a need to know basis?' Tristan says, with another wink.

'Absolutely.'

Sparkle and I stay for a lunch of homemade pizza, cooked on stone in the oven outside, served with a fresh herb salad, all grown in Bart's wonderful garden. All too soon it is time to say goodbye. But it's a sweet sorrow. Sparkle is warm and sparkly and seems so much happier for seeing Cahira and Cormac. Not like last time when the response was more nuanced.

On the way home we talk about how good it has been, and when the next visit will be. I apologise for the delay in getting Sparkle together again with their siblings. 'It was partly to do with them leaving the other placement and having to find a new one,' I say, rather lamely. Privately I think that Richard could have told me so that I could have given her, sorry *them*, an explanation. That may have helped them through the last few months.

I manage to get a little information from them about Groove.

'How often do you hang out together?' I ask, as gently as I can.

A group of them, comprising Sparkle and a few year 10s and 11s, hang out at lunchtime and talk to each other in the evenings on their phones. Of course they do. They are teenagers, after all. But a bit of me is not happy at all about the age differences. Sparkle is four school years below.

We arrive home with Sparkle in what is now uncharacteristically good cheer. But my own good cheer is vandalised in seconds when Lloyd shows me the email we've received from Richard while I've been out. He wants us to attend therapeutic training to work with LGBT children.

'It's for four sessions, each of which is a day long. We both have to go.'

'What?'

I don't need to see the look on Lloyd's face to know that he is deeply unimpressed. The two of us losing four days of work each is catastrophic.

'Why do we have to do this?'

'It's to help us understand and support Sparkle and Lily. It's a new training programme that the council have paid into, apparently.'

'Due to the *massive* numbers of young people reporting that they are LGBTQ+.' His emphasis is sarcastic.

I want to be supportive and do the right thing. I know that trans-gender issues have always been there, but have been buried or unacknowledged. But, I feel like I'm under scrutiny again. An overburdened student about to be tested by intrusive examiners. I mull over the conversation I've just had with Sparkle about her friends. Should I call Maria's sibling Groove, even if her own parents don't? I've known them since they were tiny as 'Alina'.

I detect a little seed of rebellion growing in me.

XIV

After a night's disturbed sleep, I'm still fuming about the imposition of four days of training. Why do I need to go through this? Why four whole days? After all my independent research (I dread to think of the hours already spent), a one-day event must be enough to deliver the key bits of information that we need to hear. Surely?

I think about what I could get out of four days spent doing an art course of my choosing, and when I might ever have the luxury to do that. Then I think back to the course we had to do in order to become foster carers in the first place. That was three days. *Three days*. In total. So why would it take four days to understand the principles of LGBTQ+? This can't be an efficient way to allocate funding in an already overstretched sector.

As a cynical ex-educationist, where one of my roles was being the author of new courses at the university, I have an answer. I am well aware that the organisation delivering the programme would be charging significant fees. They would be financially better off if they ran a four-day programme rather than a one-day event.

'It's not happening,' I declare, first thing in the morning. 'I'm not doing it.'

'Well, not yet, you're not,' says Lloyd. 'We don't have an actual date. They need enough people to sign up to all four days before it can take place.'

'Which they won't get. There's a serious flaw in this thinking. Foster carers usually have jobs and we both know that an employer isn't likely to let their staff off for four days LGBTQ+ training. I bet it won't happen anytime soon.'

'So we're off the hook?'

'For now.'

I'm a researcher by nature, qualification and career, so a dig into the culture, history and law is something I will do for myself, regardless of the requirement for four days of training sessions.

Not least because I'm still confused by much of what I see here. I have enthusiasm for the changes that society needs to make in terms of attitudes towards gender and sexuality. I also have my doubts. I *always* want to support the young people I look after, but I also need to know what the 'rules' are, because anything that has that many labels must be bound by a fairly rigid ethics code, which will translate into codes of conduct for us and them. I hate saying that: *us and them*, but that's what it feels like. There is an element of aggression in amongst

149

all of this that I am struggling with, alongside what feels like counterintuitive elements. We have been set a hard task in having to re-learn our language, and if we make mistakes the punishment is harsh. So far, if any of us forget to use the correct pronoun, we are belittled and shouted at. That can't be right. Especially when we're trying to do the right thing. As an educator, this seems not only unreasonable, but illogical and counterproductive. The most successful teaching and learning outcomes arise from clarity, support and kindness. I'm not getting any of that. Oh, and let's not forget the biggy: a sense of fun and joy in learning. There is no joy thus far. Only punishment and ridicule for making an error. And it's not as if I'm just an out-of-touch Boomer. The boys feel intimidated and get shouted at, too. And they are peers. It's all too much.

At breakfast, Vincent and Jackson announce that they want to eat at a different time to the thems.

'We're fed up with being shouted at if we make a mistake with a pronoun,' Vincent declares. He has apparently been appointed as the official spokesperson for the boys' deputation.

'The *thems* have made plenty of mistakes about stuff too, and if any of us comment, they storm off,' Jackson adds.

'So it'll just be easier if we avoid *confrontation*,' Vincent finishes, evidently pleased with the way he has concluded his argument.

'I need to think about this,' I say, at a total loss as to how to handle the situation.

None of this is healthy for family life. I want to have dinner with the boys, too. It's their home. Lloyd has already implied that he would rather eat with the boys as it's more fun. 'They don't want to bite my head off.'

I'm not sure what to do. I can't do two shifts for dinner every night.

Sparkle seemed happier yesterday after seeing her brother and sister but her mood has already deteriorated again.

Over the next few days things disintegrate further, at an alarming rate. Sparkle continues to struggle to get up in the mornings, presenting like the member of Nirvana that never made it. Each day it is like she had a really 'heavy' night before. But she is still only 11 years old and this troubles me.

Her appearance also changes. She is a child and yes, all children experiment with their appearance, but hers is a sudden shift and quite dramatic. When she arrived, there was a trace of having a trendy or alternative family background in the way she dressed. But this new look is since she began to spend time with Groove. It is both dark and colourful at the same time. The clearest manifestation of it is in the way that she colours her hair. For Christmas I bought Lily some hair chalks, with strict instructions that they were only to be used at the weekends and during school holidays. The school has made it very clear that, as part of their uniform policy, only natural hair colours are allowed. Of course, I have seen some girls push that to the limits with red hair dye and blonde lines at the front, and they get away with it.

Not Sparkle.

Sparkle has used Sharpie pens to colour her hair in rainbow colours. I don't imagine this is going to go down well. But, as ever, I try to be supportive.

'Would you like me to get you a rainbow flag and a few other artefacts to decorate your room with?'

This is a quick way to signal not only that we support her choices, but that we want to give her the space in our home to be herself, whatever 'being herself' means with such rigid descriptive labels.

I'm hopeful that we can find a balance of some sort.

I catch Lily at a different moment and ask her the same question. 'Would you like some rainbows for your room? Flags? Or any other LGBTQ+ merchandise? Maybe a poster?'

I'm surprised when she answers, 'No thanks.' Her tone is flat.

I frown, thinking that I have misheard her. 'Are you sure?'

She looks past me, out of the window for a split-second to avoid eye contact. 'Yeah. No thank you.' She turns away and heads to her room.

Later at dinner, which for the time being I'm still insisting is a group arrangement, Lily is noticeably quiet. Sparkle attacks nearly everything that is said. Poor Lloyd seems to be their (Sparkle's) main target. They go on and on about trans rights and who is now Pan or Bi or this or that at school.

Then Sparkle announces, 'I'm going out with Cassie.'

Cassie is a little girl who came to play with Lily when Lily first arrived with us. Cassie's mum is a nurse and used to live a few houses along from here. When I first told her about the arrival of Lily she jumped straight in to help. Lily and Cassie were good friends for a while, until Cassie moved to the other side of town and went to a different primary school. She and Lily met up again in year 7 when they started at secondary school.

I'm beginning to wonder if there is something in the water.

I can see that the boys will almost certainly refuse to eat with them again. Lloyd, I think it is fair to say, is being persecuted for the dual crimes of being male and a Boomer.

'The world is dying because of you and men like you,' Sparkle hisses, menacingly.

Out of desperation because Sparkle is being so challenging, I pipe up to intervene.

'Can you say all this with a clear conscience, yourself, Sparkle?'

'What do you mean?'

'Did you turn off your bedroom light before you left for school this morning?'

She is silent.

'No,' I answer for her.

'So?'

'Have you chosen to purchase goods that don't come in plastic?'

She really does not like any come back at all, because she screams, 'Fuck off, you transphobic cunt.'

That pushes Lloyd to the edge. I've watched as he has taken weeks of Sparkle's snide remarks and verbal abuse on the nose. Tonight he doesn't.

'Sparkle, will you shut up please. Do not use that language in this house.'

With that, Sparkle stands up, scraping her chair on the floor tiles. She looks directly at Lloyd. 'You're a cunt.'

She storms off before anyone can say anything else.

Lloyd looks tired. 'I can't cope with this abuse in my home any more.'

Vincent says, 'I'm not eating with her again.'

I hear myself correct him. 'You're not eating with *them* again.'

He gives me a funny look. 'Whatever.'

There's a pause. Then he says, 'I don't know what all that Cassie stuff was about. I saw Sparkle kissing a boy at school. Go figure.'

He stands and throws his own chair back. He's not usually one for walking out in a huff, but tonight he does just that.

Jackson stands up more quietly, pushing his chair back neatly underneath the table, but also walks out of the room.

I stand up to stop them, then sit back down feeling sick. I can't remember when I felt this unhappy.

'I've had enough,' Lloyd says. 'She can go.'

I don't correct his pronoun usage.

The mood in the house feels thick with everyone's combined anger. Lloyd goes to his studio and shuts the door. A few seconds later I hear The Cure playing loudly. I decide it's best to leave him to settle down. I go to check on the children, heading to the highest room in the house first. When I knock on Vincent's door, he is sitting on his sofa bed with his headphones on.

He throws me a scornful look which breaks my heart.

I sit down heavily on his bed and look at him. He lifts his headphones away from his ears a fraction.

'I'm sorry, Vincent. This is tough, isn't it?'

He flicks the headphones down around his neck, his face softening a little.

'It isn't right, Mum. She's a liar and a bitch.'

I don't flinch at the words as I might ordinarily do with that kind of use of language.

After a short pause, he says, 'And she's as gay as I am.'

I smile at that. 'So. Is there something you want to tell me?'

Vincent voices something I thought earlier. 'It's like there's something in the water, and it's doing my frickin' head in.'

'Hmmm.'

'I'm not gay, lesbian, pan, bi, demi, omni, poly, queer, trans or them, they, it. And I'm not a squirrel,' he adds for good measure.

'I know what you mean.'

'She's angry, but not because of all that. She's just angry about her life.'

He can be perceptive at times, can Vincent.

'Making us all suffer,' he continues, 'by hiding in the fricking LGBT stuff isn't fair. She's doing it because she knows we're – or at least you're nice – and will try and be supportive.'

He smacks his hand down on the duvet. He is carrying so much anger and frustration of his own. I don't want to see my son like this. It's not fair.

'I'll tell you what else. At school, Groove and their little gang bully other kids by accusing them of being gay or straight or whatever. They followed Tim around.'

Tim is an old friend of Vincent's who is quiet and shy around school.

'They kept saying sexual things to him and freaking him out. He's too scared to repeat what they said so he's refusing to come in, pretending to be ill.'

I keep looking at him, knowing there is more.

'Groove is a freak, Mum.'

Again, I wait.

'She and one of their other loser mates – who says he's gay but he's just ugly and stupid and wants to fit in – they pinned Tim up against the wall by the swimming pool. Then the gay-not-gay one grabbed Tim's dick and said he wanted to-'

'Okay, that's enough,' I say. This is all worse than I imagined. I sit back further onto Vincent's bed. I feel despairing. I don't know what to do. This is very serious. What I'm hearing from Vincent amounts to abuse and bullying, and it's sexual harassment.

This isn't anything to do with the LGBTQ+ community. This is about unhappy children hiding in it and using it as a way to exert power over others. These are children that need help.

The emotion I feel, overwhelmingly, is a deep sadness. Children's childhoods are becoming shorter and shorter all the time. None of them need this.

'Thank you Vincent. I needed to hear all of that. I appreciate you telling me.'

I wait until he is settled again. Actually, if I'm honest, I wait until I'm settled again. He slips back into another, less-complicated world when he puts his headphones back on, and picks up from where he left off in his game.

He raises his hand to wave at me as I leave. He's still not smiling. This is horrible.

I wander up to Lily's door next. I knock and when she says, 'Yeah?' I open it gently.

'I just came to see how you're doing. Are you okay?'

'No, not really,' is her reply.

This is breaking my heart. I hate it when any of them are unhappy, but all of them at once feels too much to bear.

Lily gets up from her bed and moves to stand by her window. She looks out without turning to me. 'She's trying to take all my friends.'

'Can you fill me in a bit, so that I understand what's going on?'

She sighs. I can see a tear trickling slowly down her face. She still won't look at me.

'Every bloody friend I have, she and Groove try and take away from me.'

'How? Do they try and convert your friends?'

She hesitates. I can tell that she's not entirely sure what I mean.

I rephrase. 'Okay, do you feel that Groove and Sparkle approach your friends to see if they are part of the LGBTQ+ community? Or if they want to be.'

She nods.

What she says next shocks me.

'I'm not. I don't want to be there. I don't feel right.'

'So don't.'

The lone tear turns suddenly to a sob.

'I don't know how to escape.'

How do I deal with this? I'm finding it so hard. This is another form of bullying hiding behind the LGBTQ+ community.

I feel devastated for her. If this was sexual harassment

from a male to female I could call it out. I could go to the school and it would be managed. Because this is an LGBTQ+ matter, I daren't say anything in case I'm accused of phobia.

Bloody hell, I need some help.

'We'll sort it. I don't know how, yet, but I'm working on it. We'll sort it.'

I continue my rounds, getting to Jackson's bedroom door next.

He is also gaming. I think he's gaming with Vincent, even though they are in different rooms of the same house. Life is surreal.

'How are you feeling?' I say.

He doesn't hold back. 'I wish Sparkle would shut up. She's a bully. And that's it, end of.'

Not much I can say to that. Jackson is straight back to gaming.

'Loser!' he calls out to someone online, very possibly Vincent.

I just don't know what to make of life at the moment. Children and teenagers can bully each other. School life can be very cruel. But what's the line? Is Sparkle bullying the others? What does she – whoops, and I've been so good – what exactly does *they* get up to at school? I know the grammar's wrong there.

I need a plan.

I check on Lloyd. He's still working, or should I say 'hiding' in his studio and doesn't want to talk. There is one person left to go and see. I go back upstairs to see Sparkle. I knock on her door, now feeling more than a little tired, physically and emotionally, but I choose not to mention the way she spoke at dinner.

'Are you alright?' I ask instead.

She is sitting on the floor with rather a lot of make-up on.

I walk towards her.

'Yes, thanks. I'm fine.' A short pause. 'I'm going out.'

I am a bit taken aback and stop in my tracks. Time is pushing on. I look at the clock. It's already after half past six, and it's a school night.

'Not tonight, Sparkle, you've got homework and it's late. Perhaps at the weekend.' I keep my tone light.

'I'm going out and you can fuck off,' she says, looking me in the face, her eyes full of challenge. I'm sure that she never used to swear this much. She really has embraced the Year 7 transition vocabulary.

'No,' I say, more firmly. 'And where did you think you were going?'

'I'm going out with Groove.'

'Perhaps I'll text Groove's mother and explain why I'm not letting you this evening,' I say, knowing that I'll have her in my phone as something like Maria/Alina's mum.

'Don't you fucking dare.'

I'll text who I like, I think. Who are you to tell me who I can and can't communicate with? I can't help but conclude that I'm being attacked and have few defences here. I keep being wrong-footed. Again I feel that I'm being made to go along with this new world order. This is not about anyone's gender. This is about what's safe and appropriate on a school night.

I feel very old all of a sudden. Then I stop berating myself and remind myself once more that it's not just age because the boys don't buy into it any more than I do. And, given the conversation I've just had with Lily, I rather suspect that Lily doesn't any longer either.

If I speak out, or even think privately in ways which are critical about what is happening, am I being phobic? How do I separate the different elements of what is going on here without falling foul of accusation? I am lost. If I contemplate anything other than obeying these new world rules, I am in trouble. Not least, I'm in trouble with myself because I have a conscience, and my conscience prevents me from wanting to contribute to any injustice to an individual or a group of people. My feelings are compounded by the knowledge that this particular group is one that I have previously supported. I supported the culture and lifestyles of gay, lesbian and bi friends and advocated for their rights when they were a minority. I would absolutely have thought of myself as an ally.

Now I'm not sure if they are even part of this new movement. It seems like they aren't really, or at least not according to Tristan and Bart, who hanker after privacy and just want to be left alone to get on with living their lives without fanfare.

When I was teaching at the university I knew a trans woman, an individual who had transitioned from the male gender assigned to her at birth. I haven't heard from her in a while, but I think now would be a good time to catch up. I'll email her and run some thoughts by her. Perhaps ask for advice.

Meanwhile, I bring my thoughts back to Sparkle. In a funny sort of way I think that they might be glad that I have said 'no' to going out. I can't quite put my finger on it, but something just gives me that impression. Their resistance is performative rather than the result appearing to be genuinely upset that they can't go out.

'So, let's get the homework done, and then you can watch some TV.'

She rolls her eyes. 'TV! Ha. What are you like? No one watches the actual television anymore.'

Oh, don't they? Did I miss that memo?

I think I give an eye roll myself as I leave Sparkle's room.

But, with the household all occupied in their separate spaces, I have some space to set about implementing some plans. First, I send an email to Richard, suggesting that Sparkle may need some extra support from their counselling services to help her feel better. I'm not sure where Richard stands with the LGBTQ+ issue. I never want to presume, and now I'm awkward about the whole conversation, if I'm honest. In a way that I simply wouldn't have been three months ago. But, there we are. They've manoeuvred us into an impossible position. Next, I send an email to Sparkle's tutor and a safeguarding teacher. There are five safeguarding teachers listed on the website, so I'm not sure which one to choose. It isn't clear if they have specific specialist roles. I look at their pictures and end up choosing the one who looks the most friendly. In my email I ask if we can have a chat about some concerns I have for Sparkle. The last thing on my list is to email my old colleague, Iris, who transitioned.

For now, I feel better. It's amazing what writing a list and ticking some things off it can do. At least I feel as if I'm taking some action. I text Bart and Tristan with a little update about tonight's shenanigans, explaining that it's a pretty hostile atmosphere in our house right now. They message back and make me feel much better. Tristan makes me smile.

Speaking as a fully paid-up member of the Boomer gay man club, I'm well aware that younger people will think everything I have to say is nonsense, but I remember the difficulties at my old workplace in the 80s with Mrs and Miss. Do you recall the assumption that a woman was either married or unmarried?

He sends a follow-up message:

The simple and permanent solution was to give women a third choice, 'Ms'.

Oh, yes! He's so right. There *will* be a way through this. We just need to find a path through this tangled-up jungle of language and ideology.

XV

It's been a few days since I sent those messages, and so far I haven't heard back from anyone who I thought might be able to help me. I suppose I don't blame Richard: he's already confirmed how busy he is due to the ridiculous size of his caseload. It takes years of battering to develop a skin thick enough to survive the extremities of organisations like children's social care. I drift around Tesco's searching for inspiration for tonight's staggered eating regime while thinking about the three different types of social workers I have met over my time.

I categorise as 'Good' the ones who genuinely have empathy for the children and their families. They want to help make a positive difference to children's lives and always go that extra mile. Then there are the 'Benign' ones. These manage the emotional pain of the role by having boundaries. They go home on time and do what they can within their limited means. They don't cause too much conflict or pain.

Then there are, sadly, a few 'Malignant' social workers. They seem to have an absence of conscience, and a psychological need for power. Perhaps there is something in their own lives that makes them like this, or perhaps they become institutionalised over time, worn down by the sheer weight of their work. Richard is a 'good' social worker, but I suspect that he will shift to 'benign' as time goes on, as a strategy for coping with the trials and tribulations of the job. Many of the good ones leave. I suspect Richard's lack of response is simply because he is snowed under.

The school, I'm sure, is just busy. Like children's social care, there aren't enough staff to do the things that need doing. Safeguarding is a priority, but there will be more 'acute' needs elsewhere.

I'm most surprised that I haven't heard back from Iris, my friend from the university. Perhaps she is also just too busy. I have noticed that my colleagues in publishing and the art world tend to get back the same day. Communication is business and money. In education and care, where people have been most affected by cutbacks, anyone who has a job is doing the work of three people, it seems. Maybe it's a sector thing.

My trolley is still fairly empty and I'm near the bakery section when I spot Maria and Alina's mum. I can't remember her name, but I recall her well from their primary school days. We'd always smile at each other in the playground, share a few words as we waited for the children to come out in the afternoon. I give her a nod of acknowledgement and begin to push my trolley towards her to say hello. It would be good to know how she and the family are.

But she shoots off in the other direction, darting down the next aisle, and has completely disappeared by the time I get there.

I *know* she saw me. That is a bit weird. Lily and Maria are friends – or at least I think that they're still friends. I feel a bit hurt. She definitely saw me and recognised me. It's really decidedly odd.

At first, I detect a little paranoia about what I might have done that she feels the need to avoid me. Then I pull myself together, determined to get to the bottom of what's going on. There is so much more to this than meets the eye. Tonight will be the night. I become instantly more decisive. I pick up some pizzas for the boys and Lloyd, and a bag of salad that I can add to, perhaps some feta cheese and lovely black olives. They have removed the meat counter and replaced it with a deli counter. It's costing me a fortune. I'll keep it simple for the boys, but do something a bit more special for Sparkle and Lily. Perhaps if I cook the thems a fancy dinner tonight and there are no men around to cause offence, I can use my metaphorical tweezers to glean some insight into what is going on for Sparkle right now. I see that gnocchi is on special offer and the supermarket has a recipe card to go with it, encouraging us to serve 'vegetable gnocchi with beurre blanc'. Well, well. Move over Raymond Blanc.

Asparagus and peas are just warmed through in a silky butter sauce in this beautifully seasonal dish. The fresh spring veg is weaved through a generous bowl of pillowy gnocchi... I head back towards the vegetable aisle. It's not quite the height of asparagus season, but there's some on the shelves. It's probably come from Peru or somewhere. I daren't think about the food miles. I'll also grate some hard cheese that they can sprinkle over the top, and maybe get a garlic flatbread to tear and share. I cheat further and buy a vegan trifle for pudding. Sorted.

After school, I let the boys know that they will be having their dinner earlier, at 'first sitting'. I have a supply of sweets for them to take to their rooms and nibble while gaming. I suggest to Lloyd that he does something similar while I try to have a 'them and me' dinner. He is delighted by this arrangement. After his pizza he grabs a bottle of beer from the fridge and reaches for a glass. (He's very civilised these days.) Off he heads to the world of sci-fi.

I clear their plates away into the dishwasher and prepare the table for Sparkle and Lily. Pleased with my efforts, I call them down from their rooms and Lily is first in.

'Oooh, this looks nice.'

I smile. It's so good to hear that. There is a trace of the old Lily in her words.

I can hear Sparkle bounding down the stairs. She must be hungry. I show her to her place with mock formality and, as if I'm a waiter in a smart restaurant, I pull out her chair with a bow. I manage to catch myself before I say the word 'madam'. Instead I say, 'Sparkle'. Best to stick with names as often as I can.

I still panic about pronouns. I think it's partly because I was hardly at school when they did pronouns and verbs, and other parts of speech. I'm still not entirely sure about exactly what a pronoun is. I was no help whatsoever during all the language preparations for SATs exams when the children were younger. For now, I seem to consult frequently with my research assistant, Google. I'm a bit cautious of even mentioning the word 'pronoun'.

Names are best.

I've known this from very early on, having navigated the minefield that is mentioning birth and adoptive mothers. I was so scared to call either of them anything in case I offended them or got it wrong. I had to think of sentences that included their names not their descriptions.

I think the pronoun war that has been happening in this house has upset me more than it should, because I feel as paralysed by words as I did then.

This time, thankfully, I'm not pulling my hair out. Well, not yet anyway.

I lay the red and white gingham tea towel over my arm with a flourish and rush around them making mocktails and serving a few nibbles to start. My heart warms as I watch the girls. No, I'll say 'young people', enjoy the attention and relax.

After the nibbles, I put the big pasta bowl in the middle

with two 'big hands' that are the servers and dish up the gnocchi. My word, that goes down well. I have toasted a few pine nuts and seeds, and put them in a little dish to try out with the gnocchi. They love it. Louise's Italian Restaurant is a huge success. Perhaps they can leave me a review on Tripadvisor.

As I busy myself in the background, the 'young people' chat away. My ears are flapping when they talk about Groove. It's amazing how I just become the 'background noise'. Perhaps it was my very convincing impression of a silver-service trained waiter. They pay no attention to me. Lily talks about the group of friends that have fallen out with Groove because Groove apparently, according to Lily, 'is a bitch'.

I am once more confused. So, can a girl who is now gender-neutral and whose pronoun is 'them' be called a bitch? Or is that a form of deadnaming? Deadnaming, as my wonderful research assistant informed me earlier this afternoon, is calling someone by their birth name after they have changed their name. So when I think of Alina rather than Groove, because that is the way I've always known her, that is deadnaming. I wonder how Alina's mother, she who swerved me in the supermarket, feels about the name she chose with love and care now being her child's deadname?

And there it is!

Sparkle calls Alina a bitch too. Then agrees, 'She's been a right cow.'

I butt in gently as I step away from the fridge door to reveal the deluxe trifle that is just for them. The children, because they are children, regardless of what other labels they insist on, both stop talking for a split second while they cast their eyes on the treat that is being presented from the fridge. Both light up like happy little suns. I wave my hand across the pudding and say, 'Anyone for a little trifle?'

'Not just a little!' Lily says.

Thank the lord for clever packaging that lets me dish up the dessert as if I am a domestic goddess who has been busy creating all afternoon.

(For the record, the domestic goddess thing is as far beyond my reach as a Mars astronaut is, but never say never.)

'How's Maria?' I ask nonchalantly.

Lily says that they are friends again. 'And I'm going to meet Maria in town at the weekend for a Costa-lot.'

'Excellent. Is she still in some of the same classes as you? How is she getting on at school?'

'She's in the upper band, she's really clever. Especially at science.'

'Wow, good for her. That's wonderful.'

Sparkle has shed her prickly skin and seems a little more like an 11-year-old should be. She joins in to explain that Maria doesn't speak to her any more.

'That's a shame. But try not to let it worry you too much. *One* can't be friends with everyone.'

Gawd. I sound like Queen Elizabeth II in the height of her received pronunciation days.

'How's Groove?' I say, as if I haven't heard them talking about Groove just now.

'Alina?' Lily is quick to say. 'Oh, she's a cow, no one's speaking to her.'

This just sounds like normal bitchy-girl behaviour, switching allegiances. But of course I don't say this. This conversation is too fragile to interrupt with my uninvited opinions.

'So, what's Alina done that warrants her being deadnamed?' I say, as if I've been using that language all my life.

Both of them look at me for a moment, then at each other, but say nothing. Ha, I'll show them!

'Well, she's been filming people around school,' Lily explains. 'Then she put animal heads on them and posted them with evil comments.'

'Oh, really? That's not nice.'

They look at each other and evidently decide that if they are in for a penny, they're in for a pound, because Lily continues, 'They, I mean, she, did one of you.'

I'm shocked. 'Me? What? Why me?'

Then I frown. 'And, sorry, but how?'

Sparkle grins, but it's not a nice grin and Lily looks worried.

I think back over the last few weeks. I vividly remember

the night that Alina came here, when the 'thems' were all in Lily's room with the door closed and I couldn't get in.

'Did they, she, sorry, did Alina take the picture here?'

Lily nods.

I know I felt horribly uncomfortable that night. In fact, that's when all of this started. Alina came with a bad vibe. I don't often say that I don't *like* a child, but Alina seemed to have an energy about her that I found negative and untrustworthy. I don't remember ever having that same feeling from Maria. I wonder if their mum knew about the photograph, and perhaps that's why she shot off in the supermarket.

'How horrible.' For a moment I contemplate asking to see it, but then change my mind. I don't think I want to.

More importantly, I need to understand where these girls/thems are in their worlds. Are they still weaponising gender identity and sexuality against us.

'So, if not Groove, who are you hanging out with now?' I ask, directing my question at Sparkle.

I hear a whole load of names that are unfamiliar. Some obviously nicknames, and some deliberately non-gendered names. Some, I have to say, sound ridiculous. But then I am the adult in the room, so of course they do to my old-fashioned Boomer ears.

I ask if either of them are going to the LGBT group at school.

'LGBTQ *plus*,' says Lily.

Sparkle says that she's going most days with 'Lol'.

'Is that Lol Laugh out loud or Lol Lots of love?' I ask.

I don't get an answer. Evidently a question like that isn't worthy of response.

Lily looks at me across the table, and as Sparkle looks down to tuck into the trifle she mouths 'Sarah' to me.

I nod. I know who Sarah is. I sigh quietly and wonder who hasn't become part of the LGBTQ+ community at school.

Lily says she's not going to the group anymore. Instead she's going to a sports club at lunchtimes. My, how the world can change in a short space of time.

Out of genuine curiosity, and perhaps running the gauntlet just a little, I say, 'Do any males go to the LGBTQ plus group?' I clarify. 'I mean, original birth males?'

Lily shrugs. Sparkle says, with as much enthusiasm as I've heard from her in some time, 'Yeah, a few. Codey and Ryan are queer. And Mason goes.'

I stop her and ask, 'Which Mason?' as I know of four.

'Mason H. He's Pan. Yeah, he goes.'

'So, is it the same teachers in charge? Do you like the teachers now? I thought that you didn't approve of them because they were straight?'

'Well, we've been looking on their Facebook pages and can see that Mr Simmons is gay because he was standing next to a man in a photo, and Miss Everett is too old not to be married, so she's definitely a lesbian.'

Hearing her speak like this reminds me how young she is, in spite of the way she tries to look. How much she still has to learn about life, even though she thinks she knows it all now. But also, if this were a scene in a cartoon instead of my kitchen, then my doppelgänger would be standing next to me and we'd have just looked at each other, raising both eyebrows while a question mark appeared over our heads. Because, surprise, surprise, I'm confused again. Did I or did I not just hear two accounts of presumed gender, sexual identity? Isn't that everything that the LGBTQ+ community battles against? More than ever I'm convinced that they can't have it both ways. This is the very definition of having your cake and eating it, isn't it?

But of course, I don't say any of that. While Sparkle has been talking, Lily, with no explanation, has nipped up to her room and returned with her make-up bag.

It is just as if I've missed several episodes of a television series. When did this communication happen? Without saying a word, she gets a clean tea towel out of the drawer and puts it around Sparkle's front, and proceeds to do her make-up. Like Mrs Overall from *Acorn Antiques* I do a humble half-curtsy while I clear away the dinner and get back to my duties.

XVI

A new day dawns, and for once Sparkle rises for school with far less bother. Dare I hope that today is going to be a good day? It isn't exactly all peace and light and harmony. The boys are still staying away from the other young people, and until Lily tells me otherwise she is still 'them'.

'Until' could well be 'Saturday', judging by Lily's face when Jackson asks if his friend Marcus can come for a sleepover then. I wonder how much hair and make-up will be attended to prior to his arrival.

When I go to my studio, I discover that I have an email from Iris. I'm delighted to hear from her, but she is very amusing in her reply to me about my confusion and dilemma. (Though she confuses me even further by adding more letters onto the LGBTQ+ community name. LGBTQ2S+. What? I get back to Google immediately. 'LGBTQ2S+' is an acronym that stands for Lesbian, Gay, Bisexual, Transgender, Queer or Questioning, and Two-Spirit. I am completely bemused.

What the devil is two-spirit? That sounds very 'New Age' to me. The irony there being that 'new age' is fifty years ago now. Back into Google I go. *Two-spirit (also two spirit, 2S or, occasionally, two spirited) is a modern, pan-Indian, umbrella term used by some Indigenous North Americans to describe Native people in their communities who fulfil a traditional third-gender (or other gender-variant) ceremonial and social role in their cultures.*

Wow. I had never even thought of indigenous North Americans as part of the LGBTQ+ community. More evidence of the way that trans-gender-issues have always been there, but have been hidden by dominant ideologies. My knowledge is expanding and so is my scope of awareness and understanding. I carry on reading. Those who embody both masculine and feminine spirits are highly regarded in Native American communities, where intersex, androgynous people, feminine males and masculine females, are held in high respect. I am fascinated. It is a language complexity once again. Of course, why would any oppressed community accept an identity label being imposed on them. I just want to find out more and more. The LGBTQ+ identity is so much more than I had originally thought. So many layers, and it's so important that people like me or any of us, have the decency to learn.

After I feel more learned and in a much better and humble state of mind, I reply to Iris with a few more details, explaining that one of my young people has identified as pansexual and my other young person has identified as pangender. Though I also admit that I have a feeling that Lily may be an LGBTQ+ tourist.

I hit send, slightly worried that by using that term I'm being disrespectful. Iris replies instantly. She finds it hilarious and says that she's going to use it from now on. Phew!

Because we are older, perhaps, we're happy to use email as an instant messaging service. It would be easier to pick up the phone, but we at least share that reluctance with the younger generation.

How did the transition go? I type. *How are you feeling?*

To my surprise Iris says that she decided to slow it down and not go to surgery. She has spent a lot of time in therapy and had to work through a lot of her childhood issues first.

Iris has, in the past, shared with me that when she was young, 'something bad' happened at scout camp. Iris is also married with three children, a whole other layer of responsibility and concern for Iris and their family.

Iris is very open with me, discussing some of the complexities of her situation. At work she identifies as Iris, and the university has been incredibly supportive – as have the students and her colleagues. At home he is Robin. Iris is a respected academic, and I remember when she used to present as Robin all those years ago. He was a lovely man who always had time for the students and deeply cared about them, a lecturer who always went the extra mile. It must be nearly impossible to play one role at work and another at home.

That sounds very hard. How are you managing the dual identity?

Her reply comes straight back. *I hate it. I just want to be Iris and hate having to be Robin. Although, as far as men go, Robin is very understanding and a great lover.* This last part is accompanied by a winky face emoji.

I appreciate her openness, but perhaps this is a little too much information, especially in an email. It's interesting to hear, nonetheless. I ask about the therapist. Was it a good experience? Iris replies that her current therapist is much better. The last one was 'dangerous', (her word) and sent Iris into a deep, guilt-ridden depression, stirring up some of the childhood abuse responses that she had tried to forget.

But I wonder as I always do, was that a bad therapist, or a bad fit? It might have been due to where Iris was on her own journey. Whatever the answer, I'm overwhelmed by the realisation of how complex and difficult it must be to navigate emotions for those who feel so strongly that they are in the wrong body. With what I have learned from Iris, I feel more sure that Sparkle's issues with identity, and alignment with a community that is struggling to exert their human and legal rights, may be linked to feelings that Sparkle has about herself. Iris desperately wants to live an authentic life as a woman. Sparkle seems to want to suppress her womanhood. I think back to our first conversation about periods, and Sparkle's comment about them being 'another thing' that women have to deal with. This child has never been comfortable in her own skin.

Another email pings into my inbox. They are like buses. It's Richard:

Morning Louise, I just wanted to let you know that I have spoken to the emotional welfare team about Sparkle's needs. They would be happy to work with Sparkle, but would like to have a meeting with both you and Lloyd first.

This is good news indeed, and something that makes me feel hopeful. Because Sparkle sees us in the parent-adult role, this affects the way she feels about speaking to us. To have some external expertise is brilliant. I'm so pleased and email straight back with much gratitude and positivity.

When I go in to tell Lloyd, he shares my optimism. At last we can help Sparkle in some very practical ways. She deserves that. Moreover, after talking to Iris, I feel empowered and more sure of the territory. We will do all we can to help Sparkle get her sparkle back.

A few minutes later I hear back from the school. These emails really do come in threes. It is not good news. The school suggests that they have had some concerns about Sparkle. She has missed a few self-study sessions, so there are unaccounted gaps in the register. But she was seen in school at the time and attended lessons before and after as normal. This is the first I've heard of her bunking classes. I had no idea. Given the circumstances they consider this a safeguarding issue. Oh dear. That was not what I wanted to hear at all.

To distract myself, I pop out to the shops, intending to

get some good comfort food for later. I decide that I'll cook a vegetarian meal for everyone to enjoy. I do a mental list in my head of who likes and dislikes what. If I stick to that we will eat nothing at all so I compromise with extras. I decide to make pancakes with cream cheese fillings, and for pudding I decide to make, yes, pancakes with fruit and ice cream. A double-dinner. Perfect!

My creativity pays off and all in all it's rather successful. We manage to steer clear of pronoun mishaps and angry gender wars are kept to a minimum. After everything is cleared away, I go upstairs and knock on Sparkle's door, wondering in what order to tackle the various communications that today has brought.

I receive the usual young person response of 'Yeah, what?' which I used to find irritating but have now learnt to ignore because they eventually grow out of it. One day I hope I shall be greeted with a charming 'Hello' accompanied by rays of sunshine and fairy dust as they warmly welcome me into their bright, spotlessly clean and tidy, just-aired bedrooms. We can but dream. Sparkle's room is a mess. It smells decidedly stale and unpleasant, and is very dark, due to their insistence on keeping the curtains drawn all day and all night. While they are at school I rush around all their rooms and open the small middle windows and pull back curtains. The boys do it automatically for themselves now, and Lily sometimes dos, though she is more hit-and-miss. But living in that level of filth cannot be good for the mind or soul. I'm unhappy about the state of it, but I'm well aware of the wisdom of choosing one's battles. The room can wait.

'Do you mind if I come in?'

She shrugs and sits back at her desk.

'Can I sit on the bed?'

Another shrug.

'What are you working on?'

She covers it up. 'Nothing.'

'I bought sweets for later,' I say, 'if you're interested.'

She is still young enough to be more than interested in this news. Although, having said that, so was Lloyd when I mentioned it earlier.

'So, a couple of things to talk about. Richard called me earlier with some good news.'

Sparkle looks puzzled, but not particularly engaged or excited.

'Yes, he said that he'd spoken to the emotional welfare team and they would like to help you.'

A spark of interest. She turns her chair slightly towards me.

'How?'

'Now, that is a damn good question.' I say. 'I suppose that will largely be down to you. But this is a step forward, and it's good news because it means that you will get some control back in your life.'

Little do I know as I say these words that I will live to regret them.

'You'll have the chance to talk to professionals about how you're feeling,' I explain.

'When?'

'Well, Lloyd and I are having a meeting with them first, tomorrow morning, to share what we know and our *wishes and hopes* for you. The follow-up meeting with you will be shortly after. I'll let you know as soon as I have something confirmed. But soon. It will be soon.' I try to be reassuring.

She gives a kind of upwards nod. Dismissive. I won't tackle the school situation straight away. Sparkle is so volatile and I don't want her to become aggressive because of something I say.

'Helping you feel better is the main aim.'

Right, I'm nearly done talking in Unicorn and, though that has gone relatively well, I need to get back to reality. I must remember to mention to the emotional welfare team that because I feel that she can be volatile, it has made me cautious about upsetting her. I've stopped communicating properly.

I close the door and realise that I have not referred to her as 'them' once in my thinking. I am still tuned into 'her'. It's hard-wired. But I know it's important and I must work much harder. Rethinking something as fundamental as language, which is like breathing, is very hard indeed. I need to retrain my brain.

In the morning Sparkle is slow to rise once more.

I stick my head around the door several times. 'Sparkle?'

'Are you moving?'

'Are you awake?'

The other three are crashing around, moaning at each other to hurry up in the shower. There are two showers in the house, but the walk-in power shower is the popular choice, not the one that's in the bath. That is reserved for Lloyd and me. It's a much smaller experience. More of an electric dribble-shower.

I go in again. 'Are you alive?'

I regret saying it as soon as the words are out of my mouth. If I had said that to any of the others there would not have been a bat of an eyelid. Certainly no offence would have been taken. And none would have been meant.

But today Sparkle screams at me, 'What would you care?'

It's an unbalanced response from Sparkle, in my opinion, but then I seem to have lost the ability to articulate my opinions. I feel a little that we're under a Sparkle cabal. I have to be so careful about what I say.

I go downstairs to find Lloyd sitting in the kitchen, drinking coffee and looking at his phone. One of us likes to be on hand in case any of them needs anything before school. It's usually sports socks or pens.

'So, Sparkle isn't moving.'

'Any particular reason?'

'Not sure. I wonder though. I told her last night that we were speaking to the emotional welfare team today. Perhaps she wants to overhear what we say.'

It's one of those catch-22 situations. On the one hand, I'm a huge believer in telling children the truth about what's going on, and including them in decisions about their lives. On the other hand, everything feels different with Sparkle. Her volatility and aggression mean that it will be easier to talk without her. I'm so uncomfortable with this whole situation. It feels intense and fragile. And the feeling that it's me who's losing my rights is unnerving. Particularly since they are 'rights' that I have not previously given a second thought to: basic rights like the ability to speak my mind in my own home and the ability to communicate fully with the people in it. Moreover, the ability to properly look after Sparkle. I feel as if these things are being compromised.

I phone the school and let them know that Sparkle will not be coming in today. The answer phone invites me to give a reason for the absence, but I can't really give that information. I just say that I hope she will be in tomorrow.

Once the others have left and I've cleared away their chaos, I email Richard to let him know that Sparkle is not at school today. I admit that I'm not entirely sure why, but share my hunch that it may be to do with the fact that Lloyd and I are due to talk to the emotional welfare team. It's only natural that she doesn't like being talked about. I get that. And I've been on the receiving end myself as a child. But we need to find a way to manage this because, sadly, children in care are talked about and written about a lot. We need to help her feel safe and reassure her, but she can't just not go to school. I write some words to that effect, and then ask Richard in the email if he can help us with managing this. She might feel more reassured if her social worker helps her feel safe.

Morning admin done, I manage a little work for an hour or so, then pop upstairs to see Sparkle. She pretends to be asleep.

I keep my tone light, but explain nicely but firmly that if she is ill she needs to stay in bed. I go over to her window and open the curtain.

She moans.

'It's daytime and there is a world out there wanting to say "Hello Sparkle" to you.'

A grunt.

'Are you feeling any better? Would you like some breakfast?'

'Yeah.'

'Please?'

A pause.

'Right, well, if you are well enough to have breakfast you need to come downstairs and eat it. I'm not bringing it up here so you can eat in your bed. I believe your legs still work. Would you like an omelette? Or croissant? I've got some of that dark berry jam that you like?'

'Oh, alright,' she says and wriggles out of her bed.

I have a familiar, slightly sinking feeling that I'm not going to get much work done today. I head downstairs while

Sparkle huffs and puffs and manages to indicate that she is doing me a huge favour by coming downstairs to eat her breakfast.

Once she moves about and has a drink and something to eat (opting for the omelette *and* the croissant), she begins to brighten up.

'Would you like a nice bubbly bath?' I ask.

I'm mindful of my own child-off-school rules, the first of which is that you mustn't make it too nice or they're likely to bunk off more often. In Sparkle's case though, I suggest the bath because she really does need to freshen up.

She also thinks this is a good idea and follows me upstairs. I fuss over her, offering a choice of bubble bath. We decide to make a vanilla, coconut, lemon and pine blend. I actually begin to see a smile. I fuss around a bit more with two fresh fluffy towels: one for the hair. I hope that will encourage her to wash it. I take a selection of shampoos and conditioners down from the shelf and position them close to the bath. I run down the stairs to get the speaker out of the kitchen so that she can listen to her music.

'What shall I listen to?'

'Reggae. Try Reggae.' I think she might enjoy it. I select some tracks and press play.

'Have a nice bath,' I say, as I go towards the door.

I hear a much-missed tone of sweetness in her replying 'thank you.'

Our meeting with the welfare team, comprising Zoey and

Alexander, takes place via Zoom. It's convenient, but means that it's much more difficult to get a handle on what people are like. Zoey sounds American, or perhaps Canadian. I'm not very good at accents, and I don't want to ask or assume anything, so avoid all conversation relating to travel. I'm assuming 'them' but we haven't talked pronouns. I *know* that I'm wrong to assume, but I don't want to ask. This is exactly how I end up tying myself up in knots by working very hard to create sentences that do not need genders – mostly because I feel like some sort of a fraud saying 'them'. It doesn't come naturally yet. Aaagghhh!

I know that I just need to get used to it.

I think like a child, sometimes. A child learning something new, like riding a bike. They make a few mistakes but get it with support and encouragement. If their adult says they're an idiot or shouts at them it will put them off learning to ride the bike. I have been shouted at so much by Sparkle that I feel like that. I don't feel at all confident about riding my pronoun bike. I am self-conscious and scared that I'll fall off and get bullied or laughed at.

Zoey is a large character, in both size and personality. She is very chatty, and uses a lot of unnecessary words to describe things. 'I'm so glad, Louise, that we are able to have this communication through computer interface today.' Far too many words. Big words that are also somehow empty. I only need to listen to every twenty or so words to keep up with the gist of the conversation.

I take a sip of my tea and imagine her talking about a teacup. She would probably say it's a 'dual-facility artefact that offers the user a lifestyle choice that depends not only upon the selection of the cup and saucer, but also the content and how it was supplied, including the water or whatever choice of liquid has been chosen.

'The user of the cup is entitled to spend as much time drinking or not drinking or sipping, or if their choice is to slurp the liquid from the cup as the user wishes, though when the user consumes the liquid, it may be either with or without milk or possibly a choice of fruit or herbal extraction. Just because it's a tea cup doesn't mean we exclude coffee or any other liquid, if the user feels that's the right choice for them. Though the cup and saucer are traditionally used together it does not mean the user has to conform to that practice. In fact, if the user wishes, they can drink the liquid from the saucer.' That gives a good flavour of how she speaks. And makes just about as much sense as anything else she might have said. Lloyd tunes out entirely, judging by his facial expression. I have to nudge him to remind him that some of his non-verbal responses can be seen on screen.

Alexander is a young man, in his twenties, perhaps? He has curly red hair that covers his ears and makes him look rather Roman. I can't tell what colour of eyes he has via Zoom. He waves his hands around a lot and seems to say all the right things. I think that perhaps he may still be at that 'transition stage' that some young people have, where they don't yet have a real understanding of how they are using other people's time. It is a long meeting.

Lloyd does engage, and explains in some detail the ways in which Sparkle seems to have become quite militant.

Both Zoey and Alexander seem to bridle a little at that description.

'Sparkle can become aggressive if we slip up on the pronouns,' he says.

They talk about practice making perfect. 'Perhaps you could both benefit from the four-day training programme?'

I nod with lots of enthusiasm, knowing full well how unlikely it is to happen.

I give them the bit of background information that we had gleaned via Richard, and from Tristan and Bart, though I am careful not to reveal where the details have come from since foster carers must not share information. Yeah, right. How else do they think we raise our game and sharpen our skills?

'Okay, Louise, so thank you for sharing, there. We appreciate that. The next step in the process is for us to arrange to meet Sparkle and draw up a plan from there. That's great progress. Well done us. Well done you. We'll take on board everything that has been exchanged between each of us as stakeholders here today.'

I like to think of myself as a 'parent' and a 'carer' rather than a 'stakeholder', but I smile and nod and say goodbye with a cheerful wave, while nudging Lloyd in the ribs and encouraging him to do the same.

Lloyd turns to me once their faces have disappeared from our computer screen. 'Was that like talking to two children's TV presenters?'

I nod and laugh. It's the best description of the bubblegummy, too-toothy, over-enthusiastic and, if I'm honest, slightly patronising exchange we've just experienced.

I need not have worried about Sparkle being home while we talk to the emotional welfare team. In fact, she's still in the bath when we finish. I run upstairs in a panic and knock on the door, worried that something might have happened.

'Are you okay in there, Sparkle?'

'Yeah, thanks.'

I'm not convinced about the value of any outcome from what we've just been through. I can't help but feel a little suspicious sometimes about counsellors. I know that it is a listening role, and not necessarily an advisory one, but the whole notion is complex. Before I wrote my first book I had, along with a number of colleagues, been made redundant from the university. As part of our redundancy package, we were each offered six free counselling sessions. I not only understood and accepted the redundancy, I was, in some ways, actually quite relieved about it.

Sometimes a change is powerful, even if there is a little pain with it. So I thought I would take the counselling, but use it to support me through accessing my adoption files. A good plan, I thought. I had held on to the file quietly for a few months but I wasn't ready to look at it by myself. Nor did I want to go through it with Lloyd. This seemed like the answer. The counsellor was nice. Her office was a rented office in a big hall that had previously been a call centre, but I do remember the sound of bird song as I followed her inside.

It was when I pulled out a copy of an old letter that things started to go wrong, although not in a way I could have foreseen. I had written the letter to my birth mother asking for her help when I was nine years old. It was a very sad and disturbing letter for so many reasons that I have covered elsewhere. When I looked up at my counsellor she was crying and working her way through a box of tissues. I ended up comforting her when I should have been processing my own emotions.

It has heightened my awareness that sometimes counsellors and therapists inevitably bring their own baggage to a session. Moreover, the well-known phrase, 'Physician heal thyself', attributed to Jesus from Luke's gospel, comes to mind. I first heard it from a friend years ago and it has stayed with me. I wonder if some therapists, and maybe even some social workers too, are consciously or unconsciously, there to heal themselves.

My suspicions are confirmed with bells on when we receive 'the plan' a few days later. (Before they've had a chance to meet Sparkle, I might add, in spite of Zoey and

Alexander's assurances that a meeting would be the next step.) I read a very long section which begins: *Louise Allen presents as...*

Turns out that the way Louise Allen presents isn't described in the most complimentary of terms. It isn't so much a plan as a personality assassination of us. Mostly me, but also the rest of the family.

If I had hackles they'd point up to the sky.

'What the fuck?' is my first response. The second is, 'They can fuck right off.'

The f-word is used in several more creative ways the further down the page I go. I read recently that Dame Judi Dench admits she loves Shakespeare because of his use of expletives. I do, too. It's so liberating. And probably a reaction to hearing, the whole time when I was growing up, 'That's not very ladylike.'

Lloyd stands next to me, reading the long text that might as well be entitled 'Destroy Louise', with his mouth open. He isn't usually as sweary as me, but he joins in the swear-fest with some gusto. I read and read again, getting crosser each time.

Lloyd only gets a single paragraph of critique. I wonder how he always gets away with the least complaints from children's social care in comparison to when my name is mentioned. It seems very unfair, even after I've gone over it a few times to try and digest it all properly. Zoey and Alexander, who I remind myself only met me for about an hour on Zoom and did most of the talking, seem to have been able to give me a full psychological review.

And then I see why. They have drawn heavily on the fact that I'm an ex-care-system child myself. They must have been rooting around in our files to discover that. It certainly didn't come up in our conversation. How dare they? I am not under investigation for anything, so why did they think it was okay to dig into our file to look for things to judge me on? My blood is boiling.

It seems to have sent them into a spin.

I share some of the best bits out loud. Verbatim:

Louise's 'say it as it is' personality-type could be offensive to Sparkle.

Where the hell are they getting that from? They haven't even met Sparkle for her to say anything negative about me yet. How do they have any idea of what might be offensive to her?

Louise may revert back to her own childhood trauma if challenged or triggered by Sparkle, and her needs may overwhelm Sparkle's.

I say it again. 'What the fuck?' What qualifies them to decide that I might 'revert back'? I'm an adult who has spent years processing what happened to me. I draw on those experiences to help me support the children in my care. I'm furious. Beyond furious. I don't have words to adequately describe the rage that I feel.

Lloyd attempts to lighten the mood. 'They got all that in an hour from a Zoom meeting? It took me years to see all that!'

I throw him a filthy look.

'Oh, hang on, there's more. Louise may revert back to her former traumatised self and create conflict and difficulties for Sparkle.'

I have the NUPFC (National Union of Professional Foster Carers) on speed dial. While I'm waiting for them to answer I dissect more of the 'I hate Louise' document.

The 'recommendation' from Zoey and Alexander is that *Lloyd and Louise should attend therapeutic counselling to enable them to work through their prejudices and biases from early life experiences to enable a positive relationship with Sparkle.*

They also recommend that Jackson and Vincent attend counselling. Lloyd isn't looking so smug now. I'm not sure which bit I react to the most. I think it is the recommendation that Jackson and Vincent need intervention. On what grounds are they making this judgement? Jackson and Vincent weren't even involved in the Zoom call. Lloyd gives it the full Judi Dench and doesn't hold back in his ranting and swearing.

Every thought in my head, every bone in my body and every fibre of my being shouts 'NO!' This should not be happening. I will not let it happen.

How dare they?

My call connects, but I'm placed on hold at the union. My anger doesn't dissipate. I have not been this angry for years. How can we look after a child and meet their needs when we ourselves are being threatened like this? It dawns on me that this is dangerous territory. Would I have a mental health check and therapy recommended if I was looking after a child from another culture, perhaps a refugee?

No, they would probably say, 'Here is the email for a voluntary group of asylum carers, in case you would like some additional support.'

I think my head is going to explode. Who the hell are those people? I wouldn't trust them to make a sandwich, let alone assess ours, and my sons' mental health. This is an utter abuse of power. How did they get that much power?

This experience is having the opposite effect than they intend in terms of me supporting Sparkle. In fact, my initial reaction is to say that I want to give the 28-day notice and for her to leave. And that's not her doing, it's theirs. I want to rage at the injustice of everything that those idiots wrote.

After a while, I manage to get through to the union and speak to a representative. It's simple. It's not mandatory, it's a recommendation, and therefore our compliance is entirely voluntary. I pace about the kitchen waiting for my rage to settle down into something manageable.

I watch Lloyd, who is buttering and then rapidly scoffing crispy thins in a kind of frenzy. One after another disappears. It's quite a remarkable sight. I have a kind of envy of him being able to find solace in anything. 'Do me one,' I demand, like he's pouring double scotch.

I look up at our clock which has moving cat's eyes that

always make me smile. Like Baldrick to Blackadder, I say slowly, 'I have a cunning plan!'

Working as a union rep at my old university had its plus points. One thing it taught me was that sometimes you just have to play the system. I grab my laptop and compose a response.

Hi Zoey and Alexander, I type. *It was great to meet you the other day. We appreciate you giving your time to help us support Sparkle.*

(This is simply blowing smoke up their wot-nots. It's their *job* to speak to us.)

Thank you for your observations and recommendations. (I resist saying 'it must take a great talent to glean so much in a one-hour Zoom, especially about me.') *We asked the boys if they would like to take part in the counselling session. They wondered if they could have a bit more time to think about it?* (We didn't ask, and they will not be attending counselling sessions with those two.) *If you could suggest some dates we will see when we are available to attend a mental health assessment.* (That will be never). *When would you like to see Sparkle?* (This is where I tell an even bigger fib than those which have gone before). *Sparkle would like to come to you if that's okay. She likes a drive and to listen to her music and talk if she feels comfortable.* (What I really mean is, we don't want you in our home and Sparkle would benefit from seeing the reality of institutions like yours, and the council office environments. So would I, but for different reasons.) *We look forward to hearing from you soon, Louise and Lloyd Allen.*

I wait until the morning to send it, so that it's more

convincing. And that, dear readers, is how it is done! A small deception, but I feel much better for it.

XVII

A week passes and we have not heard back from Zoey or Alexander. I wonder if they ever work alone, or if they always exist as a double act. They were very quick to try to give Lloyd and me a spurious diagnosis, but so far nothing for Sparkle, who is the one needing the mental health review. From where I'm sitting, it feels like their priorities might be slightly skewed.

I told Sparkle that they were going to help, and I told her that in good faith. I believed it to be true, otherwise I wouldn't have given her that expectation. But we have not heard a peep out of them. I think it's wrong to keep children dangling, especially children like Sparkle who have so much going on in their heads and hearts.

I do notice that once the other children are aware that Sparkle is due to have some counselling support or therapy, the atmosphere in the house relaxes a bit. It's amazing how much faith we all put into mental health services, hoping that they will be the silver bullet and fix the problem. Perhaps our expectations need to be managed, but I wonder how. We're so desperate to help Sparkle find her sparkle that we are clutching onto anything that might help.

But the help doesn't come.

Another week passes.

Each school morning, Sparkle struggles to rise. Each morning I approach the issue in as light and creative a way as I can. I quickly run out of strategies and methods, and find myself repeating them, even when they haven't worked before. I try cajoling, bribery, warnings, cheerful promises, flattery. Even the things that do work quickly become stale and do not seem to have any effect a second time.

Her mood is low, and getting lower.

Everyone is engaged in the 'cheer Sparkle up' game at the start of the day. Most mornings I end up driving her to school, which is a ten-minute walk away. She gets there either just in time or is late and has to sign in after the school gates are closed. I have to go into reception every time and explain that she is struggling. I know a few of the teachers and the senior management team. So many of my foster children have attended this school that I know many people and I'm a familiar sight. But I've never visited as often as I do at the moment.

In the evenings, we all tiptoe around Sparkle, scared that we will upset her. We are all careful about what we say, fearful of making her angry or even more sad.

Another week passes. As each day goes by, I feel further and further out to sea, with a sinking feeling that I can't really explain. I wonder if it's because I believe that I'm failing and that we, as a family, are failing Sparkle. It seems like we're all stuck in Groundhog Day. It's crushing.

One day, more than a month after the strange Zoom with Zoey and Alexander, I get back home from the unnecessary but necessary school run and do the usual rush around the house, flinging windows open, shaking out duvets, collecting damp towels from unlikely corners and picking up the discarded clothes from bedroom floors, giving them the sniff test: fabric conditioner or person. While I'm in Sparkle's dark pit I open the curtains and notice that there are marks on the linings. I look a bit closer and see that it looks like smudged blood. I inspect both the curtains properly in the light.

Blood.

Not drops of blood, but smears and wipe marks.

No, no, no, no, no.

We've been here before with other children, sadly. I knew Sparkle was in a bad way. I didn't realise we had reached the stage of self-harm. She must be cutting herself. My heart sinks even further with the realisation of what is going on.

I go to the desk and wonder what it was she was hiding. I know it's an invasion of privacy, but I also have her welfare to think about in the light of this discovery. I pull out one of her drawers and, not too hidden, is a pile of notes and drawings.

I sink down into her desk chair and cry as I read each

page and look at her drawings. There are over thirty A4 pages of what I can only describe as utter despair. It's her story. Her sense of the world.

Her pain.

God, I feel utterly lost. She has presented it like a Year 5 English assignment. It even starts with 'Once Upon A Time' and it nearly kills me to read it.

Once upon a time lived a young princess called Lois. She was the most beautiful girl in the world. Then one day she met a prince called Luke. They fell in love and married. They lived in a castle high on the hill where they had servants and parties. But one day, a bad knight turned up at a party and hurt Lois. This made Lois very sad.

The drawing that accompanies this text, at the bottom of the page, is of a woman with bright red hair bent over with a stick in her back. Or maybe, I think, her bottom.

There is nowhere further for my heart to sink as I look at the words and the pictures. I don't know what to think. I flit from am *I reading too much into this?* to *am I not reading enough into this?*

I look around her room with fresh eyes. This is the room that, when Sparkle first arrived, she seemed so pleased with. For a few days she showed some pride by arranging the welcome gifts and other objects on the shelf. I remember how she made her bed and folded her clothes.

It began to go wrong when Groove appeared on the scene, or am I reading too much into that as well? I'm projecting blame onto another child.

But I can't help myself, because it went a bit wrong for Lily at the same time. The difference is that Lily seems to have come back to us.

What is the connection between Groove's influence and these images? Is there one? No child's story is a legal document. They have their own truths, their own hidden messages, their own story to tell. I keep reading, fascinated and horrified. Why doesn't she call Lois and Luke 'mum' and 'dad'? Are they one of the several families that I have come across where the children call their parents by their first names?

It was a bit of a thing when I was a child in the 1970s, growing up in Oxford. I remember having friends who called their parents by their first names but they tended to have parents who were connected to the university and were a bit 'out there'. It's always seemed strange to me. Another trapping of language, perhaps.

I keep reading. There is something about the dog. Sparkle mentioned before that she had a dog and she does enjoy the company of Doug and Dotty. Maybe she misses her dog. I can't make head or tail of this bit but it looks like a man is doing something wrong to an animal, maybe a pig? Hurting it?

I take the drawings downstairs and show them to Lloyd, interrupting him in the midst of an issue with one of his clients.

'What's wrong with people?' he says, looking with the same horror at this bizarre manuscript.

'That's exactly what I was going to say.'

I point out different things that have struck me in the pile of drawings and text.

Like me, he is deeply saddened by the whole, sorry mess. Then he says something which sends a chill down my spine.

'She needs help, Louise. This is seriously messed up.'

It sends a chill because I know that he's right. I just didn't want to acknowledge it in such stark terms. I go back upstairs and return the papers back into her drawer roughly, not disguising that I've been here. Part of me suspects that she *wanted* me to see them, so a bit of me wants her to *know* that I have.

As I slide the papers back under a book, I see a number of sharp objects. The blade from a pencil sharpener, a compass and several paper clips unravelled into points, lie together in the drawer. Next to them are blooded, crumpled-up tissues.

Oh, Sparkle, Sparkle, Sparkle. This changes things even more.

I take the paperwork back and head off to my office where I take pictures of every page in the order that I found them. Then I return them for a second time, and take a picture of what was in the drawer.

When I walk past Lloyd's door, I explain flatly, 'I'm sending pictures of her work and what's in her drawer to Richard and the emotional welfare team.'

I don't know where else to turn. It's times like this when

you really need your supervising social worker, and we still haven't got one. That makes me feel vulnerable.

Lloyd dashes up to Sparkle's room to see what I found in her drawer.

I Paste all of the pictures into a single Word document and send it on to Richard, copying in Zoey and Alexander, too. I explain that, after finding these images and texts in Sparkle's drawer, the blood on the curtain linings and the sharp objects, it looks like Sparkle is self-harming. I add that we still haven't had a date for Sparkle to meet with the emotional welfare team. As I write this, I realise that this has happened since I told her that she was going to receive help and so far, she hasn't. This is it. She is crying out for help.

I was already cross with Zoey and Alexander, but it was a selfish sort of cross. I was angry at feeling targeted by them. Even when we were on the Zoom call something about their methods and attitude did not ring true for me. But now, I'm angry again, and this time it's on Sparkle's behalf. Why haven't they helped, like they said they would? I decided a long time ago that help of this kind should always be straightforward. If it isn't, then we need to ask what particular agendas are preventing it from being that way.

In my experience of working with children's social care, both the councils and the independents, there are always the same three gremlins that get in the way: greed, power and insecurity. It's clear to me that Zoey and Alexander have their own agendas, and from what I've seen so far, supporting children doesn't seem to be their number one priority. Things have changed dramatically given what I've discovered in the last hour. It makes their personal attack on me seem even more petty and misguided.

I feel desperate. We can't keep going on like this. It's been five months since Sparkle arrived. Her mental health is in constant decline and I know that her mood is infectious: we're all suffering. But she is suffering most of all.

Richard calls me back within the hour. He's driving to another meeting and speaks to me from the car on his hands-free set.

'I saw your email, Louise. I'm escalating everything. This is urgent.'

Hallelujah! At last. Although there is, of course, little to be triumphant about in this situation, at least someone is finally listening.

'I know. I think Sparkle is feeling desperate because there hasn't been any help, and I did tell her that basically help was on its way, because I genuinely thought it was, but that was five weeks ago!'

'Have you managed to have your mental health review?'

'No, we haven't, we've been too busy. But that shouldn't stop them from seeing Sparkle!'

'You're right. It shouldn't.'

I leave it with him to chase them.

'Let's make sure that Sparkle gets the help she needs sooner rather than later.'

When Sparkle gets home from school, I carry on as usual. In between photography, phone calls and fighting my own fears, I managed to zip out to the local shops and get loads of fruit for the several fruit bowls around the house, and a bag of custard doughnuts.

The latter is definitely the children's preferred choice for now, but I'm hoping that the healthier option will kick in soon after.

The house is still on edge. I can tell that the boys are keen to shoot off to their bedrooms for safety. Lily is a little more supportive of our collective endeavour for peace and love and domestic tranquillity. Her efforts are theatrical but well-intentioned.

'Would you like me to make you a hot chocolate to go with your donut?' she asks Sparkle.

Sparkle's reply is flat, but she adds a 'please', which is nice.

'Have you read my school report, Louise?' Lily asks.

'Not yet. I saw that something had been emailed through from the school but I haven't had a chance to look. Do they give you a hard copy?'

'They do!' Lily pulls a piece of paper from her school bag, which is precariously balanced on the edge of the kitchen table. I can tell from the pattern of colours and codes that she is doing just fine.

'Did they give you yours, too, Sparkle?'

Sparkle reluctantly pulls out the piece of folded paper.

Her colours are more varied. I can see in an instant that she is excelling in some subjects and not in others. But there are definitely some positives here. I want this child to feel good about themself, not to be harming themself. Praise is the order of the day.

'Oh, well done. You clever, special, brilliant girls!'

Lily beams at what is intended as a compliment.

I don't think about what I have said until Sparkle storms out of the room, shouting wildly.

'I'm not a fucking girl, you stupid, phobic bitch!'

XVIII

Lloyd comes into the kitchen, just as the door slams to Sparkle's bedroom. He holds up his arms in a questioning gesture. I stand there, speechless.

Lily doesn't help. 'You shouldn't have said *girls*. You should have said *people* or something!' She bursts into tears.

I know that she is finding this really hard. We all are. I don't know who to attend to first.

Vincent chooses this moment to make his entrance behind Lloyd. He looks at Lily. 'What's up with you?'

Lily cries harder. Vincent sits down next to her at the kitchen table and looks at me. 'Mum.'

It's one word, but the intonation speaks volumes. It's a plea. It says, 'mum, we can't keep doing this,' and he's right.

I give him a flat smile. But I don't have an answer. I do know that I need to get to Sparkle, though. She can't be on her own right now.

'Can you stay here with Lily while I pop upstairs to see Sparkle?'

Vincent nods.

'And why don't you finish making the hot chocolate?' I say to Lloyd, who clearly needs a job to do to prevent him from feeling like a spare part.

I bump into Jackson as I go up the stairs. He's evidently heard all the commotion and looks concerned. 'What's going on?'

I shrug. I don't know the answer.

I knock on Sparkle's door. There's no answer so I walk straight in to find her sitting on the floor underneath her window, crying. I walk right up to her.

There's blood on her thighs.

'Sparkle?'

It's too late to call anyone. Richard will be finished for the day.

I sit down on the floor next to her. I don't mention the blood. 'I'm sorry, Sparkle. I forgot to use the right pronoun or noun, or whatever part of speech it was. I'm supportive of your decisions, I really am. I hope you know that. I was just caught up in the moment and was so proud of you both. The word just came out. I didn't mean to use it, and I didn't mean to offend. I just wanted to congratulate you on the report, and I am sorry.'

I hear these words on the air and wonder just how we ended up here.

I need Sparkle not to behave like this just because I have a linguistic slip. This reaction is way out of balance. It's wrong.

Even though I am sad for Sparkle, and I know how much she is hurting, I think that the hurt runs much deeper than pronouns. Her war is not a gender war. And a new emotion is developing inside me. It's like something breaks. I'm done. I refuse to pussyfoot around in my home, scared of speaking.

I know that some people will be critical of my next actions. I stand up and say, 'I'll leave you to it, Sparkle. I'll call you for dinner but if you're not hungry it's no problem.'

I walk to where I know her blades are and I remove them. I know she will find other things, other ways to do what she feels she needs to, but I don't know what else to do.

Then I turn around and I leave.

I think that in some way we've been feeding this behaviour by giving it so much attention. My emotions are high, but slipping up on a pronoun does not warrant this level of behaviour. This self-abuse is also a kind of house-abuse.

I go downstairs and get out the pots and pans. Somehow, I start to conjure up a meal, throwing onions and garlic into a pan. I don't know what it's going to be yet. If they eat it, they eat it. If they don't they can have toast. I find that I don't care. Something has switched in me, and I think it's called finding my own bloody voice and identity again.

There is no doubt I have felt repressed and oppressed by all of this.

This is our family home. There are five of us bending

and crouching to the needs of one. One child, who should be receiving the help she needs from the people who are there to provide it. This one child cannot control us like this. She is in pain, of that there is no doubt. But, my word, is she transferring her shit onto all of us. It is not fair, nor is it right. We are just a regular foster family, not miracle workers.

The smell of onions and garlic cooking away on top of the stove puts me in mind to make a sauce for penne pasta. That's about as good as it is going to get this evening, because amongst all this I have lost so much time, including time to do a big, proper supermarket shop. I'm not resorting to the take-away trap; that's for weekends and emergencies and, regardless of what Sparkle thinks, behaving like that because I got a word wrong is, in my opinion, not an emergency.

I feel strong. I feel brave. I feel better. And I will get that child the bloody help she needs and deserves, by hook or by crook.

Just as I start to lay out the pasta bowls, with everyone else already seated, Sparkle comes into the kitchen, sits down at the table in their usual place and, without saying a word, eats a big bowl of pasta. Once finished, they walk silently back upstairs. (I get some of the pronouns right, some of the time, even if it's in my head.)

I can also deal with silence. That is fine.

Which is a good job, because nobody else speaks either. The others haven't picked up on my new-found 'power', and the default setting is silence because not speaking is the safest option around Sparkle.

No, I think. Not anymore. That cannot be the 'safest' option from now on. Leaving Sparkle the option to join in or not is how it should be. I will also remove all the sharp objects from the drawer and from around the house. Sparkle's identity is their own and is out of my hands. What I can try and intervene with in a supportive way is their desire to self-harm or self-abuse or self-injure or any other description that the social scientist or therapists want to call it. From now on we will be discussing the cutting, and the professionals can work on cutting, family, possible abuse, and LGBTQ+, because that is a long list and much of it is out of my remit and beyond my skill set.

The next day I email Sparkle's teacher and the PEP/ SENCO (personal education plan, special educational needs coordinator) lady, and the headteacher who I copy in for courtesy's sake and for insurance. Frankly, I have no time whatsoever for staff getting sniffy about 'going over their heads'. This is a child in a crisis and they need help. No more pussyfooting around means just that. Not just around Sparkle, but around everyone connected with them. That help must start now. I ask directly for them to receive counselling and a referral to an educational psychologist. That makes me feel marginally better.

Next, I email Richard, Zoey and Alexander. I get an out-of-office reply from Richard explaining that he is *currently on annual leave.* I didn't see that one coming. He didn't mention it, and I'm inclined to think, given the urgency he spoke of yesterday, that he might have done. Is he on annual leave, or is he possibly off on sick-leave? A friend of mine who is a social worker in a county in the north of England told me that they are not allowed to be, and definitely not allowed to say, '*off sick*'. The management, perhaps understandably, does not want people to know that their staff are struggling. Language, once again, is the first casualty.

A few hours later, Sparkle's teacher emails back and tells me that she has arranged for Sparkle to see the school nurse next week. Ideally, she will see someone a bit more specialised than the school nurse, but right now we'll take what we're given. At least it's a start, and hopefully the school nurse can refer Sparkle to a specialist. I think to myself: it's only five days and we can keep going for five days. Then we can move on to the next stage. I *still* haven't heard back from Zoey and Alexander, who sound more and more like a clothing range at a supermarket every time I say their names together like that.

I decide on a new approach. I will send different emails to them separately, to see if they can respond independently. Or at all.

On Saturday I take Sparkle and Lily out for a walk. We head towards the park. It's cold although it's sunny; that sun is deceptive. No warmth comes from it. Both teenagers wear black hoodies and jeans. I am far less discerning, throwing on as many layers as I can find in an effort to keep warm. The wind is fierce and biting.

Sparkle and Lily take a dog each as they walk along the road, while I walk behind watching. It still amazes me how the simplest things can bring such joy. Despite all that has happened, watching them walk with the dogs, being dragged to good sniffing spots and laughing and smiling reminds me that they are still children. Inevitably that leads to a question: what the hell are we, by which I mean society, doing to our children to make them want to cut themselves or starve themselves or think about their sexuality way before they are sexually active? They should be enjoying their childhoods.

I still haven't worked out what was going on with Groove at the start of term, now 'deadnamed' back to Alina. I have done so much reading about the LGBTQ+ movement and it occurs to me that the movement itself is meant to be about gender. The problem is that it's become about sex. The children are selecting their sexuality by thinking it's about gender. Has it occurred to them that not everyone has sex all the time? I suppose, if you're as young as Lily or Sparkle are, then because you haven't experienced sex yet, both good and bad (or as most of my female friends have said over the years, boring and dutiful), then all your ideas are second guessing and in the realms of fantasy.

We arrive at the park. 'You can let them off their leads now.'

I take the leads from Sparkle and Lily for safekeeping.

Both of them can be a bit forgetful or clumsy at times and a lead might easily be dropped or mislaid. It's not a criticism. It's absolutely normal for their age and why they need 'parenting'. They are developing. Works in progress. Why is someone who only received their pen licence a year ago, and still gets excited by sweeties, trying to work out their gender identity? This is a crazy world.

We walk together along the path. The thems chat about going into the closed-off play area to go on the swings. It's easier to think of 'them' when there are two of them and they are plural. I am trying so hard to get things right in front of Sparkle and Lily, but still regularly think of Sparkle as 'she', and for some reason I can't explain, but perhaps because I have known her for so much longer, it's even harder to reject the 'she' label for Lily. There are inconsistencies in my thinking, I know.

Just before they reach the swings. Doug shoots off to say hello to a friend of his, a West Highland Terrier called George. The owner waves to me. He's a lovely old chap whose name I can't remember (because I know the dogs' names but not the names of their owners). Even though I don't know his name, I like him for his cheerful greetings and good old-fashioned manners. I wave hello.

Suddenly Douglas runs up to George and starts humping him. I walk quickly over to the rampant pooches and call Douglas away. He does this every so often. No rhyme or reason. He was 'done', in the sense of being castrated, years ago. But there is a big Rhodesian Ridgeback called Elsie who he also tries to do this with, but to be successful he'd need a step ladder; it's quite a sight. I step in and pull Douglas away by the collar. I think we're safe and let go. Douglas is still enamoured and charges straight back to George for some more humping activity. I hear laughter behind me. The thems are watching and are in hysterics.

'Thanks for the support!'

This time the nice man uses his walking stick to try and separate Douglas from George.

'I think he fancies George,' I say, feeling a little embarrassed by my dog's antics. Douglas keeps going back to George's derrière. I give up and get the lead, attach it to his collar and pull him away with a stream of apology. 'I really am so sorry. I would have thought he was too old.'

The old man laughs in a good-natured way. 'Clearly age is just a number for Douglas. But you would have thought he'd lose interest once he remembers that George is a boy.'

When I unite with the thems before they go through the play area gate, I suddenly have a thought. 'Do you think Doug is pangender or pansexual?'

Lily laughs. 'He's a dog, Louise.'

'Yes, I know that, but they have sex. How do you think they have puppies?' I can see Sparkle cringing, but I carry on. 'Do you think Douglas thinks about his gender or sexuality?'

'Of course he doesn't,' Lily scoffs. 'Like I said, he's a dog.'

'So why do we?' I ask.

What comes next is one of the most astute and interesting things I think I've heard a young person say, and it comes from Sparkle.

'Because if humans didn't, we would live in chaos.'

'Do you think our genders and sexuality are actually controlled by society and religion?' I'm pleased with myself. That will make them think.

Lily responds, 'Yes, definitely.'

Sparkle shrugs.

I congratulate them on their great comments.

They go off to the swings and climbing frame to lark around while I do a few laps of the park once George has left. Sparkle's comment stays with me.

If humans didn't think about gender and sexuality, we'd live in chaos.

XIX

Sparkle refuses to get up. Point blank refuses. The others are almost out of the door on their way to school, but she is still not moving. Children refusing to get out of bed and go to school when you're in a hurry and have to be somewhere can test your patience to the limit. Fortunately, today I'm working from home with no plans to go anywhere apart from the fields with the pooches. I have looked after enough school avoiders to know that it's a complicated process and if I allow myself to get wound up by it, I won't make the process any easier. As I go towards Sparkle's window to pull back the curtains I see some fresh blood on the lining. I get the desk chair and move it to the window. I chat away as I do this. 'I'm just going to wash your curtains.'

I stand on the chair to unhook both sides and fold them over my arm. I put the handful of hooks on her chest of drawers. With my other hand I take the chair back to her desk, all as if this is a perfectly normal part of a morning routine. The daylight pours into the room more than it normally would now that there are no curtains, just the bare window panes. 'And I'll just open this top window to let in the fresh air. There we are.'

I have often wondered if there was any data for the positive effects of fresh air and clean bedrooms for teenagers.

'I'll head downstairs now to try and remove the blood stains from these.' Again, just as if it's the most typical thing in the world.

I lay out the curtains with their lining sides up on the kitchen table. I apply baking soda paste (two parts baking soda to one part water), a good trick to help lift blood stains. I leave the paste on for a good half an hour, just as the trusty 'research assistant' advises.

While I wait for the paste to work its magic I call school and tell them that Sparkle will be late today, and may not arrive at all. I make sure I do that well away from her earshot. I don't want to give her 'permission' to have time off. I clear up the kitchen, let the dogs in from the garden and shove Hetty, my vacuum cleaner, around the 'high traffic' areas downstairs. Next, I empty the fire grate from the log burner and plump up the cushions. I have a quick shower, then hang upside down to dry my hair. When I stand up my fringe is sticking out like a shopfront awning.

The dogs start barking because someone's at the door. I rush downstairs to answer it. It's my Amazon order for Sparkle. I haven't told her and really, I would like her to have been at school for the day to receive a present. I don't really want to reward the school-refusing. I take it into the kitchen and see that most of the blood stains have faded. Good. I blot the areas of blood with kitchen roll then add another solution, this time of distilled white vinegar.

While this second concoction is seeping into the fabric of the curtains, I open the package. The first item is a graphic novel about a teenage girl finding her gender identity. I found it on the New York Times recommended LGBTQ reading list for LGBTQ children and teenagers. There's also a picture book that I liked the title of because it has echoes of the writing that Sparkle did, *A Princess of Great Daring!* by Tobi Hill-Meyer, illustrated by Eleanor Toczynski. There's a non-fiction guide, *The Every Body Book: The LGBTQ+ Inclusive Guide for Kids About Sex, Gender, Bodies, and Families* by Rachel E. Simon, illustrated by Noah Grigni, and a collection of short stories, *This Is Our Rainbow: 16 Stories of Her, Him, Them, and Us* edited by Katherine Locke and Nicole Melleby. The parcel also contains a black T-shirt with a picture of a door opening out with a rainbow and the words 'Better out than in' in a circle around the door. I leave them all on the side in the box. I can't decide if I should give them to her today or not. I don't want to condone or reward the school-avoidance. On the other hand, I do want these books in her hands.

The vinegar solution seems to have done the trick. I put the curtains in the washing machine at 30 degrees. I open the windows even though it's cold because the kitchen smells like a chip shop after all that vinegar.

My phone rings. I don't recognise the number that flashes up. It's a mobile. I pick up.

'Hello. Is that Louise?'

'Yes.''My name is Pat Evan. I'm the business manager here at the Emotional Welfare team. I'm calling to book you and your husband Lloyd in for your mental health review?'

I quickly push my first reaction away, and manage to avoid saying, 'bloody hell' out loud. In all the time that we have fostered, the one thing I have definitely learnt is that normal human reactions and behaviour are not the best way to deal with people who work in children's social care. I think it best to always err on the side of caution. They could be writing down what you say. They can certainly misinterpret what you say. It's not beyond my experience that they may even be trying to catch you out. I'm aware as I write this that I sound paranoid. That's because experience has taught me that that's probably the best thinking when it comes to these guys. Zoey and Alexander have not filled me with confidence. Lloyd has referred to them as 'the children's TV presenters' on several occasions, which sounds harmless enough, but there is something sinister about them. Everything in my 'listen to your instincts' armoury says 'tread carefully'.

With a super-friendly voice I thank her as sincerely as I can. 'Hi Pat, thank you for calling me.' I then deflect away from that awful question of hers by saying, 'I'm so glad that you called. We are very worried about Sparkle, who is not coping very well and is off school again. You may or may not have seen the reports that I've sent, but Sparkle is beginning to hurt herself.'

I keep going with some of the detail until I hope that Pat's original brief of getting Lloyd and myself in for a head-test fades.

Bingo! It works. Pat doesn't get a day or time from me, and I have put her number in my contacts so I will have pre-warning next time she calls. That way I can avoid speaking to her and just correspond via email instead. Hopefully she will get back to me soon, as I suggested, by email. Social workers seem to me to be getting younger and younger. That's only natural as I age. But the average age of a foster carer in the UK is 54 years. I'm not sure that's always taken into consideration. There is a perception that foster carers should be like teenagers, glued to our phones just waiting for them to call us, as if that's all we have going on in our lives. If they knew anything about me they would know that my family call my mobile phone 'the static'. It's a long-running family joke. I hardly take it anywhere. It collects dust. Pat, frankly, hit the jackpot with me answering at all. Still, I've had a result myself in the sense that I think I've managed to kick their request for us to have a mental health review back into the long grass. What I can't understand is why they are so focused on Lloyd and me. Well, mainly me. Sparkle is a child. The emotional welfare team is part of the 'corporate' parenting. They have a responsibility towards Sparkle. Why aren't they asking to see her?

I begin to accept that I am losing my day to Sparkle's issues, and in my head begin to make other plans. In reality that means staying up late tonight to work. I love that bit of the tax office questionnaire where it asks you how many hours you work per week. As a foster carer I am categorised as self-employed. There are many holes in that category. If I really was self-employed I could advertise my services elsewhere and work anywhere I got work. Of course, that's not quite how it is once we sign our Fostering Agreement. And, even though it's not recognised legally or morally by the local authorities as a contract, it counts as such in financial terms. It's just one example of how the local authority bends and twists rules to suit them. To all intents and purposes it *is* a contract but, if they actually said it was, that would give us some rights. Heaven forbid that should happen. They don't want those pesky foster carers having rights and getting above their station. On my darkest days the work and pay has felt to me as though it resembled modern day slavery. Is it any wonder there is such a shortage of us?

I go back upstairs to check on Sparkle. It's time to see how she is getting on. How they are getting on. I mentally correct myself again. It just won't come automatically. When I'm really thinking hard about it I can remember to say '*they*', but inside my head Sparkle is still 'she'. Perhaps I could cajole her into doing some school work. Perhaps, indeed, that's a good way of justifying giving her those books on a day when she has refused school.

When I get there, Sparkle is pacing about. They remind me of Dotty when I've taken her bedding out of her bed to wash. She paces about looking for something else to sleep on. Sparkle is unsettled, I think it might be as a result of all the light in the room. I suspect they're in the habit of cutting themself while sitting on the floor in the dark with headphones on, probably listening to Nirvana or My Chemical Romance, or some other old, loud rock music.

There is something hectic and wild about harming, even though it appears to be calculated and controlled. I wonder what else we can do for them. I try to think in terms of little changes we could encourage Sparkle to make to improve their life. Things that may help them to feel lighter, freer. I know it's a cliché but I wonder if they could try Yoga, or swimming, or more walking.

I wonder if I should write an outline of what we think is going on for Sparkle. A combination of observations and suggestions. Maybe the Emotional Welfare team might respond faster to some helpful suggestions.

'How are you doing? Would you like some breakfast now? Or perhaps we could go out for something to eat.'

They shake their head. 'I'm not hungry.'

Sparkle pauses and then looks up at me. Their face is pale beneath the flop of thick blonde hair that they wear stiff against the side of their face. The side that was cut has grown into a wavy effect and it looks better. She looks tired. *They* look tired. So tired, and lost. I just want to help this hurting child to find some peace.

'Come down for a drink at least, perhaps a little piece of toast?' I touch her arm.

Sparkle pulls it away. She, they, look small and vulnerable as she folds her arms around herself as if she was hugging herself. The 'them' just falls away from my mind as she rubs her hands up and down her upper arms. As she makes the movement, her pyjama sleeve reveals some cuts on her lower arm above her wrist.

I feel sad. And further defeated. I want to give her a hug. I want to help Sparkle. I want to do something! Distract her, at least.

'How about we go out for a drive?'

To my relief she shrugs. 'Yes.'

This is wonderful news. My own mood lifts straight away. 'How much time do you need to get ready?'

I love going out with one child on a drive. They behave differently to when there are a few of them. When there is only one they share their music and I can talk about the lyrics and ideas and even sing. When I was a child I would have to sit in the back of cars on my own as I was shipped about by my adopted mother, Barbara, or social workers. Barbara didn't have a radio. It was always just silence when we were driving, but I loved looking out of the window at the fast passing sights of fields, trees, houses and other cars.

I found it comforting. Soothing, somehow. Perhaps Sparkle does, too. Some social workers I travelled with would keep the radio on. I remember listening to *Brown Girl in the Ring* by Boney M and finding it cheering. Music has so much power to move us into other moods and places.

'I'll be downstairs,' I say. While I wait for Sparkle to get dressed I begin to tap out an email to Zoey and Alexander.

Hi Zoey and Alexander,

I hope that you are both well?

I wanted to share with you a few thoughts, observations and ideas regarding Sparkle who has now been with us for nearly six months. We feel that we have got to know Sparkle and have, in the short time that they have been with us, seen them grow in many ways. They are a lovely young person who has shared our lives and home; though this has not always been easy.

We have seen changes that do not always feel good. For example, recently Sparkle has been self-harming. This behaviour has escalated and is causing us concern. The cutting has increased in recent days. Sparkle wipes the blood on the lining of the curtains in her room. They are due to see the school nurse soon. We are waiting to hear and we wondered if you would be able to meet Sparkle and discuss with them what therapies are available to them...

I stop typing when Sparkle appears, standing in the doorway of my studio, clearly ready for a drive. She looks like a teardrop. Her shoulders are slumped and round. I'm sure she looks thinner. I pull the lid down on my laptop and stand up and walk over to Sparkle.

I say, with an exaggerated American accent that in my head at least would work in *Thelma and Louise*, 'Let's go, Honey.'

We walk past the pooches. Douglas and Dotty want their walk. 'Later, my little four legged friends,' I promise. Right now I have a child who wants to have a drive. We walk through the back of the garage. I give Sparkle the keys to press the unlock button. The car lights flash and we get in. I pass Sparkle the cable to attach to her phone. Off we go.

'I thought we'd head up-country,' I say.

I head towards the M5 and keep going. The late autumn sun is fierce. Some of the trees are clinging to their leaves. The world is all deep amber and red, burnt browns.

'Isn't this just beautiful?'

Sparkle smiles and nods her head.

They play a bit of Reggae which feels good. I'm heartened, because it's the same tracks that I put on when they had their bath that day. Light and poppy Reggae, but a good introduction to the beat and rhythms.

'What would you like to listen to?' Sparkle asks. Again, I'm touched. Thinking of someone else hasn't always been top of Sparkle's agenda. The first thing that jumps into my brain and I can't explain why, is Queen's *We Will Rock You*. Thanks to the wonders of technology, there it is in a flash: *You got mud on your face, you big disgrace*.

I look across at Sparkle who is tapping out the beat on her knees and smiling. Win! I love this. I know that I need to keep this connection going. I ask for Nirvana. 'Teenage Spirit.'

'It's *Smells Like Teen Spirit*,' she laughs.

We both sing the words. I nod my head and shout out at the top of my lungs. 'Here we are now, entertain us. A mulatto, an albino. A mosquito, my libido, Yeah, hey, yay.'

Sparkle looks at me in some surprise. 'How do you know this?'

'I've heard you and Lily play it often enough and I hate to break it to you, but I do remember when it first came out.'

Sparkle shrugs, adjusting to this new idea.

I smile to myself.

We pull into a service station and when I get back into the car, Sparkle has lined up another Queen song. *I Want to Break Free*. We sing as we go. We don't talk about how she feels, or what sort of therapy is best for her needs. We laugh! On the way home we have Pink Floyd *The Great Gig in the Sky* on repeat, four times in a row. The vocalist, Clare Torry, sings with so much meaning but without meaningful words.

'I remember the first time I heard this. I was reduced to tears and it still affects me.'

Sparkle nods.

'That's the power of music,' I say.

Sparkle nods again.

On repeat number five Sparkle sings along too, and I am moved again. I let out a little gasp, actually. Their voice is beautiful. The volume is up so loud that I think they forget that I'm there. I watch Sparkle, eyes closed, palms flat on their knees, leaning forward to hit those notes.

Tears begin to pour down my face while I drive. While they are singing there is no gender, no cutting, no depression, just release. Pure release. I want the drive to last forever, Sparkle suspended in the safety of the song. But of course, real life intervenes and we must return home.

When we get back inside I tempt Sparkle with peanut butter on toast. 'I've made enough for both of us.'

Sparkle seems a little lighter in mood. Dare I think that they are a little happier? I reach for the Amazon box on the side and hand it over. Sparkle places it carefully on the kitchen table, opens it and lifts out the books.

'Thank you.' The thanks sound genuine and are accompanied by a smile.

They hold up the T-shirt and read the blazon out loud. 'Better Out Than In. Cool.'

Then something happens which hasn't happened before. Sparkle walks over to me and gives me a hug. I am off again, a blubbering mess. She comes back in for a second hug, because I'm now the one clearly in need of comforting. We stand like that, together in the kitchen for a minute or so.

When Sparkle pulls back she looks at me and laughs. 'Louise, you really need to sort out your face.'

I go back to my studio and get back to the email for Zoey and Alexander, picking up from where I left off:

Even though Sparkle is experiencing many challenges, I strongly feel that they want to be themself, to feel free, liberated. I think it's very important that we all try to understand Sparkle's past and jigsaw together what we can to get a picture of what their earlier life was like. None of us really knows, and we can only do our best, but I am mindful that we need to share what we all know to help Sparkle as much as we can. I have gleaned from their drawings and text (I shared with you in an earlier email) that life has not been straightforward, and there are some glimpses into their past that I am concerned about.

Sparkle is an intelligent, creative child who I think would benefit from a therapeutic programme that involves the arts. Today we went for a long drive and listened to many genres of music and I heard Sparkle properly sing for the first time. It was beautiful. I wonder if we could look into music for easing the symptoms of depression and improved motivation? I believe there has been some research into associated benefits. I've been reading about... (I check Google again) *Binaural beats. I wonder if you have some knowledge of this as a therapy? I look forward to hearing from you soon.*

Best wishes,
Louise

I hit send and sit back in my chair, Sparkle's haunting rendition of the Floyd song still playing in my head. We've made a breakthrough today.

XX

Richard is due round later today, after school, to take Sparkle out for a coffee. He will also look at their room. All good. He needs to see it. I am no longer the foster carer who feels judged by what social workers think of my house.

In the early days of my fostering journey, I felt that a foster child's mess was my failure. Now I think, 'this is reality'. The only child I have ever known to be clean and tidy and spend time in their bedroom vacuuming and dusting and arranging furniture to optimise the space was me. Every weekend I rearranged my room and cleaned it from top to bottom. Even my adopted mother said to me one day, 'It's not normal to do that.' I wonder if my obsession with my room was a way of controlling something, when everything else in my life seemed out of my control. Was it, ironically, a form of 'dis-order'. Using that word makes me think of eating disorders. I have noticed, a couple of times now, that Sparkle is becoming thinner. They are still self-harming or 'self-injuring'. I can't remember which term we're using at the moment. Social science language seems to come and go in circles, like hemlines. Speaking of terms, I'm getting a little better in thinking in terms of them-they pronouns. It's not easy, and I still make lots of slips. My subconscious still reverts to 'she', but I'm trying.

Sparkle has not wiped any more blood on my curtains. I haven't hung them back up, but replaced them with blinds for a while in order to remove temptation. But it doesn't mean that they have stopped cutting themself. When they were following me around the house a few weeks ago, they were in the guest room where my airing cupboard lives. It's my 'safe space' in the house. Sometimes I wish I could hide in there amongst all the clean fresh linen and towels. Every Christmas I plant more presents of bars of lovely gift soap amidst the tidy folded piles of essentials. I was taking some fresh bedding out and asked them to hold out their arms to become my shelf while I went through the cupboard. I noticed how they inhaled the aroma of lavender from the soaps that were slotted in the pile of bedding. I pulled out the bath towels and dropped a red hand towel on the floor. Sparkle asked if they could have it, and of course I said yes. Now Sparkle uses the red towel to blot her blood. Every few days I pick it up and wash it so that it's back in her room when she comes home from school.

Once again I feel that we are stuck in limbo. I don't know what to do for the best. Sparkle was meant to meet with the school nurse. After two failed meetings we learnt that the school nurse has actually left the school, and is yet to be replaced. Unfortunate circumstances, but for Sparkle it has been awful. It made them feel worse about themself, as if they were somehow to blame for that. The paranoid path of thinking that they didn't matter, that there was something wrong with them.

After that news she cut herself again. Argh, see. After a bunch of 'theys' I slipped back to 'she'.

I have tried removing everything in the room that I find that's sharp. And I have made everything I can think of inaccessible in the house, anything that could be used to inflict injury, but there is nothing to stop them popping into Poundland or anywhere else in town to find something sharp, even a pack of screws from the DIY shop will do the job. On one occasion they used a ripped bit of a plastic cup that they found somewhere on the street. After, they showed me how they had cut it into sharp shreds and stored them in a sock in the bottom drawer.

It's very hard trying to balance the sad realities of life with Sparkle's needs. I was hoping that the school nurse would be able to stimulate some action. Now I'm beginning to return to the idea that I'm failing them because I can't seem to make anything happen. I still haven't heard from Zoey and Alexander. When I see Richard later today I will push him on this stuff. As far as I can see we still haven't got anywhere at all, in spite of the 'urgency' of the situation.

This child needs help, and they aren't getting it.

The children pile in from school. As usual they all head towards the bread bin to see what the cake fairy might have bought today. That fairy has surpassed herself and they aren't disappointed. Custard doughnuts and a multipack of Monster Munch are nestling in there. With the speed and agility of pickpockets, bags disappear into blazers as they pass. Lily prefers pickled onion and the boys nab the spicy ones.

Sparkle hangs back.

'Which would you like, Sparkle?'

'No thanks, none for me,' is the reply. The tone is flat, and they head off upstairs to their room.

I call up after them. 'Sparkle, remember that Richard will be here at 4.30pm!'

I hear back a defeated, 'Yeah.'

I hope that they are getting changed out of their school uniform. My worries for Sparkle grow daily. Each day they are thinner and more cuts appear on their arms. This child is so, so unhappy and struggling. None of this is their fault. Every child deserves better than this. Sparkle deserves better than this. The feeling that I'm letting them down increases. I want to help. I want to give them answers.

The dogs bark, alerting me that Richard is at the door before he knocks, so I pull back the latch and welcome him in like I was in wait.

He smiles, 'Hello, Louise.'

Quietly, so no one else can hear me, I say, 'We need to talk.'

He nods. 'We'll catch up when I get back from our coffee. I can update you on events.'

'Have you heard anything from the Emotional Welfare team yet?'

He smiles. 'Yes, I have.'

In spite of his smile, something inside me feels that their action is not going to be the action that I've been hoping for.

'Let me know if they eat anything,' I whisper. 'I'm really concerned about their weight. They've stopped eating any kind of snack, and is eating less and less at breakfast and dinner.'

He nods and smiles again. 'Will do.'

As we begin to talk about the traffic on the B road into town, Sparkle appears. They are in skinny black jeans and one of the several uniform black hoodies. I notice that their legs are thinner than ever, outlined in that black silhouette. I think Richard notices too.

Whilst they are out I prepare dinner. The boys gravitate back to the kitchen when they smell the onions and garlic. I'm making caramelised garlic spaghetti with homemade garlic bread, proper 70s style. Sliced baguette with crushed garlic butter jammed between the slices wrapped in tin foil and placed in the oven for thirty minutes. The bread comes out crispy, but oozing in garlic butter. A bit of that with the caramelised sauce is amazing. I cook the sauce and leave everything else ready to go so that I'll be able to serve up quickly after Richard has gone.

Richard and Sparkle are less than an hour and return to more barking from the pooches. Sparkle looks angry or sad, or both, and goes straight up to their room. I hear the door shut and the sound of Nirvana.

The other children vanish.

I have foster carer's paranoia.

'Is Sparkle okay?'

Richard sits down. I pull up a chair opposite. He says, 'I had to tell her about her parents.'

I look at him with a frown, not bothering to correct his pronoun usage.

Whatever he has told Sparkle, why didn't he warn us that he was going to do it first? A heads-up would have been nice.

Lloyd comes in, closes the kitchen door behind him and pulls out a chair.

'Sparkle asked to see her mum and dad, but something has happened that means that she can't see her dad.'

He pauses.

All sorts of things flash through my mind, but I wait patiently for the news.

'A few parents have complained to the police that Luke was gaming with minors. Their children. And he has been inappropriate online.'

The way he says it tells me that there's a euphemism if ever I heard one.

'Are these children friends of Sparkle's?'

'Most likely, yes, I'd imagine so. But I can't say definitely for now. The fallout is that it's been decided that for safeguarding reasons it's best that Sparkle does not have contact with her dad for now.'

That's hard on so many levels. 'Does Sparkle know the reason?' Children deserve to know the truth, or the most suitable version of it, or they are left wrangling the wrong emotions, and blaming themselves, just as Sparkle did with the school nurse.

'I haven't told her all of it. I said that there had been a problem with Luke gaming with children online. That's all.'

'What about Lois? Can Sparkle see her?'

'Not easily, no. Not in person. She's currently in America.'

'On holiday?' I ask, slightly incredulous.

'Lois is visiting her boyfriend, someone she's met online, with the idea that she may move out to the US.'

This is hard for me to hear, let alone Sparkle. This poor kid. I feel so much pain for them.

A thought occurs to me. 'What about the grandparents? They're still around, aren't they? Is there a chance that Sparkle could talk to them or meet them for a lunch or something? We could invite them here if that's easier?'

'We've thought about that. I think it's unlikely. Prior to Luke being questioned for inappropriate conversations online with children, his parents had bought him a new house in a different area with the view that it would be a fresh start for Luke and Lois.

'As it turns out, Luke's parents are no longer speaking to him, as Lois is doing her thing and Luke moved a different woman into the house. The relationship has become fractious. The grandparents are concerned that this is also inappropriate as the young woman is just 18 years old and Luke is in his mid-40s. They've made their feelings clear.'

'They're washing their hands of their own grandchildren? Are you sure?'

I feel my own heart plummet. And if I feel awful on her behalf, what must Sparkle herself have felt? This is a deep abyss of rejection.

Richard shrugs.

I repeat it, because I want to clarify. 'So, Sparkle's grandparents are refusing to see Sparkle? And the siblings?'

He nods. 'The grandparents have stated that they withdraw support and no longer wish to be connected with Luke or the children.'

I need somewhere to channel all this hurt, and I feel myself starting to get angry again. It isn't the grandchildren's fault that their parents are so stupid. Why are they punishing the children?

In the heat of the moment, I'm not able to articulate this. Richard fills the gap as I search for words.

'Look, I'm trying to work with them so that they'll see Sparkle and her siblings, but at the moment the grandmother is refusing. The step-grandfather seems far more reasonable and we hope that he'll help her feel more positive.'

'But how can they just abandon them?'

'Under the circumstances, I can understand that it must be difficult for them. The grandmother is very angry with Luke. There is a piece of work to do there.'

I begin to tune out as Richard sounds more and more like he's embarking on a student project. This is so much more than a 'piece of work'.

I hear the words, 'school nurse' and I zone back in, ready to hear what comes next.

'The school nurse wrote a report on Sparkle.'

'Hang on, I'm going to stop you right there. The school nurse never met Sparkle.'

Richard looks a little confused. 'Really? Well, that's strange because there's a report from the school nurse.'

'There can't be. The school nurse cancelled their meeting twice, then we heard that she left.'

He is determined to read out her report. I lean in to hear this. I am already fuming, but it gets worse.

'The, err, report states that the nurse believes that Sparkle has ADHD.'

'Leaving aside the fact that she didn't meet Sparkle, she's a nurse, not an educational psychologist.'

Richard explains that now it is becoming standard practice for teachers and school nurses to make assessments about children's needs.

I have to breathe deeply not to react to this.

Lloyd reads my face and body language and decides to try and take over my part of the conversation in an effort at diplomacy, but I'm not having any of it. I am Furious. The capital F isn't enough to denote how Furious I am.

'A teacher and a nurse are not qualified to diagnose a child who may or may not have special educational needs. It isn't fair on them as professionals to be put in that position, however 'standard practice' it might be. Nor is it fair on the children. They may well be misdiagnosed.'

Richard nods.

I'm starting to resent the nodding and smiling. He seems to nod even when he's disagreeing, like we won't notice what he's saying if it comes with a nod.

'But we are where we are,' he says.

And that simple utterance makes me snap. It has to be one of my most hated phrases. 'We are where we are' dismisses the fact that we could be somewhere else if others were not so stupid. It's a ridiculous statement, especially when it comes to children. As adults we should do everything we can to ensure that our children are in the best place, not just, 'we are where we are.'

I try to establish facts as calmly as I can. Which isn't very. 'Richard. So, are we now thinking that Sparkle, who struggles to get going on a daily basis and would prefer to be *quiet* in her room, has ADHD? Is that actually what we are saying?' I can't keep the sarcasm out of my voice.

I pause and Richard looks like he might be about to speak. I cut him off before he has the chance.

'And that *diagnosis* was created by a nurse who never met Sparkle and has now left? And we're all OK with that?'

To give him his due, Richard swallows rather than nods this time.

'Richard, do you know Sparkle?'

'Yes of course I do.'

'And are you aware of the signs of ADHD?'

'Yes.'

I know my kitchen table isn't a court of law, but I'm on a roll now.

'What would you say those symptoms are?'

'Well, things like having a short attention span and being fidgety and easily distracted.'

'Anything else?'

'Um, not being able to listen or follow instructions. Forgetful, clumsy, that sort of thing.'

'And you've just said that you know Sparkle. She is none of those things. In fact, she is the polar opposite of those symptoms. I'm not qualified like the school nurse who appears to be able to see into her crystal ball and can make a diagnosis telepathically, but in my opinion, you know, from living with her for six months and seeing her every day, watching her not able to drag herself from that bed every morning, Sparkle is possibly, if we want to give it a label, suffering with Sluggish Cognitive Tempo.'

My trusty research assistant has been hard at work. Richard looks bewildered, so I bring up the notes I have saved on my phone.

'SCT is a syndrome related to attention deficit hyperactivity disorder (ADHD) but distinct from it. Typical symptoms include prominent dreaminess, mental fogginess, hypoactivity, sluggishness, staring frequently, inconsistent alertness and a slow working speed. That is Sparkle. Not the symptoms you've just described.'

Richard nods. More slowly this time.

'And, about the Emotional Welfare team. When exactly is Sparkle likely to get an appointment with them?'

Richard looks uncomfortable. 'They said that they are unable to properly support Sparkle until you and Lloyd have had a mental health review.' He swallows again. 'And the boys and Lily.'

Lloyd and I share a look of utter disbelief. I have absolutely had enough now.

'Okay, and I would like Zoey and Alexander to have a mental health review in order that we, as professional foster carers, feel satisfied that they have the experience, qualification and integrity to be able to offer Sparkle anything at all.'

If Lloyd and Richard thought I was ranting a moment ago, now I really launch.

'Mine and my family's mental health is not part of this. It has nothing to do with it. Sparkle came here as a placement just over six months ago. You and your colleagues matched her. You matched her to us knowing who we are. You made that decision. If there are any concerns about our mental health, they come from the stress that we are experiencing as a consequence of the total lack of support from your organisation for Sparkle!'

I pause for breath, but nobody looks like they are going to interrupt me now.

'We know from bitter past experience that when foster carers speak up and advocate for their children they can be punished. That punishment can come in the package of an allegation. So, shall we expect an allegation from someone in Emotional Welfare soon?'

Richard, like all good social workers, knows exactly what I am saying, even in his fledgling stage.

'I've heard lots of shocking things in my time, but for a child to not receive the help she needs because the foster family refuses to attend mental health reviews. Well that has to be one of the most perverse things that I have heard for a long, long time.'

Richard ends the conversation, or makes an attempt to, by standing up and pushing his chair underneath the table, and saying, 'I hear what you're saying, and I'll log your concerns.'

I wonder which one day training course that was on.

'Richard, you have delivered bad news to Sparkle and a misdiagnosis of her learning needs which was not asked for.

We need support for a young person who is self-harming. Have you seen the cuts? Do you want to see more blood? '

I don't give him a chance to answer again.

'I also suspect she is purging and in the first stages of developing an eating disorder. Along with gender dysmorphia. How many more warning signs do you need? You can tuck your chair neatly underneath my table and leave this house, and we will have a mess to try and pick-up.'

'Look, I'll do what I can to try and get the Emotional Welfare team to see Sparkle without seeing you first.'

He backs out of the kitchen, and I follow.

'Don't try and persuade them to do their job. *Tell* them to do their job. Sparkle needs help. They needed it months ago and, after your news today, God only knows what will happen next.'

XXI

Perhaps unsurprisingly, Sparkle doesn't come back down after seeing Richard. I go up multiple times to see her, finding different reasons and bringing different things with me each time. I take up a sandwich, crisps, fruit, a bottle of Coke and a glass of water. Each time I return, none of it has been touched.

I take up breadsticks. I know Sparkle likes bread sticks. They have a party trick of eating them by nibbling in one go from one end to the other. I have seen them laughing while they do it. I put the latest tray on Sparkle's bed and sit down. There is an awkward silence which I fill with a rather lame, 'Are you okay, Sweetheart?'

Of course she's not okay.

I go on to tell her that Richard has filled me in on the news about her dad and mum and granny.

Sparkle says, 'Granny? She's a fucking bitch. She was always horrible to Mum and me, she hates us.'

'That's sad and a shame. I don't know how anyone could hate you. You're so lovely.'

I wait to see if anything comes back. It does. 'My dad's a useless pervert.'

I don't agree or disagree. It isn't my place to do either. I only know what Richard has told us, and haven't seen any evidence either way but what I do understand is that the news of her father's conduct is no surprise to Sparkle.

'Would you like me to arrange something with Tristan and Bart to see your brother and sister?'

'Yes,' they say, very quietly.

'Sparkle, I can't make any of the past go away nor can you but we can try and improve today and tomorrow.'

It's not enough. I know that this child will hurt themself when I leave the room.

The other children are very down, too. The whole household seems deflated and depressed. I can see by Lloyd's demeanour that he feels the same as I do. As if someone is unfolding layers and layers of black cloth into our lives. My beautiful sunny family is being crushed by what has been brought into our house. All the children look sad.

It hurts more than I can say.

A child has come into our lives and, through no fault of their own, is pulling us all down into their sadness and despair.

After dinner, a sombre affair, I make sure that the children are up to date with their homework. I try to spend a bit of time with each of them.

Jackson is the first to say, 'Mum, are you all right?'

The fact that my son has asked me hurts me even more.

I sigh. 'I'm waiting for help for Sparkle and it doesn't seem that forthcoming.'

'Would it happen if we did the mental health tests?'

Nothing gets past these kids. We haven't even discussed it with them.

He smiles. 'We do know, you know. We could hear you talking to the social worker.'

My heart is breaking. What is going on here? My son is volunteering to have a mental health review in order that Sparkle, a foster child, receives the help they need and are entitled to. This is utterly mad and feels wrong on so many levels. It's an abuse of power. It's like my children have to donate their organs to help Sparkle get theirs. What kind of a system is this? It's wrong, wrong, wrong.

In the morning Sparkle is slow to rise. I could have predicted that. I go into their room and see that the red towel is discarded on the floor. There is some dried blood on the towel. I smile brightly at Sparkle.

'Would you like some breakfast? I'll take you to school. I've got to pop out anyway.'

(I haven't.)

By the time she comes downstairs the others are just on their way out.

Jackson, being friendly, nods, 'All right?' to Sparkle.

He may as well have said something incendiary because

it triggers an explosion in Sparkle. Their reaction is entirely out of proportion. They stand in the hall, shouting their head off.

'You fucking fat cunt. You ugly bastard. No one fucking likes you. They hate you.'

Lloyd emerges from his study, also shouting. 'I'm in a bloody meeting! Will you all shut-up?'

I watch Jackson's features seem to fall apart as he bolts out of the front door. The other two have already left via the back. I am mortified. There is no need for Sparkle to talk to Jackson like that and, if I have ever heard transference, that was it. Huge, ugly, sad transference of their own pain onto Jackson, who last night was offering to help Sparkle by donating a metaphoric organ to save them.

Sparkle goes into the sitting room, sinks down onto the sofa and cries and cries and cries. All the tears in the world seem to spill from that small, pale face.

I sit next to them holding their hand.

I notice Sparkle's bony knees prominent against the fabric of their black tights.

'Sparkle, love.'

They pull their hand away and place it on their lap. Then they stand up. I stand up, too, to follow them out.

'Sparkle please don't take your anger out on Jackson. He only said *all right*.'

Before I know what is happening she whips her arm towards me and, with the back of her hand, hits me hard in the face. I stand still in shock. When I put my hand up to my mouth, it comes away with blood on it and the salty blood taste enters my mouth through my cut lip.

Sparkle stands by the door, their body seeming to pulse in a primal rage, fists clenched, arms bent at the elbow, feet pushed into the ground. Then the screaming starts.

Scream after scream after scream, mouth wide open as the anguish pours from it.

Lloyd flies into the room looking absolutely shocked at the picture he sees: I'm standing behind Sparkle with blood coming through my hand and my eyes watering. Sparkle is in a trance-like state, in an unworldly place of despair.

Lloyd is pale and upset. He looks past Sparkle directly to me and whispers, 'We can't do this anymore.'

I cry.

XXII

It feels like hours but it's only ten minutes later when I sit back down with Sparkle. This time they succumb to my proffered arm, the physical need for another human being overtaking them. I hold them and rock them while they cry and cry.

Their body, their thin, too-thin body trembles. Again it's a jolt to realise quite how thin and bony they have become. Physically as well as emotionally fragile. They morph back into she in my arms. She becomes the Sparkle I recognise as the young girl who arrived here months ago. I gently hold her wrist with one hand. With my thumb I smooth over her cuts on her wrist and lower arm. I can smell her breath. She has halitosis. I can only assume that it's a result of purging.

This poor child. I am at a loss to know what to do. Her pain is huge. I can see why she is in this much misery. It's obvious to anyone. So why can't we get her the help that she needs? Why are those people, Zoey and Alexander, delaying the help? What the hell is really going on here?

Lloyd brings in a tray with a couple of pieces of dampened kitchen roll for me to put on my face. I have a brainwave. I mouth to him, across the top of Sparkle's head, to take a photo of my face. This could be just the evidence we need to show the children's TV presenters how bad life is becoming for us and may get Sparkle some help. Lloyd takes a few pictures. Sparkle is still crying. I don't think they noticed Lloyd and his phone amidst all the emotional pain.

I have a headache myself from all the drama, and I think, despite Sparkle's current physical state, they managed to hit me pretty hard in the face. I hold the damp kitchen roll to my mouth and begin to pat the area to wipe away the blood. I think I should look in the hall mirror and assess the damage. I let go of Sparkle and stand-up. I pull all the cushions from the sofa and armchairs to surround her like a big, warm, squidgy hug. I wipe the wet hair off her face and give her another hug. I kiss her on top of her hair and say, 'I'll be back in a minute. I'm getting you a drink and some tissues.'

She slumps forward and breathes in more than cries, as if she is breathing in her own tears.

I divert from the route to the kitchen to the hallway to look in the mirror. I know that any injuries to the head always look worse but I do look like I've been hit by a heavyweight boxer, not an 11-year-old girl.

I find Lloyd in the kitchen making coffee. I decline the

coffee and go for two paracetamol and a glass of water instead. I put the kettle on to make a cup of tea. I pour a glass of water and dampen some more kitchen roll. I go back into the sitting room to find Sparkle sparked out on the sofa. It's as though they fell over and slept where they landed. I try to make them comfortable by gently lifting their feet and placing them on the ottoman foot stool. I move the cushions around so that they slip into a more comfortable position. I get a couple of blankets out of the large chest in the corner and lay them over them. The dogs have stopped looking scared and have dug themselves in as closely as they can into the sides of Sparkle, doing their bit to keep them safe and warm. I place the glass of water on the table by their side. I can't do any more for now.

I leave them there while I have a cup of tea and Lloyd has his coffee.

He looks up at me. 'I mean it. We can't keep doing this, Louise. I know she's in pain but it's bigger than us, she needs help.' He rolls his eyes, knowing the futility of it all as well as I do. I ignore the pronouns.

'I'll email Richard. He was the one who sparked this event by telling Sparkle all that negative stuff without any warning to any of us. So how could we help them? I'll copy in Zoey and Alexander.'

Lloyd scoffs at that. 'What, those muppets? As if that's going to help.'

The state of Sparkle is depressing enough without

thinking about the state of mental health support for traumatised children.

'It's messed-up! We are failing Sparkle. How is any of this good for any of us?' I reach for the laptop. I report, as dispassionately as I can, on the latest developments. I code-switch, back to 'they-them' pronouns as I type.

Cc. Richard, Zoey and Alexander.

Hi All,

We just wanted to update you on Sparkle. After you left yesterday, Richard, Sparkle stayed in their room. I went to see them a few times but they didn't want to engage in conversation. I shared with them that we are sorry to hear about their family news. I was struck by just how not shocked they were by the news of the accusations against their father. Nor did they seem surprised that he was not allowed to have contact with them after parents reported inappropriate online behaviour with their children. Sparkle expressed that their grandmother hated them and their mother. This was sad to hear and articulated thoughts that I suspect are contributing to Sparkle's pain.

This morning Jackson (my birth son), said 'All right?' in a kind, friendly way and Sparkle became verbally aggressive. Sparkle stood in the hall shouting, 'You f******g fat c**t, you ugly b*****d, no one f*****g likes you, they hate you.' Then, after the children bolted for school, I was in the sitting room with them and, while in a *state of distress, Sparkle hit me in the face. Please see attached photo. After this event I sat with Sparkle and comforted them. I went to the kitchen to get them a drink and cool damp cloth for their face. When I returned they were fast asleep. I have left them on the sofa to rest. I have telephoned school to let them know that Sparkle will not be coming in today.*

Both Lloyd and I are asking you if you can get the help for Sparkle that they need. Their mental health is affecting all of us and we are struggling to help Sparkle and keep them safe. They continue to self-harm (please see earlier emails), and more recently, Sparkle has begun to not eat. I would say that Sparkle is showing signs of being at high risk. We feel that as mainstream foster carers the support Sparkle needs goes beyond our remit. We also have to balance Sparkle's needs with the needs of the three other children in our home and our own needs and commitments.

We would like to arrange an urgent meeting with you all to discuss a way forward for Sparkle. We look forward to hearing from you at your very earliest convenience.

Best wishes,
Louise and Lloyd Allen.

I hit send.

XXIII

It's the weekend and more than ever I need a lie in.

Sparkle's mood and aggression have taken its toll on all of us. I've noticed in the past that when Lloyd and I are struggling with a placement and we need a bit of me-time to ourselves we end up going to the shops, not for any particular urgent purchase, but a gentle mooch and lunch. We are so desperate to get out for half an hour, or maybe stretch it for 45 minutes. I have been known to drive into town to buy a tube of toothpaste when there are three already in the bathroom cupboard. I know that our house is in trouble when we resort to doing this. I recognise these signs. I know we are overloaded and demoralised. It seeps into everything. There is the loss of joy in our work, more negative thoughts and feelings than good ones. There is loss of sleep, exacerbating increased anxiety levels. I find that we also now don't feel as naturally empathetic. I hear myself say, 'For God's sake, Sparkle!' when she has a pronoun outburst and rants about all of us being phobic again. This latest time it was completed by the suggestion that we 'all deserve to die.' Not my favourite way to start a Wednesday. After saying it, Sparkle stormed out. Anyone who feels the need to strop or storm off has, as far as I'm concerned, lost. They are out of control. There are no answers, there are no strategies, there is only aggression and hurt.

Every day feels relentless. We all walk around on eggshells. No one should have to do that at work, and especially not in their own home, their safe space. I am more and more worried about the other children and the effect that Sparkle's behaviour and needs are having on them. There seems to be no joy, no laughter. I'm worried that we're beginning to shut down, to remove our heads and heart from Sparkle. When it's this hard we need help. We need a break.

Things were tough enough already, but they have become dramatically harder since Sparkle learnt about their family.

I make sure that I never pass judgement in front of Sparkle, but their dad has been an absolute idiot, in my opinion. What grown man in his forties wants to game online with children? Especially when he has children of his own. Children who are now in care because he can't meet their needs. His behaviour is irresponsible and inappropriate. What are his boundaries? What did he do to his children? From what I've heard, Lois seems like she is running away, leaving her children behind, but running to whom and where? Is this man she has met online safe? Or even real?

You hear so many stories of violence and abuse against women in her position. Is she safe? She's vulnerable because it sounds as if she has been abused herself. On the rebound and looking for love, whatever that means.

I'm cross with the grandparents, too. They compound this whole, ugly mess. What are they doing? Why aren't they stepping in? It's unbearable to watch this play out in the context of all of Sparkle's emotional trauma. They have money, and, if they've retired from the antiques business, time.

I wonder what else has gone on in their household in the past. These scenarios do not emerge from nowhere. What kind of abuses were happening when Sparkle was living in the thick of it all? It's always the poor children who get the short straw when the adults around them make poor decisions. All my resentments are heightened because now my own children are suffering as a result of Sparkle's family's problems.

We *still* haven't got a supervising social worker. I think this has been the longest sustained period in my long fostering history. We nearly had a temp who was going to come out of their retirement to help with the backlog but that didn't materialise. We had a date and time for a Teams meeting but it was cancelled. I wonder if the retired social worker looked at the workloads and thought better of it. We keep writing logs and sending them to Richard, who I know is overworked, quite possibly out of his depth, and firefighting. I have sent several more emails to Richard, Zoey and Alexander, keeping them updated with each act of aggression that takes place and disintegrates our home further. I have been explicitly honest and told them that we are struggling, that the whole household is struggling, that even the animals are struggling as we tiptoe around Sparkle.

This weekend we need a rest, and we need to find a way to regroup. I plan a film night after pizzas and ice cream for Saturday evening. I ask Lily and Sparkle if they would like to go shopping in Big Town, our affectionate name for the nearest proper town centre to the village, to look at clothes and have lunch. It would give Lloyd and the boys a little space and I have never known a young person not like to go clothes shopping. Lily is straight in with a 'yes' and 'what time?' I explain the times that I am planning to leave. If it was left to Lily we might just about get there as everything closes. She has always had a tendency towards the slow.

I knock on Sparkle's door, take a deep breath, and walk in happy and smiling to try and set the mood. I see hair sticking up out of the duvet which isn't quite right because yesterday she had long hair and it would not have achieved the spikiness it has this morning. I pull up the blind. I still haven't hung the curtains back up. I don't want to put temptation in the way.

Although, perhaps wiping on any available fabric is a thing for the girls. I have noticed that Lily has been experimenting with foundation cream and has decided to wipe her hands and face on her cream dressing gown that hangs on the back of her door. One of my step-daughters would wipe her hands and face on the throw I bought her to cover the futon in her room. Nail polish, lipstick, foundation and smudged mascara. I bought her face wipes, boxes of tissues, but she kept doing it. The tissues she scrunched up and threw on the floor, the bin stood empty. I was much younger then, and newly married, and I saw her behaviour as a way to target me and make me angry in order to cause problems between Lloyd and me. But other teenage girls we have fostered have done similar.

When Lily started wiping makeup on the dressing gown, I decided that it was pure laziness. It does drive me up the pole but as I always say, 'pick your battles'. I have always considered it a female trait. Perhaps I should turn it around and see it as society throwing all these products at women to necessitate the wiping.

I begin a conversation with the hair sprouting from the top of the duvet. 'Fancy some shopping in Big Town later?'

They grunt, 'No.'

Strange, I think. Why not? I explore a little further with my delicate tweezers. 'So, you don't want any new clothes or treats?'

'No.' A pause. 'I'm going out.'

This is a surprise because they haven't asked permission, and I haven't agreed to anything. I keep it light and casual, though. 'Oh, who with? And where do you plan on going?'

Sparkle pokes their head out from beneath the duvet.

Oh dear, I think to myself. Sparkle has what I can only describe as a mullet, and not a good one either.

I have a flashback to when Sparkle told me that hairdressing was a first choice of career. There might be some way to go there.

I ask them again, 'Are you sure that you don't want to come shopping?' *And find a hairdresser to sort out that mess*, I want to add. 'I thought we could go and see the new Head Shop that's just opened.' It's a big rainbow-coloured, LGBTQ+ oriented, alternative, trendy shop. I spotted it while I was doing a food hygiene training session for foster carers while in town a few weeks ago. 'It looks good. Next to the museum. Though obviously we won't go *there*,' I say, lest Sparkle thinks that I'm trying to make this educational.

But, no, they do not want to come.

'Sparkle, what is it that you *would* like to do today?'

Now they sit up properly. I can see that, thankfully, there are no new fresh cuts on their arms. I can't see any bloody smudges on the pillows or the part of the sheet that's showing, either. Good news, perhaps, but I will look more closely later to make sure.

'I'm going out with Groove and Tex.'

I'm not thrilled with this idea, nor their casual assumption that it is okay to go without asking first. I have had my concerns about Groove as an older influence on this young person and, because Groove hasn't been mentioned for a while I had hoped that the friendship had run its course. Evidently not. I haven't a clue who Tex is. Makes me think of Tex-Mex. Perhaps it's an American child. I can't think of any American families at the school, but it's a big school with nearly 2000 students who come from all over the area, so what do I know?

I agree that Sparkle can go, because, frankly, short of locking them up, what choice do I have? If I'm honest, I feel a bit of pressure is off my shoulders because they'll be out of the house. Funny how, with the return of Groove, the 'they' pronoun comes more easily to me in relation to Sparkle. Then we get down to logistics.

'Okay, well you can go for two hours-'

'Fuck that, I'm going for longer and you can't fucking stop me.'

I say, 'Before you bite my head off, I was about to say you can go for two hours and then call one of us to tell us where and what you're up to. If all is okay, you can stay out a little longer.'

They look daggers at me.

I go on. 'Sparkle, no matter what you think, you are still a child and it is our responsibility to look after you and keep you safe. It's not about restricting you. We need to know your whereabouts in order to make sure that you are safe. Do you not understand that?'

Sparkle mutters something rude under their breath and I pretend I don't hear it.

'So, what time are you leaving?'

They look at their phone and move quickly out of bed to get ready. 'Half an hour.'

Blimey. It would be great if they could move that fast on a school day. I refrain from saying that, too. While Sparkle is in the shower I have a look at the bedding. There are a few smudge marks at the bottom of the sheet and duvet. I wonder if they have been cutting their ankles instead of their arms. I'm hypervigilant at the moment. The red towel looks unused, though. Another good sign. I'll wash everything once they've gone out.

Lily is also busy getting ready in her room when I go in. She stands in front of the mirror and carefully ties a rainbow scarf around her head. It leaves her looking like a little WW2 land army girl, but lovely nonetheless. I check on the boys, who are clearly not leaving their rooms until the house has emptied of conflict and they know it's safe.

Perhaps I'm overthinking that. The reality is that they are fine, and I doubt if it's the fear of Sparkle's possible conflict. Probably more to do with being cosy and in a game. While Lily and Sparkle flutter about performing urgent ablutions and sartorial adjustments, I wait in the kitchen by the coffee machine. I look out of the window and try to predict the weather. It's grey and looks damp. A clouds-set-to-stay day. Lloyd comes in, rather cautiously. Perhaps his caution is nervousness about inadvertently encountering Sparkle.

'It's okay, the coast is clear.' I turn to switch on the coffee machine.

Lloyd is reading a news update on his phone when Sparkle appears. I pray that he offers no reaction at all to their new, slightly unfortunate hairstyle. My prayer is answered when he smiles and says 'morning' before heading out to the conservatory to pretend to get something.

'Would you like some breakfast?' I ask Sparkle. They look at me as if I have asked them to eat the insoles of Jackson's trainers.

I suggest that they wear a coat, or at least take a raincoat with them as the sky looks so dark.

Sparkle says, 'Na. I'm good,' and walks out.

The front door slams and they have gone from the house before I get a chance to do or say anything else. The good news is, I have Groove's mum's mobile number because of Maria, so Sparkle hasn't gone totally rogue. Though the attitude suggests that they are pretty confident that they have. I text Sparkle: *Have a fun time. Remember to check in in two hours xx*

No reply. I'm 'left on read', as Lily would say, meaning that my message has been seen but not responded to. One of the biggest insults to their generation.

Lily herself is in good spirits and I can feel that she is enjoying our one-on-one time. I go out of the way to ensure that our day is great fun. We have lunch in a street-food fast-food place which is great. Utterly delicious, and we manage to find something vegetarian that she likes: a steamed bao bun filled with a cheesy filling served up with salad and peanut powder. She skips most of the salad, but the bun is a hit.

It begins to rain. Really rain. It's 'the rain from hell' as we all say in our frequently-flooded town now.

I text Lloyd to remind him to fix the flood gate. It doesn't take long for the rain to rush off the fields and divert from the ditches that haven't been dug out for about twenty years, down the lanes and into our homes. When it rains like this it feels unsafe. I wonder if we should head back before the flooding closes the roads home. We look at each other with a grimace as we fight to put umbrellas up.

On the splashy dash to the car we grab some cakes from the lovely old-fashioned cake shop. They sell bread-and-butter pudding in thick slabs, and Vincent's favourite, spiced apple cake. We run to the Head Shop and I see something for each of the boys: bracelets with skulls and bits and pieces. I pick up some rainbow bunting for Sparkle, and Lily sees an embroidery set that spells out, 'fuck this'. She pays for that herself. I enjoy her ability to see the joke in that, but I would not feel comfortable about Sparkle having something like that for several reasons. I hope it's for Lily herself and not for Sparkle. There will be needles in the kit. I will need to check.

We take our goods and run out of the shop. The downpour is so heavy that it hurts our shoulders and backs as it pounds onto our coats. The puddles are swelling and the drains are pushing the water back up. Our highways drains can't cope with this amount of flood water. We head towards the car, parked outside the big Tesco superstore. I open the door and get Lily in the car. Her rainbow headscarf is stuck to her face. In just the few minutes I spend putting the shopping bags in the boot, I am drenched. The umbrellas became pointless after we left the Head Shop. I sit in the driver's seat and shut the door fast, as if we have escaped a chase from wolves. I pull down the mirror and laugh. I have wet hair and a fat face, the look no woman of my age really wants at all. I reverse out and head home. It's like we're in the *Twister* film from the 90s, with Helen Hunt, chasing storms in Oklahoma. The difference is we're flood running. There is an end-of-days feeling. We need to get home before we aquaplane, or end up stuck with no signal for help.

Others have exactly the same idea as us. The single track road out of the car park is jammed. I'm panicking inside, but trying very hard not to scare Lily.

'Could you text Lloyd and ask him to contact Sparkle and find out if they're safe?'

Immediately a text pings back. Lloyd reports that Sparkle is at Groove's house. Without telling me, Lily messages Maria. After another ping, Lily says, 'Sparkle isn't at Maria's.'

Right. I am not impressed. Where the hell is she/are they then? The 'she' slips back now that I sense I might have a lost child on my hands.

I drive carefully home through the country lanes, questioning my decision-making this morning. Not that I

266

even felt as if I had much choice. Sparkle had made up their mind and that was that. But it now feels as if it was not such a good idea to let Sparkle head out on their own. Should I have been more insistent?

As we drive over a stone bridge by the Mill House, the water is already up to the top of my tyres. I've become quite skilled at driving through flood water in recent years. I drop into first gear and drive as slowly as possible while keeping the revs up high by slipping the clutch. It's crucial to find the balance between stalling and creating a wave of water that might flood the engine. The last thing I want is to have the engine cut out and leave us powerless. The windscreen wipers sloosh backwards and forwards at top speed and it isn't enough to keep a good visual on the road. I have to concentrate on getting us back safely before I can channel my thoughts properly onto Sparkle and where the hell they might be.

When we get home, Lloyd is outside on the footpath sweeping the continual cycle of debris from the drain covers. It is crazy but just a few leaves or bits of litter can block the grid and cause the water to divert. Water always takes the easiest route. Our house is on a hill so the water flows to the bottom. So far, the flood water has not run uphill. I park and we make a dash to the back of the house to get in the back way. Both boys, who are completely unaware or uninterested in the potential problem outside, are eating toast and talking about Pokémon cards.

Within the next half an hour there are two claps of thunder, one outside which tells me that the storm is passing and one in my head as I see a text from Sparkle.

I'm staying for dinner at Tex's.

I ask the children who Tex is. None of them know.

Lily says, 'I don't remember hearing that name. I don't think it's anyone from the LGBTQ+ community at school. I know most of them. Not in our year anyway. It must be a friend of Groove's from outside school, or maybe someone in Year 11?'

Lily quickly texts Maria to see what she knows.

'Is Maria still part of the LGBTQ+ community?' I ask.

Lily shakes her head. 'No, definitely not. She hates them.'

Strong choice of word, I think.

A moment or two later there is another ping on Lily's phone. She reports back that Maria thinks that Tex is indeed a 'them' in Year 11.

'Can you find out any more?'

Lily's fingers are already tapping at the screen of her phone.

'Tex's birth name is Elenora.' She names a nearby town where Tex lives.

'Anything else you can find out?' I push.

More tapping.

'Elenora was moved from her last school in Year 10 because of bullying.'

I say. 'Oh, that's sad. I hope your school is managing it better than their last school, then.'

Lily is still reading. 'No, they were the bully.'

Nice.

I ring Maria's mum then and ask if she knows where Sparkle is, 'Because Sparkle said that she was with, err, Alina,' I explain. I'm not sure if Alina's mum knows that Alina is Groove. She is very nice on the phone, if perhaps a little guarded.

She tells me that she will collect the girls from Elenora's when the weather has calmed and the road to her town has cleared of flood water.

'What sort of time do you think that might be?'

'I'll aim for 6ish?'

'Brilliant, thank you.' I am glad. I am glad that Sparkle is safe, but I am even more glad that she is not here right now. We need a break from the drama.

Maria's mother is as good as her word. Whatever they got up to during the day has worn Sparkle out, and they claim to be hungry when they get home. Given the eating situation at the moment, this is good news.

'Would you like to eat pizza and ice cream with us?'

They grunt, 'No thanks.'

So I heat up a margherita pizza from the freezer with some sweet potato chips for them. I'll do ours later. I watch Sparkle, hopefully without them knowing that I'm watching them. I compliment them on their new style.

'Hair looks nice, Sparkle. Will the colour come out before school on Monday?'

Sparkle looks sort of at me, not quite making eye contact. 'Don't care.'

Sparkle, or someone, has coloured their hair with Sharpies in rainbow colours again.

They sit with their coat still on at the table.

'You must have got caught in some of that rain, like we did. Can I take that coat off you so that I can hang it up on a radiator to dry out?'

They completely ignore me.

One by one at intervals, the rest of the household walk towards the kitchen, see that Sparkle's back and turn around and go away again. It's awful. This is not how we live. This is not who we are.

After Sparkle finishes eating the pizza, they stand up and walk out upstairs. No word of thanks or acknowledgement.

I note that Sparkle's trainers are wet and muddy and, if I'm honest, for the sake of my floors, I'd rather she took them off before going up the stairs. If it was anyone else, I'd ask them, but I don't ask Sparkle. And the reason I don't is because I am scared of her, them, they.

I start to feel the pronoun slippage again. And I've worked so hard at it.

The rest of the weekend is horrid. Sparkle insists on going out again on Sunday and leaves before I have a chance to do or say anything. I can keep some tags on them through

Maria's mum but she's not what I would call 'helpful'. I can feel myself letting go, abdicating some kind of responsibility in a way that I wouldn't do with another child.

I don't know what we can do. Sparkle has set out their stall.

I have attended training on 'compassion fatigue' or, as some call it, 'blocked care.' This is when parenting a child with trauma causes significant stress in the parent or carer to the extent that they are unable to connect with the child. Prolonged stress suppresses the capacity to sustain loving and empathetic feelings towards the child. Both terms are used by social care professionals to describe the same thing.

Often these kinds of terms are invented by social scientists or business people and can sound clinical and inhumane and don't help us, the parent carers, understand what is happening, or allow for the fact that it is a vulnerable child who is being discussed. There seems to be tons of research and guidance around subjects like these, and of course the advice is well-intended, but it doesn't include the elephant in the room: the lack of support for the parent or carer and the child. The feelings of instinctive self-protection for self and one's own family are regularly described by these terms of 'compassion fatigue' or 'blocked care', but rarely is adequate support put in place in time to offer meaningful help, or even enough help to keep the child in their placement. It's usually when the placement is breaking down that the descriptions are used, and it can take weeks, if not months for anything to be put in place.

Even when something is put in place, it might not work. I know full well that Sparkle's behaviour is part of a broader attempt to mask their fear and confusion, but that doesn't stop it from being extremely challenging. I feel that I certainly, and perhaps the rest of the family are, consciously or unconsciously, separating ourselves from knowledge of their trauma and only reacting in the moment to the aggressive behaviour that is disrupting our family life. That feels like failure. I don't want a professional to arrive after the horse has bolted and tell me that I'm suffering from compassion fatigue. It will feel like criticism, not support. I know what's happening and I know I want to protect us from the wrath of the social workers, as well as get the help for Sparkle that they need.

But I've run out of options. I've tried everything. I'm not sure if we have the energy left to keep battling with the system, and I'm certain that badgering Lloyd and me, and our children to have mental health reviews is not helping. In fact, it has entirely the opposite effect. They feel like the 'mind police' and I have no evidence of what Zoey and Alexander's actual experience and qualifications are to enable them to make those judgments. Important details like those tend to be skirted around.

If I ask for help again from the Social Work and Emotional Welfare Teams, I will be the one who is scrutinised further, and

I do not want to be told that I am reliving my own childhood trauma. That's not fair. To me that feels like bullying. I can't say to them when they say something or do something we don't like, 'Oh that must be because of your childhood trauma.' That would be inappropriate and unprofessional. Why are they able to do that the other way? When I have been a foster carer for years and years. It isn't right.

I go round and round in circles. I need to protect Sparkle, and us, but try and get the right support for them at the same time. Yet those people are the gatekeepers to that support and, as far as I'm concerned, they are failing miserably in their responsibility. I begin to look for other avenues, other networks, I'll see if there are groups for parents and carers with LGBTQ+ children.

God, I feel disheartened and exhausted. I hope things improve for all of us soon.

On Monday morning I receive an email from Lily's tutor at school. Ms Birtwistle tells me that Lily stayed behind for half an hour after tutor time today.

Lily was very teary and said that she doesn't like coming home because of the problems at home.

My mind is instantly sent into another tailspin. The wording of her email feels like a criticism, though I'm sure it's not. But, that's where I am in my mindset. I feel so tired and worn down. Now we will have to meet with the teachers and if I say that the social workers aren't supporting Sparkle they may side with the social workers.

Not for the first time I consider the ways in which we are now vulnerable. The social workers could make our lives very difficult. We had a placement a few years ago, Sky, whose mother kept meddling in our lives. We ended up having the police in our house. We had another instance where a social worker threatened that our sons might be removed. My mind goes wandering through all the dark places. I feel so unprotected. I am exposing my family to all sorts of risk. I talk to Lloyd, whose smile I miss now that he looks so sad most of the time, but he is sensitive and snappy, as am I. Again I think: *this isn't our life, this is not who we are.*

I know that I need to take some action. I take control of the areas I think I can handle. I decide to head off the Lily situation and try to make sure that it doesn't get out of hand. These things can fly off in terrible directions if too many people with too many opinions feel that they know what's happening and what's best for the child.

We know what's best for Lily. She has lived with us for so long, she really is one of our children. I email her social worker and cut and paste the teacher's email to me. I would have cc'd our supervising social worker but, of course, we still don't have one. I explain briefly that we have been having problems and that we have tried to support Sparkle and are trying to keep our home safe and calm but it isn't that easy.

My mobile goes just minutes after I hit send. It's Lily's social worker and I dread what she will say, bracing myself for further condemnation. That's how low I feel. That's what happens when you are being manipulated. And when I try to put the whole situation into perspective, that's really how it feels: as though we are being played by Sparkle. And even as I have that realisation, I know how ridiculous it sounds when she is an 11-year-old child. People tend not to believe that one child can have such a negative effect on this many people, but it's true, they can.

To my surprise and relief, Lily's social worker is kind.

'Thanks for laying it all out,' she says. 'To be honest, I had a good idea about most of it already. Lily has told me quite a lot about the situation. She's been very good at keeping me up to date.'

I don't feel betrayed by Lily. I feel glad that she's had a friend in all this.

'Thus far I've tried to not interfere with Sparkle and her social worker, and the rest of the Emotional Welfare team, but now is probably the time to step-in and push for help.'

'I'm so pleased to hear you say that,' I say.

'I don't know this social worker. Richard, is it?'

Fair enough, but I'm surprised. Children's social care is a relatively small world.

'But I will be emailing Richard, Zoey and Alexander to express my concerns for Lily's placement. I'll make it clear that I'm doing this in a supportive way, and I'll add my voice to the petition for support. Something is required to help keep the household stable. '

I am grateful for her support, I really am. But when I

put the phone down I feel somehow even more exposed and vulnerable. This is my family being discussed here, by people I don't really know.

I update Lloyd, and wonder what I should get for dinner. I'm not able to focus on anything. I am too tired. Too worn down. I'll take the dogs out instead. I look in the hall mirror on my way out with Dotty and Douglas and catch myself: a haggard version of the me I used to know, I look older, I look weary.

As I walk around the fields it occurs to me that no one really knows what to do.

The school set up an LGBTQ+ group that not many go to. It's not their fault, they're trying to set up channels of support, but children like Sparkle are very negative about the staff and their intentions. The pronoun wars are, I feel, abusive and unhelpful. Sparkle is waiting to catch us out, and of course we make mistakes. Sparkle assumes that it's a deliberate act of sabotage against their identity choice, and that we are undermining them on purpose. We are trying to learn a whole new language. If I was learning French, a native speaker would forgive a pronoun slip, surely? It goes against speech patterns that we have previously learnt that are so ingrained that in some ways it's even harder than learning a new language from scratch.

There is no clarity from any quarter.

I wonder if the reason Zoey and Alexander are so resistant is because they don't really know what to say or do either. Given the maze and the lack of clarity, it's easier to pick on and punish the foster carers for who they are rather than try to understand the children. Do some children, like Sparkle and Groove, use the LGBTQ+ banner as a weapon and an excuse to be unkind? Some days I feel like we need a solicitor to intervene, not emotional support.

The lines are too blurred and I have no idea where I actually stand. And this is our home and Sparkle is still a child who has been invited into our home.

When I get back from the dog walk I see an email from Zoey and Alexander. Why can't they work independently?

I read it and reel.

Their plan for Sparkle is that we all have 'Resilience Training'.

Give me strength!

I haven't got the energy to walk to Lloyd's studio so I call out like an old fish wife.

'Lloyd?'

He can tell something's up. 'What now?'

'You'll never guess what the children's TV presenters have advised us all to do,' I call.

I hear his chair scrape the wooden floorboards and he walks to my studio.

'What? Go on!'

I look at him and say, 'Effing resilience training.'

He looks furious, as I knew he would. 'You're kidding me?'

'Nope. That's their solution.'

He walks back to his office grumbling to himself. I catch the odd expletive in his muttered monologue.

This isn't the first time that we've encountered 'resilience training'. When the flooding first began a few years ago, I wanted to set up a group of voluntary flood wardens to help our community when we flooded. We wanted to find a way to pull together while the council and other agencies like the water companies developed a strategy and did the work. But the council decided that we needed to set up a resilience group. At first, I thought okay, there may be other things that, as a community, we could help with. So we got involved. And learned that, apparently, resilience groups *promote the many systems that contribute to a community's overall health. This approach builds on disaster preparedness by adding features like social connectedness and everyday health and community systems. Community resilience also has a factor in climate resilience.* We train for disasters such as terrorism, plane crashes, bush fires and flooding. I hear teachers and business people all talk about 'resilience'. It's all over the school website and it's become a bit of a buzzword. We need to be more resilient. We need to learn how to be resilient.

But I also repeatedly hear social workers say that 'children are resilient.'

How can both things be true?

How come adults have to learn this but children are somehow in possession of innate resilience? They're not.

And yet it is assumed that they are. The more I think about it, the more I come to the conclusion that I've never heard such rubbish. As my thoughts travel down these rabbit holes I need to remind myself that I am tired, very tired. I also tell myself not to let it bother me, but it does.

So, my next thought is to wonder where the call for us all to be more resilient is coming from? It does not take long to trail it back to the council, and from there to local and national government. By asking, encouraging and then expecting us to be resilient, responsibility is subtly shifted. It abdicates the need to improve services because, by being resilient, we can just take whatever crap they throw at us. It's not working for me at all, this idea from Zoey and Alexander. So, because they are sitting on their hands not knowing what to do because the government hasn't actually issued any guidelines, the answer is to blame the parents and carers and probably the teachers too.

Oh, I am so cross.

Young children like Sparkle, who are identifying with the LGBTQ+ labels are perhaps not dealing with their choices as easily as the labels suggest. If their behaviour is poor, they can point the finger at us and expect it all to be all right because they put us on training courses for resilience. That means in turn that if we are not resilient and are struggling, it is us who are failing and simply need more training. Where is *my* representation here? My family's representation?

When I taught at the university I became a TUC-trained

union rep to support staff who were being bullied or harassed. The management didn't get rid of the problem bullies. Instead they let good staff be bullied out, after costing a fortune in legal fees, payouts and sick leave. The bullies were asked to do some training. Bullying continued. I have a feeling of déjà vu. I'm beginning to think that no one knows what to do about any of this.

When I try to extrapolate the thing that I'm struggling with the most, it is just that: no one has a grip on this. Children are moving into heightened states of anxiety and depression because we all seem to have forgotten who we are and what we know to be the world. Children are being allowed to do as they wish. I'm guilty. Look at the way I let Sparkle just disappear off for the day on their say-so. A child of 11 years old. A vulnerable child of 11 years old. I've never done that before with a child so young.

It's the easiest thing in the world for adults who look after children like Sparkle to be advised to support them, as I have done. But I want to know *how* to do that. It's got to be more than buying rainbow bunting and T-shirts that say 'Better out than in'. The professionals are too scared to do or say anything that doesn't look and sound 'woke'? Is being woke another way of doing nothing? Someone told me that they were woke, a few weeks ago on Facebook. She knitted some unicorns and said that she was handing them to people to make them smile 'because being woke means that you love everyone'.

I understand the sentiment, but, in reality, how damaging and unhealthy is that as a philosophy.

You can't love everyone. Children who were abused should not be expected to love their abusers.

The whole thing is confusing. I'm not sure what to think.

Ironically, when I try to book the resilience training (which I don't do because I have any faith in it, I'm only worried that the 'children's TV presenters' will use it against us if we don't), I discover that the next training session isn't available for another four months. I'm not sure that we will make it through another four months with no help. I don't have the resilience.

I decide to have a quiet call with Tristan and Bart. I need a friend or two right now.

What I learn is that the grandparents have said that they will come and see Cormac and Cahira.

'They've said it, but have made no indication of when that will be,' Bart explains.

'And what about their mother. I heard she was in America?'

'She's not there yet, I don't think. Lois has called a few times but has not actually seen the children. Tristan had quite a long chat with her, though. I'll pass you over and Tristan can explain.'

'Yes, she's going to fly out there shortly. Sadly, I suppose, she has no intention of getting back together with Luke. She said that she'd been deeply unhappy in that relationship. She had nothing good to say about him. He exploited her and abused her. She was quite open about the fact that Luke had certain 'sexual tastes' that she now realises were abusive. She has decided, quite rightly perhaps, that she deserves better. And of course she's met this chap online who she thinks will be that better.'

Tristan's tone suggests that he himself has some doubts about that.

'So she's going to fly to America to meet him and spend some time with him, and if he is everything that she thinks he is and it all goes well then the plan, ultimately is for her to take the children too.'

My stomach jumps as he tells me.

'She's kidding herself. She hasn't got a hope in hell of taking the children under the circumstances. Bart and I are going for permanency.'

I began to tell Tristan, who now puts the phone on speaker so Bart can hear too, about our experiences of late.

They are aghast. And they also have some views on the 'cult of wokism', as they call it.

I'm surprised. I had assumed, I think, that because they were gay and from London, they would be championing woke.

'Not a bit of it, Louise. Oh Bart, tell her about the nativity.'

'You have to understand a little bit about this village,'

Bart explains. 'It's full of media sorts who have come from London to buy up the big properties.'

I wonder if they include themselves in this description, but no; they have quite a different lens.

'So what about this nativity?'

'It's in the village square in front of the memorial.'

'Oh yes, I remember the memorial.' I clocked it when I took Sparkle to visit.

Bart now starts squealing with laughter. 'Oh my, oh my goodness,' he says, in his lovely Scandinavian accent.

Tristan takes over the conversation because Bart is laughing too much.

'Instead of baby Jesus and Joseph and Mary and the three Kings they dressed baby Jesus and Joseph and Mary in traditional Palestinian attire and the three kings became the three Queens and wore drag.'

Bart is still laughing, but manages to say, through his hysterics, 'People thought we did it!' He is beside himself.

But Tristan is more thoughtful. 'To be woke is to understand things; society's injustices, but it doesn't propose a solution. To be woke is to understand the full injustice. The problem with wokeness is that it doesn't inspire action; it freezes it. To be woke is about putting yourself on display and shouting about your bloody wokeness. But it invites separation. It means building a wall between you and the problem, not finding a solution.'

What he says makes a kind of sense to me. Although I would like to see the three Queens in drag.

When Tristan has finished, Bart says, 'Oh Louise, that's why I love him so, such a clever boy, isn't he?'

I laugh and begin to feel better in some small way. They cheer me up, these two.

I explain my thinking that carers looking after LGBTQ+ children need a solicitor not a therapist. 'Because we just cannot win. Whatever we do is wrong. And you'll probably think I'm awful for saying this, but I think they know that they can beat us with a stick. They have so much power.'

I'm expecting a deathly silence but Tristan comes straight back.

'I know. How can you be expected to be confident about what to do if a child wants to change their name, use different pronouns or change their appearance, hairstyle or clothes – it's socially transitioning, it's massive! How can you, or us even, know what the right thing to do is? Each child is different and I suspect Sparkle's little group of friends are experimenting. Not as many as you think will transition and change their gender, I expect most will be experimenting with their sexuality.'

'I'm worried that socially transitioning may have significant psychological effects.'

'Of course it will.'

'So how do we know what to do?'

Then Tristan voices another thought. One that I have shared but not even fully admitted to myself yet. 'And what if Sparkle is being drawn to the LGBTQ+ movement because she is so confused and hurt about her life. What if it's a distraction from her real issues and her real pain? Have you thought about that?'

Tristan and Bart really are special people. I hope they get permanency for Cormac and Cahira. I do feel a little more hopeful. Having a laugh definitely helped.

Until Sparkle gets home from school with a new little challenge for us all to navigate. They tell us that they are no longer Sparkle. Instead they are now 'Steve.'

I don't ask about pronouns.

XXIV

Lily is not herself. She's so quiet. She isn't really eating now and it's breaking my heart.

I find a moment when we are alone to ask Steve if they knew what is wrong with Lily.

Steve shrugs, 'I don't know.' and walks off.

I don't know if I like Steve. Steve seems more unpleasant than Sparkle was. I am struggling to find anything to like. If I shared this with a social worker I would be a terrible person and I tell myself over and over again that I should remember that Steve is traumatised. I think the whole household has been traumatised by Steve's abusive behaviour. Lloyd forgot to call Sparkle Steve this morning as they ran out the door without their PE bag. He accidentally called out 'Sparkle' to remind them.

Steve turned around, grabbed the bag and instead of thanking Lloyd, said, 'dick head.'

Thinking about that PE bag, I wonder what Steve does

now when they change for PE. As far as I know, the school only has male and female changing rooms and toilets. I couldn't possibly raise it as a topic of discussion, though, even as a supportive question. So I say nothing.

Now it's evening and there is another mealtime to get through. Vincent and Jackson have taken their food elsewhere and it's now the four of us left at the table.

Lily plays with her food, pushing forkfuls around the plate. I don't think a single one makes it to her mouth. She looks around sadly at the new arrangements. The boys have taken to having trays in their bedrooms, or eating in the sitting room. Anything to avoid the kitchen. I disapprove, but disapprove of the inevitable arguments more. Jackson and Vincent refuse to sit down and eat at the table because Steve is so challenging, so angry, always. There is no conversation or debate, only arguments that we never win.

I hate this.

There is an awkward silence. Not that lovely silence where people stop talking because the food is good, but an edgy, glance-sharing silence.

The sound of cutlery clanking against crockery, instead of the chatter I have always associated with mealtimes, is harsh and unpleasant.

Lloyd is the first to try to break today's deadlock.

He smiles and looks up. 'How was school today, Steve?'

'Shit.'

Not language that I'd usually tolerate while we're dining,

but then we are way beyond what I am happy tolerating. There is a short pause, then Steve continues.

'Mr Adams is a cunt.'

It's enough for Lloyd. He erupts and shouts at Steve. 'I don't want language like that at the table. In fact I don't want language like that at all.'

There is another short pause.

Then, 'You're so fucking gay!'

Lloyd gets up and walks out.

I look at the space where he has left his chair pulled out. I don't know what to say.

I swallow. My shepherd's pie tastes like cardboard. I wonder if it will choke me.

Lloyd isn't gone long. He must remember the conversation we had when I said to them all in one of my generic 'please take heed' conversations, that people who walk off or flounce out or storm off have lost. He knows I think it is deeply immature and achieves nothing.

He comes back in after about the time it takes to count slowly to ten.

He sits back down at his place at the table but will not look at or engage with Steve. In fact, no one speaks again.

Steve tries to throw out a few nasty comments periodically, but none of us take the bait. The meal takes an eternity. I think we're done and the ordeal is over, but as I clear the plates away and put the sauces back in the fridge I see them walk behind me. I look in the reflective black control panel in the middle of the double fridge freezer and see Steve smile and stick their middle finger up at us as they walk out.

For all the sympathy I have had until now, I now think to myself only what an unpleasant young person Steve is.

It's time.

I want them to go.

XXV

Lily looks dreadful when she comes down for breakfast the next morning.

I say, 'You're not going to school today. You're staying home, and you're going to tell me what's happened.'

She bursts into tears. I stand in the hall giving her a massive hug. Jackson and Vincent make eye contact as if to say, 'What now?' and walk past us, but don't pursue it. Instead they gently and carefully open and close the front door so as not to disturb her. They are very kind and have taken to leaving for school earlier to avoid any morning conflict.

I hate what's happened to our home.

I don't feel that I have spent anywhere near enough time with either of them lately. Steve takes up all my time, if not when they are at home then on phone calls and emails.

I put my hands on Lily's shoulders and walk her into the kitchen. I give her another hug, reach for the kitchen roll and pour a little cold water onto the paper towel. I hold it out for her to press against her face, to help cool her heated head down. Poor girl, this is all taking its toll and now I'm going to have to email her social worker and update her on what's going on. I thought that Lily was generally feeling low because of the mood in the house and what's been happening. We all feel it.

But I'm not prepared for what comes next.

Once Lily is a little calmed, she sits down and begins to turn over the abandoned teaspoon on the table. She twists it round and around, as if it will somehow give her the courage to say whatever she needs to get off her chest.

Lloyd appears at the kitchen door. I use my eyes to warn him off without actually saying, 'not now, go away,' out loud. The poor man only wants a coffee.

It's clear that Lily isn't quite ready to speak.

I move about the kitchen asking if she would like some breakfast.

'Cereal?'

She shakes her head.

'Toast?'

Another shake.

'How about some scrambled egg?'

She nods. It was her favourite when she was younger. I remember I used to put the toast on the plate and use the eggs as hair and the mushrooms as eyes, nose and mouth. Perhaps that will make her smile today. She clearly needs some TLC.

Oh, my little Lily, I think. *What's happening to you?*

I talk about nothing, just let the silence fill up the space while I prepare her meal. I'm not trying to make things uncomfortable, but right now that act of saying nothing will hopefully allow Lily the space she needs to pipe up.

I walk to the fridge for milk.

She says quickly, the words tumbling into one another. 'It's Sparkle and her friends.'

I turn. 'Who, Groove and Tex?'

She looks at me and scoffs, 'Alina and Elenora, yes!'

She has dead named them. This is serious.

'What's happened?' I have the milk now, and walk to get a glass bowl from the big drawer, and a fork from the clean cutlery container in the dishwasher, waiting to be put away.

She doesn't answer straight away. I wait and see if she'll speak, or if she needs me to get my metaphorical tweezers out.

Just as I crack an egg on the side of the bowl she says, 'They're bullying me.'

I pull the eggshell apart and reach for the next one, cracking it on the side glass, symbols of what I would like to do to Alina and Elenora and Steve-Sparkle, if they're involved.

'What are they doing?'

'At school break they come and find me and Maria. They separate me out and have started saying weird stuff.'

'Like what?'

'They stand around me and say I'm thirsty.'

'Thirsty? What, they think you need a drink?'

She shakes her head. 'No, Louise. It means *I want dick.*'

'What?' I am horrified. I hold the glass bowl while whisking with the fork. 'Okay, help me out here, Lily. So, they are telling you that you need to have sex with a boy?'

Lily sighs. 'No. They are now *men*, aren't they? Steve, Tex and Groove.'

I whisk a little more. 'Are they? They look like girls to me.' Perhaps I've missed something here. 'Have they transitioned? Are they medically male? Is that what you mean?'

Lily replies, 'No, of course not. But they go around sexually harassing girls.'

'What?'

My mind is as mixed up as the eggs and milk. Scrambled is exactly how I feel. I ask Lily what happens at break times, to talk me through it.

'When the bell goes, me and Maria and sometimes a few others go and sit by the trees in the first playground.'

I know where she means: it's the other side of the vegetable garden and Forest School area, where they take children who are struggling. It's a lovely place and I can see why they like to hang out there.

'They come up to us and push the others out the way so that there are only one or two of us.'

I stop her in mid-flow. 'But isn't Alina Maria's sister?'

'Yes. And they think it's funny and call it *incest.*'

Oh, no. My head is spinning once more. Does this mean what I think it does?

'What do you mean they call it incest? What have they actually said and done?'

Elenora is the worst one, according to Lily. 'She is like a vile geezer sex pest.'

I try to find out exactly what she means. Elenora rubs her body against Lily and the other girls and pretends to have a penis.

'She has a-a thing. A sort of dick-thing that she uses.'

I am horrified. I daren't think about this 'dick-thing'.

'She keeps going on about how she wants to give me one and rape me and do dirty things to me.'

I am *beyond* horrified and see Lily's eyes welling up again. This is without any doubt sexual harassment.

'You're right. It's bullying, it's predatory, it's abuse and it's going to stop! It's going to stop today!'

I ask Lily what Sparkle and Alina do while this is happening.

'Sparkle will do anything Elenora says. Apparently they have sex.'

She's 11, I think. Jesus.

'What about Alina?'

'Oh, her too. They're all fucking sex-mad bitches.'

I let that bit of swearing go. After all, the odd bit of colourful language can be a release, and I would know.

After Lily has had her eggs, I tell her gently that I am

going to have to inform the school and that they will want to speak to her. 'Are you okay with that?'

We lock eyes. She takes a sharp intake of breath and says, 'I guess so, yes.'

When she goes upstairs and I hear her music, Birdy singing *Skinny Love*, I go and find Lloyd and tell him the news.

Lloyd is really upset. 'If it were boys doing that there would be no argument. They would be punished. But they're girls, forget all their pronoun, silly-name shit.' He is very troubled. He is a man, a dad whose daughter (because that's how he feels about Lily) has been sexually harassed at school. Because it's girls or children identifying as boys who were born girls, does that make it less offensive? Because they are part of the LGBTQ+ movement, does that reduce their crime?

'Like I said, it's not therapy we need here, it's a solicitor. Where are we in all this?'

I waste no more time in calling the school. I go straight to the top and ask to speak to the headteacher, Ms Avery, to see what she says.

She is both shocked and appalled. Straightaway she says, 'Sexual harassment is sexual harassment, male, female or non-binary, transgender or gender-fluid, it is still harassment and will not be tolerated.'

Ms Avery is very professional and clarifies all the details with me about the behaviour, asking me whether it was sexual comments, sexual jokes, taunting, or physical behaviour.

'It's all of them.'

'Is it also happening online?'

'I don't know.' It didn't even occur to me to ask Lily that.

Ms Avery must check her computer while we speak because she says that she can see that all three girls are in school today. I'll speak to the safeguarding team as a matter of urgency. And I will, of course, contact the parents of all three girls.'

I explain that Sparkle is my foster child.

This is news to her. 'I hadn't realised because the surnames are different. In that case, I will also have to speak to Sparkle's social worker.'

I give her Richard's name and contact details.

She asks me how Lily is in herself.

Good question. I explain that I have kept her off school and that she is suffering from the wrath of Sparkle at home. 'As are we all. The last few months have been very difficult.'

'Yes, it must have been. This is not easy for anyone, but we need to investigate properly first.'

She promises to get back to me after they have spoken to the girls. Her choice of collective noun. It's funny but when there are matters of gravity all the 'thems' are deadnamed. It feels as if no one is respecting their name preferences, but does that mean that we are also not taking their gender preferences seriously? I haven't a clue, and I realise that we are not going to get this right, any of us, for a long time. It's completely fried my brain and plunged me into an alternative universe which, as far as I can tell, is a hostile place.

I tap out an email to Lily's social worker and Richard and copy in Lloyd, who is still smarting. The overwhelming feeling is that we are walking a tightrope here. We're unable to express how we really feel in case we are described as phobic and punished. It's bizarre. Whatever we do, we feel will be wrong. If we do nothing, that will be very wrong.

I decide to pound the fields with my two friends, Douglas and Dotty, who seem to have the best view on the world. A simpler one, anyway. As I walk past the fields of sheep and say my usual hellos to them, I wonder what notions of gender they have. I walked past an older lady, who once made me roar with laughter as her very old dog, Ralf, tried to mount Doug. Neither of us commented on the same gender desire. She only said, 'Oh, I'm glad all that's over with. Bloody men.' I remember thinking about how I loved her honesty, and realising that perhaps some people cannot be bothered about gender or sexuality at all. What category would they fit into? When I was much younger I remember an interview with Morrissey from the Smiths who famously said, 'I'd rather have a cup of tea than sex.' He might have said it because it was true or because it was controversial. It's weird how obsessed humans are with sex. I mean, you don't get Doug and Dotty having these dilemmas. I suppose, though, sometimes I see Dotty or Doug try a bit of inter-species love with the cats. What's going on there? Honestly, you could tie yourself up in knots with all this. Today I would like to be a sheep, stand in a field and munch grass, and when my fellow sheep moves I'll move too. No thinking involved.

XXVI

Lily's social worker calls me while I head down from the hills. I like her social worker. She's a benign one, the foster carer's favourite category, and the children's from what I can see.

Today's news has, however, stirred some immediate action. She is not happy at all and has made it clear to Richard that Sparkle is jeopardising Lily's placement. Clearly, Sparkle's behaviour is unacceptable. I am never entirely comfortable with this language as once again it can make me feel like a failure as a foster carer for somehow letting it happen.

But we didn't 'let' it happen; it happened.

Lily's social worker wants Sparkle removed. I know this is the only option, and I know there will be enormous relief in our household when it happens, but part of me feels heartbroken, and awash with all sorts of emotions about the fact that we have failed. It's complicated.

We have failed Sparkle, we have failed Lily and most

definitely failed Jackson and Vincent, because this is their home. But I also felt a connection with Sparkle. I think back to our first meeting at the children's home. The way we seemed to have a connection. The moments, especially early on, where things seemed to be going well. There's no way of dressing it up. It feels like failure.

Richard calls, too. 'I'm really sorry to hear the news about Lily. I hope you're all okay?'

I explain that Lily's social worker is not happy about the situation, nor am I and I'm not sure what we should do. I tell him that I am unhappy that Sparkle has not received any support. 'What exactly have Zoey and Alexander come up with?' I ask.

'I'm going to email them now, and their manager, and mark it as an urgent action. You're right, Louise. By now, some kind of support for Sparkle should certainly have been in place.'

Hooray! It doesn't change a thing, and in recent weeks I have begun to feel that there has been a conspiracy against us. But every now and then you realise that the social workers are probably as frustrated as we are but have thirty or more other children to firefight for.

Then it goes quiet, very quiet.

By the time I get back home with the dogs, Lloyd is concerned. 'I wondered what had happened to you.'

'I just needed to get out for a bit.'

I relay the conversations I've just had.

Lloyd nods. 'Do you know what? This is because those idiot children's TV presenters, Zoey and Alexander, haven't done their job.'

I agree with him. 'They were too busy judging us. Well, mainly me, to be fair.'

He knows the narrative as well as I do, but I spell it out anyway. 'Being an ex-looked after child now involved with children's social care as a foster carer really upsets some professionals.'

I do wonder if it's because people like me are a threat. Those of us who defy the odds and grow-up to do well and become quite sound, and are able to live meaningful, mostly happy lives, seem somehow to annoy them.

I have sometimes thought that foster care is a misogynistic world, ironically because it's occupied by so many women who deem themselves professional and like to dominate the lesser-paid women, the foster carers, and emasculate the male foster carers.

Lloyd says something interesting. 'Has anyone contacted Luke and Lois about this?'

Sparkle is still a Section 20 (Section 20 agreements allow the local authority to remove a child and place them in foster care without the need for a court order. Whether or not to enter into a section 20 agreement is a voluntary decision made by the parents with the local authority.) So this is a very good question.

'I doubt it and I wonder what they would say? Has

anyone been keeping Luke and Lois up to speed with all that's happening with Sparkle?'

They're rhetorical questions. We have no way of knowing the answers. It doesn't matter that Luke and Lois appear to be preoccupied and that Luke has been denied access for a while because of the complaints from parents about playing computer games with their children. I don't know the truth about what was going on before Sparkle came to us, because I wasn't there, but nothing I hear about Luke is encouraging. I don't know what happened and I probably never will. Lois I simply don't understand, but again I don't know enough.

What I hear of her behaviour makes her sound younger than she is. I know that some women who have been sexually abused as children can revert to a mental age of the time they were abused, not all the time but sometimes. I know that was the case with my adopted mother who had been abused many times by different men in her childhood. That was a combination of World War II and poverty, and because girls and women had even less protection then. I'm speculating about Lois though. I don't really know anything. I'm thinking too much because I'm still shocked and frustrated.

Lily is in her room watching TV,

'Would you like to go out for some lunch?'

She shakes her head and says that she just wants to relax. Fair enough. I walk around her room picking up clothes and putting lids on her pens. I notice that she has been doing some writing. I ask if I can have a read. She nods from her bed, where she is wearing her onesie and looking so young. Too young to be dealing with all this. Sparkle is even younger than Lily, though it often hasn't seemed that way recently. I have a sudden flash of anger at the way that our world is sexualising our children so much. Why can't we just leave them alone to grow up at a gentler pace?

'How are you feeling?'

'Okay,' she nods. But then asks, 'When will this be over?'

I have the realisation that as long as Sparkle is in the house it will not be over. Would we be having the same conversations if one of the boys had done this? No!

'Soon,' is the most honest answer I can give.

I sit down to read Lily's writings. I squint because I haven't got my glasses on, but I can work out the gist of what Lily has written.

I can't do this anymore. I just want to be me, but people won't let that happen. I don't want this pressure, I don't want to be a boy or a girl. I just want to be me, Lily.

It seems such a heartfelt plea, and such a sensible perspective that it brings me up short. Tears prick at my eyes. I wonder again what the hell we are doing to these kids that they feel this way.

'We'll sort things out, Lily. I promise.'

The trouble is, I'm not sure if this is a promise I can really keep.

By the time I have finished my lunch, I still haven't heard from anyone, and I was hoping to have done so by now. I need to know what's going on because Sparkle will be home from school soon after 3.15pm and we need a plan. It's not going to be easy. I will need to know what's okay to tell the boys too. I like openness, but this feels like it will be shrouded in secrecy and I do not like burdening my children with secrets.

I have to do something. I decide to call the school back. Ms Avery takes my call. This is a good sign that the school is taking things as seriously as they promised.

'The girls have been interviewed by the safeguarding team. There does appear to be a problem, as you suggested. While I can't divulge every detail, I will go as far as to confirm that one of the girls did have a strap-on penis in her bag which supports what Lily reported.'

I knew it to be true when Lily told me, but it's a different kind of difficult to hear it spoken amidst this official kind of language of 'divulging' and 'confirming'.

'In view of all of this, is it possible that you might be able to attend a meeting after school today, just to go over the plan for Sparkle and the other girls?'

'Is this just for me, or for all the parents and carers?'

'All the parents have been invited, Mrs Allen.'

Ms Avery then asks if it would be all right for her to speak with Lily later in the day.

'Yes. But I can't guarantee that Lily will speak. This has been very difficult for her.'

To her credit, Lily does indeed speak with the headteacher, and quite frankly, too. I suspect that's because, like most children in care, she is used to talking to adults about 'how she feels'.

After the call to the school, I call Lily's social worker again. She answers straight away by asking how Lily is.

'Quiet. Not herself. She hasn't felt like doing much today. Not surprising really.'

I also report to her that I have read, with Lily's permission, some recent writing that told a story of how difficult Lily has been finding life and, in particular, the necessity to navigate gender identity. 'She seems to be conflating gender identity with sexual identity.'

Lily's social worker says, 'It's like an epidemic at the moment and it's causing so much pain and harm for children. I'm seeing it all the time.'

'They're too young. They're just children.'

She agrees.

'You're brave,' I say, and I mean it. 'I didn't think that professionals were allowed to say or do anything that wasn't in line with the LBGTQ+ manifesto.'

'We're all learning. It's one of the hardest things I have had to deal with and, in some ways, it feels abusive.'

'I think the situation with Sparkle, Alina and Elenora feels like good old-fashioned bullying to me, disguised as LGBTQ+.'

'It's all mixed up, I agree.'

'Unhappiness and confusion about life and being young generally, with gender and sexuality to align to before they're ready. Sparkle only got her primary school pen licence last year, and still has some of her baby teeth. She takes her teddy to bed with her and gets excited about sweeties. That all says child to me!'

I notice that I've slipped back into talking about Sparkle as Sparkle, not Steve, and as she, not he. I think it's the headteacher's talk of 'girls'.

I explain about the meeting after school for parents or carers and the children.

'Good. I've also made it clear to Richard that Sparkle needs to move on.' That sounds decisive, but then she adds, 'Who knows how long that will take? After this there will not be many foster carers willing to take her on.'

'In the meantime, how are we to manage the situation at home?'

I want to know what their ideas are for the children being in the house.

'I'll have to get back to you,' says Lily's social worker. 'I'm waiting to hear back from my manager about a strategy meeting.'

And here we go again. I feel my patience sliding away. Managers having meetings without knowing us or the children. And we are meant to hold it altogether, sometimes at any cost. Sparkle's status has changed dramatically with Lily's disclosures. She is now a predatory person.

She has committed serious acts of sexual harassment against Lily and other girls and we don't have a plan.

XXVII

The clock is ticking. As we move closer to the meeting time, I feel a little sick. I've agreed to come, but this is very difficult. There will be just about enough time to see the boys and leave them to Lloyd. They will not be impressed at all. I know it will colour any future interactions they have with Sparkle. How could it not? I have brought my sons up to be feminists, to be respectful of women and girls. This is everything that they disapprove of about 'toxic masculinity.'

It's a very strange concept if you think about it. A group of girls now identify as something else, imitate the worst behaviour of the worst men and inflict it back onto girls. It's like double misogyny and deeply hurtful for the girls who have been abused. My mind boggles.

Just before the boys are due to return I pop up to see Lily. She is fast asleep. I leave her be. Sleep is the best medicine. As the boys come in loudly and hungrily, I entice them into the kitchen with some locally-made biscuits that I was saving for the weekend, but now this seems more important. They love the crunchy chunky ginger cookies. While they forage around for drinks I tell them, 'There has been an incident at school and I have to go to a meeting.'

The excitement is too much. They want to know so I give them an outline sketch of what's happened. I name Alina and Elenora, and ask them what they know.

The boys tell me that they are part of the 'outsiders' LGBTQ+ group.

'Elenora is big and aggressive,' says Jackson. 'She's angry and most people avoid her. She calls boys *c-u-n-t-s*,' which he spells out rather than says, 'and she calls girls *dicks*. She's horrible, and some of the teachers are scared of her, especially Mr Holbert the PE teacher. He walks the other way when she's around.'

Vincent corroborates, though far less articulately. 'Yeah, she's a big ugly fem Nazi.'

'Vincent!'

Oh my, how did my sons get to be so politically incorrect? That's secondary school for you.

When I get to the school I sign in at reception. I know most of the staff and say hello to the ones I see. I know the drill well and put on the visitor lanyard before I head to Ms Avery's office. I have to walk in the opposite direction to the actual school. The management offices are in a separate area which seems counterintuitive, but I'm sure Ms Avery is out and about a lot in the school. I walk through the double doors into the senior management space. Blimey, I had no idea that there were so many deputies and assistant heads: eight doors along one side and the door I want is open.

To the left of the door are three rather unhappy looking girls. I see Sparkle who is staring at her feet. I see Alina and think how her appearance has changed dramatically since I last saw her. Her hair has been cut into a short back and sides style and dyed black. It looks severe and masculine but not quite real somehow, almost theatrical.

I stand by the door and Ms Avery beckons for me to come in. Alina's mum and her dad are already sitting down. I sit down across the table from them, offer a smile and say, 'Hello.'

The atmosphere is flat. They both look sad as they say hello back.

'So, we're just waiting for Elenora's mum. She's coming from town, so I suspect the traffic is bad. We'll hang on a few more minutes before we get started, if that's okay?'

We all sit awkwardly, drinking tea and eating biscuits. I'm already on my third Nice biscuit when Ms Avery's assistant? Secretary? PA? – I don't know what they're called these days; everyone seems to have a grander title than they used to – comes in.

'I'm afraid that Ms Gibson now can't make this afternoon's meeting.'

'Ah, that's unfortunate.'

Gibson. As soon as she says the name all that pops

into my head is guitars. We used to show off our music knowledge when teenagers by talking about Gibson guitars to impress the boys. But there is nothing impressive in this scenario.

Ms Avery goes to the door and speaks to the girls. 'Please sit quietly and patiently while we talk. Elenora, I'm afraid that your mother can't make it now. We will arrange transport to get you home as your bus has already gone.'

Ms Avery is a nice woman, clearly ambitious for her school. The school recently had an Ofsted inspection and was rated as Outstanding. As a resident you know that a school's reputation is echoed throughout the area. An outstanding school helps build prosperity and puts house prices and morale up. She will be keen to sort this for all sorts of reasons, but one of them will be to preserve the good reputation of the school.

Ms Avery starts the meeting by thanking us all for attending and very much appreciates us attending. I've always liked this approach, you get so much more done by using manners and good grace. A relative of mine who is senior in the police told me that criminals are more likely to confess their crimes if the interviewer is polite and courteous. I don't know if that's true, but it wouldn't surprise me. Ms Avery skilfully outlines why we are here and the events that have brought us to this point.

'I would like to ask you to keep what is said in this room confidential.'

We all agree.

'Once we have spoken, the girls will be invited back into the room to hear what has been said. I'm a big believer in restorative justice and think it is important that the girls should understand how they have made Lily feel.'

'And the other girls?' I say. 'Lily mentioned that it wasn't just her, but that other girls had been affected by the behaviour of the three girls.'

'Yes. That's true. Although, at this stage, only one other girl has actually come forward. But, like Lily, she has reported that other girls have experienced similar behaviour. And, due to the nature of the, err, allegations-' Ms Avery pauses, searching for the right words.

I must look puzzled because Ms Avery picks up on my confusion.

'I mean, the fact that the perpetrators are female,' she explains.

Yes, and no, I think, wondering how she is going to manage this.

'The unusual nature of this particular peer-on-peer abuse has complicated things in a way that it might not have done if things were-' she pauses again. 'If things were different,' she finishes firmly.

Ms Avery then reads out Lily's statement. It is excruciating to listen to.

It becomes clear that Elenora is the leader and the dominant one among loyal followers.

Alina's parents look devastated. Her father speaks. He has a strong Eastern European accent. He shakes his head. 'We are a good Catholic family. I don't understand how this has all happened.'

The penny begins to drop. When Maria and Alina's mother ran away from me in the supermarket she was embarrassed. Perhaps she knew about that stupid image of me they sent on Snapchat. But they both look shocked.

I decide that I will take the plunge and ask them one of the many questions that I'd like answers to. 'Did you actually know that Alina and Maria were involved with the LGBTQ+ community?'

Why shouldn't I ask? Lily is at home hurting and, as far as I know, so is Maria.

Alina's mum begins to cry, 'Yes,' she says quietly. 'Yes, I did.'

Her husband looks at her in horror. 'How long have you known?'

He is trembling, as if trying to control his own emotions. It is very clear that today has rocked his world. He can have had no idea what was going on. I wouldn't want to be in their house this evening.

Ms Avery interjects quickly and brings us all back to the matter in hand.

'So, as you may know, in school we have established an LGBTQ+ group who meet at lunchtimes and attend discos and clubs after school. We have a membership of about 20 in that group, and around half of them identify as transgender, non-binary or gender-fluid.'

Alina's father looks broken as he listens to Ms Avery tell him that both his daughters have attended these groups.

'I've spoken at some length with the staff who run the group. They tell me that Maria came a couple of times with Lily near the start of term. Neither of the girls returned after that. Alina used to go with Sparkle, and Elenora turned up a few times, but caused disruption. Since we've worked hard to create this group as a safe space, Elenora was not invited back. Alina and Sparkle also made other students uncomfortable, particularly boys. They sexualised conversations and resorted to smutty innuendos, so Mr Simmons asked them not to return for a while.'

It must be difficult for a father to hear this about his daughter, especially if it is coming out of the blue, and compounded by what I assume might be quite traditional religious beliefs.

Ms Avery continues. 'I am determined to keep our school a safe place. All the students are entitled to feel relaxed and safe, and to enjoy learning. We cannot accept such predatory and negative behaviour. I have spoken with the senior management team and the Chair and Deputy Chair of Governors. We have decided to suspend all three girls, Sparkle, Alina and Elenora. We would like the girls to meet with the school counsellor when they return and a pastoral care plan will be put in place. The suspension is for five days.

The girls will receive work that needs to be submitted daily to their tutors.'

I am dreading having an angry Sparkle at home during her suspension. Richard will also have to tell her that it is probable that she will be moved on. But I'm impressed with the way that Ms Avery is handling this. Sparkle and her friends need to understand the consequences of their behaviour. Alina's parents are not impressed at all.

'We both work full-time,' their mother begins. 'I don't know how we are going to manage Alina while she is at home.'

Alina's father looks very upset. He keeps shaking his head saying, 'Ne, ne.'

Ms Avery stands up. 'So, now I'm going to invite the girls in.'

'Is it appropriate for Elenora to come in? Without her parents, I mean,' I ask.

'I have explained to Ms Gibson that the school has adopted the restorative justice approach as an outcome to poor behaviour.'

And that seems to be the end of the matter. I imagine that Ms Gibson would not have been able to argue with Ms Avery.

I nod and wait for the girls. Today they are not Steve, Groove and Tex. They are Sparkle, Alina and Elenora. We sit waiting. I smile at Alina's parents. Their body language is tense, and my best guess is that they will have an almighty row later. Again, I have the feeling that I would not want to be in that house.

One by one the students come in, not looking so confident and aggressive now. A group of young people who have behaved poorly; misguided, misinformed and misunderstood. Ms Avery welcomes them into the room using their birth names. She explains the severity of their behaviour and the punishment: that they have all been suspended for five days.

I look at Sparkle, who looks confused. What did she expect? Alina looks scared. She is definitely scared of her father; as, I suspect, is Alina's mother.

Elenora stands with her hands folded in front of her. She is a big girl, both in build and in stature. She does look a little masculine, but also rather babyish. Her face is covered in spots and her clothes don't fit properly. She is too big for the uniform. She looks like an awkward teenager. All bravado is gone.

I say to Sparkle, 'Let's go home.'

I have a quick look at my phone to see if I've missed anything. Richard called while I was in the meeting with the headteacher. It looks like he has left a message.

I need to listen to it because right now I don't know what's going on. Lily's social worker articulated quite clearly that it was not acceptable for Sparkle to remain in the house. I know that Richard will be hard pushed to find another foster placement for Sparkle.

But there is a relief in knowing that Sparkle, she, they, them, Steve, will be leaving. The weight is beginning to feel as if it might be lifting, even just knowing that she will be gone. It's been too hard, mainly because whatever we do is wrong. For that reason, it feels like an abusive relationship. I can't let five people be sacrificed for one child, albeit a child who I know has been let down herself.

I listen to Richard's message. He is on his way home and has left me an email. I suggest to Sparkle that she keeps herself away from Lily tonight until we've had time to figure out what to do. I also suggest that she stays in her room in the morning until the others have gone to school. That will not be a problem. I know how much Sparkle likes her bed.

I also say, 'I need your phone.'

She looks at me as if she is going to challenge that request.

I throw her a look in return that says, 'Do not go there.'

I take the phone from her. 'I'll keep it for now and please don't ask for it because you will not be getting it.'

I am angry and I can't hide it. I am angry with Sparkle, but I am even angrier with the Emotional Welfare team. They never helped Sparkle. They were too preoccupied with trying to analyse me and pick at me, when it was Sparkle who needed the help. They have failed her. I hope Richard has got them to come up with a support package for Sparkle because she'll need it. She will feel rejected, even though she has instigated this.

I slump down in the swivel chair in my studio. It takes me

a moment to collect myself before I can start to read emails.
I pull myself together, see Richard's email address and read:

Hi Louise and Lloyd,

*I hope that you are okay? If it's convenient I would like to come and
see Sparkle tomorrow to talk about the situation and her options. I
have spoken to my manager and we both feel that a new care plan for
Sparkle is needed.*

*You asked about support from the Emotional Welfare team. I'm afraid
that Zoey will no longer be able to work with Sparkle as she has a
personal interest in the situation at school. Alexander is still in training
so we have decided to commission an external counselling provider for
Sparkle which I will discuss with you and Sparkle tomorrow. From
a safeguarding perspective, can you do your best to separate Lily and
Sparkle in the meantime?*

I look forward to seeing you at 10am.

Best wishes,
Richard

What? I'm struggling to process some of the implications
of what is being suggested here.

I call out to Lloyd. 'Lloyd, get ere,' which is a throwback
to when we lived in Portsmouth, an exaggerated version of

the accent which is code for, 'You're not actually going to believe this.'

I wait for him to come into my studio. I point at the email. He reads it aloud.

'What do they mean, Zoey will no longer be able to work with Sparkle? She's never bloody worked with Sparkle, that's the problem.' He continues to read, then looks at me and says in amazement, 'Elenora is Zoey's daughter?'

I say, 'Yep, looks like it. That's the conclusion I'm drawing.'

Lloyd draws up my other desk chair and sits down next to me. 'The whole thing is a mess. Poor bloody children, all of them!'

When he gets to the end, to the 'safeguarding plan', he laughs at the absurdity.

'Is Sparkle in her room?' I ask.

'She is.'

'Well at least the safeguarding plan is in place.'

I have no words.

XXVIII

The wheels of children's social care turn at a glacial pace. Progress is so slow that a snail would look like Usain Bolt. I don't know that Lloyd and I have ever felt so despondent.

In the end, it is after another turbulent four weeks that we eventually say goodbye to Sparkle. In the meantime, I have to manage the household very carefully, trying to allow as much space between the children as possible. One of the first things to happen is that for the time being we return to calling Sparkle 'she', and she is happy for us to do this.

Sparkle's vegetarianism has been slipping away, too. She hasn't declared this openly, and I don't react when she takes from the family meat-meal option rather than the alternative I make for Lily. Sparkle has her dinner with Lloyd and me while the others eat together first. I can see how much weight she has lost and I know that she tries to hide the food at dinner. That's one of the advantages of Lloyd and I eating dinner with her: we can closely observe some of her behaviours around food. The oversized Nirvana T-shirt that she lives in is a good cover for stopping me seeing quite how much weight she has lost. I also think that she might be squirrelling food into a container under her T-shirt. She thinks I haven't noticed but she takes some of the food and moves it to the side of her plate nearest to her and when she thinks that we aren't looking she either gives it to the dogs, or puts it in what I think is a pencil case tied around her middle.

Her jawline has definitely become more defined. I have been researching online how to approach this, but after thinking about it, all I can do is hold her, keep her safe and calm whilst we wait. If I say anything she will flare up and go through the shame stage. I know enough about children and teenagers to know never to ask why, and never say 'you have a choice' and never say to a young person 'you need to eat, it's fuel' or 'you're not fat you're perfect' or any of the other platitudes that are rolled out. I say as little as possible. I do not want to add to her pain. I wish I could take some of her pain away.

Sparkle and Lily can't be in the same room together or a fight, either verbal or physical, breaks out. Sparkle has so much anger, so much frustration, that she cannot regulate herself. If any of us so much as looks at her she blows up. It is exhausting. I have learnt to never ask Sparkle 'why' she has done something, like throw a plate at me or hit Lily, or scream at Vincent because he reacted to her calling him something obscene. All I can do is manage the days as we wait for Sparkle to move to her next placement. I keep daily logs. Sometimes these are hourly logs recording Sparkle's behaviour. I hate it. I dislike myself when I write them, but I have to write them to create an accurate record of events to create evidence to help Sparkle get to the right placement. I don't think that she should be in a regular fostering family placement. This is not right for her or our family. Could it be right for any family? We do what we can to try and make life bearable again in the meantime.

Sparkle kicks off about her phone. She calls me the C word repeatedly and kicks the doors, along with other acts of physical protest. She wants, understandably, to be in touch with Elenora and Groove, but they are both at home on exclusion and I know that Groove's parents have been strict about communication. Unlike Sparkle, Groove has retained the name and non-binary identity. We are simply too tired to react to Sparkle's outbursts, and meet each one with a weary sense of inevitability. Because we all know that she will be moving on, we feel less pressure to create positive outcomes for her. Instead, we are happy to just get through the day.

Sparkle doesn't really go back to school after the exclusion period. She tries the odd day here and there, but she can't really cope with it. So it's a good job that we are here, working from home to make sure that she isn't alone. School has provided plenty of work and asked me to pass it on to Sparkle, but she will not do it and, under the circumstances, I can't push her. Ms Avery has been great. She reminds me that Sparkle has to submit the work by law, and then the conversation ends. Both of us know it isn't going to happen.

Sparkle does, however, continue to self-harm. There are marks across her ankles that I think we are meant to see. One evening I knock on her door to discover her in her usual spot, leaning against the radiator. She moves something beneath her leg. She quickly pulls down her leggings. I sit on the end of the bed and tell her that I wish I could take her pain away. She looks straight ahead, a tear trickling down her pale cheek. She says, 'I wish you could too.'

Richard continues not to manage to find the right support.

Every other day I call or email Richard to see if she has a placement and if we could do a staged move over a few weeks to help Sparkle. It is really hard. I feel like we are throwing her out, but I know we can't give her what she needs. She desperately needs specialist care, therapy and understanding. I also think that she should not be with boys; their presence makes her self-conscious and uncomfortable.

I feel that something has shifted. Is this the beginning of the end for us as foster carers? Perhaps we have reached the end of our fostering career. I wonder whether it was worth it. We have been treated appallingly while trying to get support for Sparkle. I'm not sure if I want to do this anymore.

I bump into Maria's and Groove's mum in town. This time she doesn't try to avoid me, but offers a conciliatory, 'Hello.'

We have a coffee together in the Portuguese restaurant. She tells me that she is okay, but that things are difficult at home.

'The children's father is not coping well with the idea that both his daughters are gay. He wants them all to move back to Eastern Europe. He thinks that England is sex mad.'

She smiles a rueful smile.

I wonder how he defines 'sex mad'.

'Perhaps that's a male perspective, from a background of faith, not understanding that young people in England and other countries are refusing to abide by their patriarchal model?'

I want to add in 'misogynistic' to that patriarchal model, but perhaps that would be cruel to a woman who is already suffering herself.

'It was all a mess,' I say instead. 'Sparkle was more naïve as a Year 7 child, and a looked-after child, than Groove and Elenora, who should have known better.'

We both agree that their behaviour was bad. It was bullying.

'But, when you strip away the power from the bully, you usually find a vulnerable person who craves control and power over others and is usually transferring their own pain onto others,' I say.

My heart goes out to the woman opposite me who, like us, does not quite know what to do for the best.

When I get back, I call Richard again to ask if they have

found somewhere for Sparkle. They haven't, and the clock is ticking. My stress is increasing. I can feel it, physically. I have been here before with the 'dangling' that children in our care are put through while arrangements are left to the last minute. The knock-on effect on our family is tough, too. I know that Richard will be up to his eyes with case work, way too many cases for any human to deal with, but I feel that my child's needs are the most important needs in the universe and she needs outcomes, not, 'I don't know'.

When I update Tristin and Bart on the madness of what's gone on, I hear that Sparkle's father, Luke, has had contact with the younger siblings which did not go well. He has made no effort to see Sparkle. This is another thing to add to the long list of things that makes me sad for Sparkle, who, in spite of everything, does want to see him. It's a similar situation with her mother. Lois has been in phone contact with Cormac and Cahira, but not Sparkle. We agree that Sparkle should not be made aware of this. I think it would simply make her even more distressed than she is already feeling. Sparkle needs her mum. If ever I have seen a child need their mum it's Sparkle, but her mum is not available. Her mum has rejected her. That must be how it seems to Sparkle, anyway.

I also learn that the children's grandmother and grandfather have been to visit them. It was arranged by the children's social worker, and appears to have been a success. I need something to help Sparkle, since that help isn't forthcoming from anywhere else.

Richard, as Sparkle's social worker, is initially resistant about contact, but I press for it, and after the embarrassment generated by the situation within the Emotional Welfare team, I find that I have a stronger hand to deal.

'We believe that Sparkle would benefit from seeing her parents or grandparents,' I say, firmly.

The arrangement is made.

We drive to their house so that Sparkle can spend a few hours with them. The official line is that Sparkle is moving on since she needs therapeutic support that the Allens can't provide as they have three other children and jobs.

A statement that is true, but belies the complexity of the situation and the struggle it has taken to get this far.

I have to put my hopes in something, and I have high hopes that meeting her grandparents again will help Sparkle to feel more connected, more grounded. I speak to Tristan and Bart again. They are excited for Sparkle to see her grandparents.

'What are they like?' I ask.

'Grandpops, as they call him, is lovely, but we think he's under the thumb.'

'And what about Luke's mum?'

Tristan responds, 'She's okay once you get to know her. She comes across as a mix between Mrs Thatcher and Liza Minnelli.'

I love the irreverent way he speaks. I get a vivid picture from his description. I combine it with the memories I have of visiting their antiques shop. I recall how she displayed the costume jewellery in a very striking way. It was theatrical and beautiful.

Not every moment with Sparkle is terrible.

Most days I let Sparkle sleep in. I won't let her stay in bed past 10am, but she seems to feel better for it; she certainly looks better. So, in reality, I can get much of my work done in the morning while Sparkle snoozes and showers. At night she asks to go to bed early, which is funny. It's been good for her too; she is naturally tired at bedtime though sometimes I wake up and think I hear her crying or moving about. When I go to her room to check on her she usually pretends to be fast asleep. It's best if we keep this arrangement. I know she is just loud enough for me to hear; she needs me to come in and see if she is okay.

The Sharpie pen colours in her hair have almost faded and, perhaps without the peer group pressure from school, she doesn't reapply them. The strange mullet-style she gave herself is growing out and her thick blonde hair is once again shining. One day she even asks me to straighten her hair. One-to-one she is fine if she is in the right mood. We have done a lot of walking the dogs together. I find that I can spend time with her like that more easily while the others are at school, so that I don't put anyone's nose out of joint. I use the afternoons to do things with Sparkle and feel like it is a tiny win every time she smiles, every time she looks like a child. Gradually her anger and violence subside and she becomes smaller and seems less volatile, more fragile.

She asks me to buy her some perfume and chooses a watermelon and citrus spray. She loves it, the light and summery fragrance brightens dull March days and it's a vast improvement on the staler smells she used to favour. But really, I don't have much left to give her. I am mostly running on empty. I know Lloyd is out of gas altogether.

Two weeks after the school meeting, I take Sparkle to visit her grandparents. Sparkle is happier than I have seen her in a long time. I do my best to make the build-up to seeing her grandparents as calm as I can. In preparation we buy a new outfit. She chooses new black jeans, some new trainers and a checked shirt.

We stop at a supermarket on the way to buy some flowers and chocolate, her Grandpops' favourite: Toblerone. She looks lovely, her face fresh and clear. I am very surprised, actually, at how clear her skin is, knowing how few nutrients she is consuming. The journey is relatively straightforward. It is also pleasant. Sparkle plugs her phone into my car and puts her music on. It never ceases to amaze me how children seem to enjoy car journeys. Or at least those that don't get car sick like Vincent. She settles into the passenger seat next to me, puts her head back, closes her eyes and listens to the music. There is something about the movement that calms her. With the sun shining through her window onto her face, she looks so young.

She doesn't talk about anything that's happened. Either the recent past or before. It's her story to tell one day when she feels like it, if at all.

We drive up a gravel drive that is tastefully landscaped and very well-kept. At the door are two welcoming people, waving and smiling at the car. Tristan and Bart's description of them is good, Grandmother does look like a cross between Margaret Thatcher and Liza Minnelli; she has an unusual hairstyle, a throw-back from the 70s. I'm sure I have seen Twiggy in old copies of *Vogue* magazine with the same coiffured style. She is wearing a pair of pale blue jeans in a fashion aimed at the more mature end of the jeans market, and a loose cream jumper that looks expensive. Her outfit is topped off by ballet flats and lovely jewellery. I definitely have jewellery-envy. She has an air of refinement. I feel myself fishing deep into my voicebox for my best version of Oxford English.

Sparkle is so pleased to see them, but a little shy. I have a sudden pang of shame that these grand people might think I haven't been feeding her. Grandpops is instantly lovely. He could have auditioned for a Werther's Original advert. Grandmother, who introduces herself as 'Alexa', puts her arms across Sparkle's shoulder and welcomes her in. I'm touched. I had a very different image of her, imagining her to be a cruel woman, unkind and snobby.

My plan was to drop Sparkle off and go into the nearest town to do some charity-shop browsing, inspired by Grandmother's fabulous statement jewellery. But no, I am invited in for tea. Into their lovely old house which, as I should have expected given their previous line of work, is full of antiques.

Grandpops sits and plays a computer game with Sparkle. He clearly doesn't have the faintest clue what he is doing, but I love that he is trying.

'Would you like a tour of the house?' Alexa asks.

Of course I would!

When we are away from the sitting room and in what she calls the 'snug' she invites me to sit down.

'Now, I notice that Sparkle has got very thin.' I almost like that there is no preamble. I wonder how much to tell her but she raises a hand to stop me.

'Bill and I have become friendly with Tristan and Bart and they've told me some of what's been happening for Sparkle.'

She moves her chair a little closer to mine, as if we are in the confessional. 'Look, much of this stems from Luke, my son. I'm not proud of my son, you know. And that's a difficult thing to have to admit to yourself. If I'm honest, I think his behaviour has been ridiculous.'

I assume that she is referring to the accusations against him in relation to inappropriate online interactions with young people, and she brings up the incident.

'You probably know that a parent reported him when he was gaming online with children. Nothing came of that and no evidence of anything untoward, just a manboy who didn't understand boundaries.'

That's quite a significant way to describe your own adult son.

'But it isn't as simple as all that. Something happened to Luke when he was a boy and I didn't deal with it well. I suppose I felt guilty and tried to make up for what I thought was my fault. That's why I spoilt him and bought him a house and supplemented his life, and that's why he has never taken any responsibility for anything.'

She is being remarkably frank for someone I have only just met properly, but I get the sense that she wants to unburden.

'I understand that Sparkle has been struggling with her gender identity.' She sighs and says, 'I wonder if this was Luke's issue too. But never mind that.' She seems to reset her train of thought. 'The last few years have been awful but they've woken me up to face the reality that I need to step up.'

I feel the stirrings of hope for Sparkle.

She talks about Lois and is kind about her. 'I understand that Luke must have driven her mad. He's still a silly boy.'

I think that he may be guilty of more than being a silly boy, but still.

'I've messed up. I feel like, perhaps now, I have a chance to sort out some of the mess. What would you think about the idea of Sparkle coming to live with us?'

I sigh a deep sigh. 'I think that would be a brilliant idea.'

'I know it won't be easy. I know that she has issues to sort out. And one thing I've learned is that I can support, but I can't sort them out for her. If nothing else, Luke has taught me that.'

I think what a profound level of soul-searching Alexa must have undertaken to reach that conclusion.

'If she was living here then she could see her siblings and make a fresh start at a new school. We've been looking at a private school that specialises in the arts.'

'I think that kind of fresh start in a supportive environment would be wonderful.'

'Let's go and break the news.'

Before we drive home, I can't resist giving Sparkle a happy hug. I am shocked anew at how thin she feels. I move a loose bit of hair away from her face. 'Sparkle, you are a beautiful girl who is loved and is going to get a fresh start.'

She blushes and with a wry smile says, 'Not a beautiful *girl*.'

'A beautiful person,' I smile back.

'I think I'm going to keep the name Sparkle, though,' they say thoughtfully.

I'm glad. I think back to our very first conversation in the car when I told them that I liked the name 'Sparkle' because it was unique, but also because it made them sound like they had fire inside them.

This beautiful person still has their fire.

EPILOGUE

After Sparkle moves to her grandmother's, I am tidying her room away when it hits me: after this experience I want to close the door on fostering.

We can't do it anymore.

We never want to put our children through this again. The support just isn't there. And I was freaked out by Zoey's determination for us to have mental health tests, especially knowing what I do now about Elenora. That whole side of things raises more questions than answers and I wonder who really needed and would have benefited most from a mental health review. Elenora is still at the school after her period of suspension.

Lily is happier. She wants to continue to explore her sexual identity and is happy to rejoin the LGBTQ+ group at school with the troublemakers now gone, although she doesn't gather with them every lunchtime. She explains how she feels as if being in the group all the time seems in some way artificial, not quite her scene. She is still questioning her gender identity but, perhaps more importantly, is determined to remain an ally to marginalised individuals. She has also joined an online youth group: Proud Trust, which seems to be good for her. I'm proud of her. She still hasn't quite found her tribe, and she worries about being in no man's land or 'no them's land' as she navigates her feelings. As time has passed, she thinks she might be attracted to girls. The feelings she had were confusing. Of course they were. We will help Lily travel, mainly by keeping her calm and safe. She still has her rainbows up in her room, and we have one displayed in the kitchen just for her. The boys are fully supportive, which manifests mainly by just carrying on as normal.

Sparkle and I share the same birthday so I will never forget them. I remain friends with Tristan and Bart and occasionally talk to Alexa and Bill and hear how Sparkle is doing. 'Much better,' is the answer. Thanks to their personal wealth they can afford very good therapy. But there was a lot to work through.

Sparkle had been denied a childhood because of the need to care for their younger siblings, and because their father and mother had their own issues stemming from their own childhoods. I found out more about Lois, Sparkle's mother, afterwards.

Luke was a university drop out. He had begun studying pharmacy but after learning to make crystal meth he went into drug manufacturing to make money. It didn't last. Luke consumed more than he sold and got into trouble. His mother encouraged him into rehab. He'd just come out of rehab when he met Lois. She was just 14 years old at the time, so Luke was nearly ten years older than her.

Lois came from a family who didn't believe in mainstream education, but didn't really offer an alternative. Lois was more or less left to roam free. Left to roam into the hands of a group of men who groomed her online.

She caught a bus to the next city to meet them, the group texting her all the time to make sure she was okay, although they were actually making sure that she was still coming. She was met at the bus station by a man who seemed charming. He walked Lois to another bus and they made another journey. She did not pay any attention to where she was or going. He held her hand and kept telling her that she was beautiful. She was taken to a high rise on the outskirts of town. She didn't leave for two days. In that time she was drugged and raped. The men filmed her and threatened her that if she told anyone they would put the films all over the internet and send them to her parents. Her mother hadn't really noticed that she had been away. Lois kept that experience tight to her chest, scared and ashamed.

While Luke had nothing to do with the group of men who abused Lois, he saw her out with friends and was drawn to her vulnerability. From the very beginning of their meeting their roles were set. She was the vulnerable child and he was the controlling man. After a few dates, Lois told Luke what had happened to her. Inadvertently, perhaps, she gave him the blueprint for how he would continue to exploit her in the guise of a relationship. She would behave like a little girl. He would love it when she was like that, then want to watch porn with her and spike her drinks. She had their three children very young, but the drink and drugs continued, mostly as a result of Luke's organisation and insistence.

If it wasn't for the regular interventions of Luke's mother, things would have fallen apart long before they did.

And that was the world that Sparkle came to us from.

As the oldest child, Sparkle was used to witnessing the sex games played by her parents. She knew to get out of the way while they amused themselves downstairs. She knew what her parents were doing: the moans, the screams of apparent pleasure, the sounds of slapping and cries of 'more'. Sparkle had witnessed things when doors were left ajar. She had seen her father in a long red wig wearing a dress. She had seen her mother wearing a strap-on dildo and having sex with her father from behind. Sparkle had tried to keep as much of this as possible from her younger siblings, but had carried the burden of responsibility for what was going on. She had also carried these images around with her in her head. She knew it wasn't healthy and knew that her mother was in a bad way. Her father was good at gently manipulating all of them. She had seen enough of the outside world before she came to us to know that their family was not 'normal'. Perhaps some of this played out in the later bullying incidents with Tex and Groove. Who knows?

Unbeknownst to us, or to her parents it seems, Sparkle hated her body. In part, she hated it because she didn't understand her body. She had seen these glimpses of her parents having sex, sometimes weird, brutal sex and seen their bodies. Those images had frightened her. Her parents' openly sexualised behaviours were coupled with the fact that they never told Sparkle what to expect as she grew up. She just got older without a clue what was happening to her. No one had mentioned that she would have a period and Luke had removed Sparkle from the Year 6 sessions on sexual health on 'religious grounds', which is ironic given what she had to witness from him at home.

She had only heard her friends at school mention periods. When the time came she did at least know what was happening to her. But in order to discover more, when she looked online she had encountered porn sites and learnt about how some men and women like having sex when the woman is menstruating. She thought that the word 'menstruating' was a Word Sandwich. Her Year 4 primary school teacher would play 'Word Sandwich' with the children in the afternoons. She loved this game, where they would take two words and make a new meaning. She had heard her grandmother say about Luke that 'men were frustrating' so she thought 'menstruating' was a play on that idea. She thought that the blood represented the pain that women experience when frustrated by men.

Her body was changing, her tummy ached and the years

of eating microwaved meals and little exercise had given her a tummy that didn't look right with the rest of her, which was thin and almost stick-like. She also developed a sloping, double-chin which also didn't look right against the rest of her; her body was skinny but flabby.

Sparkle was too young and unsettled to have been able to know who she was and what the world was about. Life was so confusing for Sparkle, at exactly the moment that her mother had her episode. If only we had known about all of this when Sparkle came to us.

Not long after Sparkle leaves, we go to 'panel'. The social care team's investigation into Sparkle's case. It feels as if we are on trial.

We go, mainly to see what is said about us. If you are a foster carer yourself reading this, you will know that the reporting is not always wholly accurate. We are here to check accuracy more than anything, and because I want to have the opportunity to speak about our experience.

The Chair begins the session by checking all the paperwork. She asks Richard, Sparkle's social worker, if he has completed the gender section. I have a copy of the documentation in front of me. I look down and read 'Gender', then the two choices: M or F. I almost laugh out loud. This tells me all I need to know. If organisations like social care actually care as much as they say they do, they would not allow details, important details like this, to go unnoticed. The forms of an organisation are as much a reflection of the underlying beliefs as the policies they keep in their offices.

I do have the chance to speak, to put our side of the narrative forward. I'm not as eloquent as I would like to be, but I make the point that LGBTQ+ rights must be upheld and supported. Of course they must. But at the same time, a balance must be struck. . I want to say that Social Services aren't taking things seriously – as evidenced by the form I've just filled in – but are then reacting unhelpfully to gender issues when they are raised directly by children. I want to say that they are pushing blame and responsibility onto carers, parents and teachers.

Of course I don't say that.

Instead I explain that it feels like children's childhoods are becoming shorter and harder every year. Sparkle is only 11 years old. A child that wants her mum and dad. 'How can a child who has only recently acquired her second teeth and not properly started her periods be able to align herself to a new gender and sexual identity?' I plead. I can't stop feeling that, and I know I run the risk of not being perceived as 'right on', but all my instincts, all my being, screams 'leave the children alone'.

'Why burden them with this, as well as navigating the minefields of social media, drugs, county lines, bullying and all the other stuff that is ripping their innocence away?'

Despite our difficult time with Sparkle, and the

complexities of what happened, we get through the panel, and are essentially absolved of any blame in what happened.

It is a relief.

It doesn't change my mind about future fostering.

Even though we are 'successful' at the panel, we still have to have the official sign-off from the 'Agency Decision Maker' or ADM. A week later we receive his report. His recommendation is that we attend a 12-week government-funded course in LGBTQ+ terminology, legislation and inequalities.

Lloyd is not impressed. Of all of the Allens, I feel he is the one who has taken the biggest hammering since Sparkle's arrival. Unfairly. He's a man with a kind heart. He is a pretty ordinary bloke, really. One who is trying his best to be a force for good in the world. Prior to Sparkle's arrival he never had a negative thought or word about anything LGBT-related. I have met many male foster carers who would not have been able to share their home with that much hostility. He is recovering. In a funny way I think Lloyd and I got such a battering because it was 'safe' to do so. We had no issues, and we are supportive.

When I try to enrol on the government's 12-week course, it tells me that I should be able to 'fit it in my own time'. Oh, I love that. Definitely said by someone without children. Completing the online form, I get to the bit about personal information. I click where it says 'sex'. A choice of two, Male or Female. I take a picture and close the lid of my laptop with a sigh. I'll not be registering. They are not taking LGBTQ+ seriously. This is not furthering the cause. It feels insincere, like they're running the course as a form of tokenism.

AFTERWORD

Before Sparkle arrived and things panned out as they did I can't remember ever having an issue with LGBTQIA+. Before I became aware of the alphabet soup war on pronouns I saw everyone as an individual. I feel beaten up and demoralised by the Sparkle experience and it's not because of Sparkle, the person. They were the catalyst for so many awakenings about the dysfunction and hypocrisy that lives within this movement, perhaps any movement. The double standards, deceit and hidden agendas.

I first began to lose faith in groups of apparently like-minded people when I was 16 years old. I was a committed vegan (before it was hip) and I spent time talking with other vegans about our collective faith in the notion that animals have the right to live. Within the vegan community there were people who were extremists. There were fruitarians. There were the fundamentalists within our group who only ate fruit and seeds. Then there were the hard core of the fruitarians who only ate the fruit that had naturally fallen from the trees or bushes, not picked by the hands of nature's exploiters, humans. I didn't stay long. Mainly because I sat in people's flats with Indian throws on sofas, drinking herbal tea, talking about fascism whilst they chugged away on bongs and roll-ups and looked terrible. Smoking tobacco; the same tobacco that was being tested on Beagle dogs in laboratories across the first world. I was about the same age as Alina, or Groove, and her friend Elenora. A natural time for experimentation and exploring new views about the world.

But Sparkle was only 11 years old.

It could be argued that the others, Elenora and Alina, were unaware of the world too, although they were significantly older. But that's why it's important for teenagers to question and to rewrite their version of the world. I feel that Sparkle latched onto the others, or perhaps they latched on to her, because she was so vulnerable. It became exploitative, way beyond children genuinely seeking to explore their gender identity.

I'm sad that this has become a thorny, gnarly issue. One that is not, in my view, always authentically supported. The other day I was in the school reception area where I saw a display board that looked like it had been done by a teacher. It was clearly there to welcome and was designed to be inclusive to the school's LGBTQ+ students. There was a picture of the former US President Barack Obama, with a quotation: *We believe in the inherent dignity and equality of every human being, regardless of race or religion, creed, or sexual orientation.* Yes to that, I thought.

There was a picture of the singer Pink, and another

attached quotation: *I think the best day will be when we no longer talk about being gay or straight.* There was one from Will Smith, the actor, stating another supportive sentence. Again, I agreed wholeheartedly with the sentiment.

But the reality for us was not dignified. It was months of abuse from someone who beat us up on every pronoun slip, while if they made a mistake we could not comment. It has been a very difficult experience. The thing about being socially conscious is that it's a journey, not a destination. There is always more to learn. There are new identities being discovered, defined, and labelled on a regular basis. I notice that the school rainbow display's heading, in big black letters, is LGBTQIA+. When did the 'A' appear? The LGBTQIA+ grouping wasn't always such a long string of letters, and I suspect it will get longer, perhaps even in the time between writing this and publication. We will continue to try hard to get it right. But as fallible humans, we may miss a letter out here and there.

What about my dyslexia? Or people's learning issues? Can we learn if we are being threatened and bullied? No, we can't. It doesn't matter how long all of us have been conscious about LGBTQ+ issues, or how many books and training courses we have read or attended. There will always be something we don't know. And we will make mistakes. Mistakes not because we are phobic, but because we slipped up. Unintentionally. Help us.

For all of us it's an ongoing path to self-improvement, growth and understanding. So, be kind if good people drop a pronoun or say something that doesn't suit your mission. People learn through joy, not threat. I feel so beaten down because of what happened. It was, as you have read, not a good experience.

I felt that almost every time Lloyd, or I, or the other children were shouted at, and called out, that it was unhelpful. Every time I was punished I moved further away. I felt like rebelling. I felt like rejecting their wants because I was sick of feeling bullied. If I too had been treated with kindness, dignity and respect, I would naturally want to support them.

It would be better if everyone agreed on how to support children but they don't because, as far as I can see, what people say to appear 'right on' and what they actually think, are two different things. I don't think this helps because it does not help resolve the problem. For me, these are children before they are sexual beings or 'genders', and just because I recognise that does not make me *phobic*.

What can I say at the end of all this? I know that some people prefer to identify outside what may be considered 'mainstream'. They wish to socially express themselves differently to the mainstream.

I love that.

Louise Allen
2023